The Church as the Extended Family of God

The Church as the Extended Family of God

Toward a New Direction for African Ecclesiology

Donatus Oluwa Chukwu

Library of Congress Cataloging-in-Publication Data

Chukwu, Donatus Oluwa

The Church as the extended family of God: toward a new direction for African Ecclesiology/Donatus O. Chukwu; foreword by Joseph Kabari.

Includes bibliographical references and index

1. Christianity-Nigeria. 2. Inculturation. 3. Catholic church. 4. Igbo (African religion). 5. Evangelization. 6. Theology

BX1682.N5 C48 2011

Bloomington, Indiana

Xlibris publication

COPYRIGHT © 2011 BY DONATUS OLUWA CHUKWU.

LIBRARY OF CONGRESS CONTROL NUMBER:		2010916127
ISBN:	HARDCOVER	978-1-4568-0511-1
	SOFTCOVER	978-1-4568-0510-4
	EBOOK	978-1-4568-0512-8

All rights reserved. No part of this book may be reproduced or transmitted in any form or by any means, electronic or mechanical, including photocopying, recording, or by any information storage and retrieval system, without permission in writing from the copyright owner.

This book was printed in the United States of America.

To order additional copies of this book, contact:
Xlibris Corporation
1-888-795-4274
www.Xlibris.com
Orders@Xlibris.com

Contents

Preface 9

Acknowledgment 11

List of Abbreviations 13

Foreword 15

Introduction 19

Chapter 1:   *The Igbo People* 29

Chapter 2:   *Images of the Church* 47

Chapter 3:   *The Quest for an African Model of the Church* 75

Chapter 4:   *The Theology of Inculturation* 97

Chapter 5:   *Toward an Ecclesio Missiocentric Theology of the Church* 129

Chapter 6:   *Leadership in the Church as the Extended Family of God* 142

Chapter 7:   *Women and the Church as the Extended Family of God* 152

Chapter 8:   *Toward an Authentic Evangelization of the Igbos* 161

Chapter 9:   *Liturgical Inculturation* 168

Chapter 10:   *Small Christian Communities as the Basic Structure of the Church as the Extended Family* 178

Chapter 11:   *Ancestral Ecclesiology* 182

Chapter 12:   *Implication of the Model of the Church as the Extended Family of God* 188

Conclusion 195

Selected Bibliography 199

Index 209

To my late parents, Janet and Joseph

PREFACE

With the end of "the missionary era" in Africa as evidenced by the emergence of indigenous church personnel and clergy, the Catholic Church in Africa could be said to have come of age. Africans are now missionaries to themselves and have even started sending missionaries to the western world. Paradoxically, the church in Africa continues to be the recipient of what Anthony Chukwudi Njoku called "Echo theology." The church in Africa, Njoku contends, continues to "echo" or repeat and practice western theology and liturgy while neglecting to develop a theology and liturgy that resonate with Africa's own theo-ontology. The failure of African mainline churches (particularly the Catholic Church) to articulate their own theology within their cultural milieu has precipitated a crisis of faith and identity and loss of members to other Christian denominations. On the contrary, African Pentecostal and indigenous churches have recorded unprecedented membership in recent times.

A critical assessment of the state of Christianity in Africa reveals a Christian faith that is far from being deep-rooted. An atmosphere of superstition pervades the world of many African Christians. The result of this phenomenon is an unholy syncretic symbiosis of Christianity with African Traditional Religion (ATR)—a Christianity that is interlaced with beliefs in magic, spirits, divination, witchcraft, etc. A seeming Gnostic dualism pervades the entire spectrum of the African Christian world.

The lack of deep grounding of the faith, in hindsight, is often attributed to inadequate missionary methodology, lack of inculturation, and the failure to recognize the fundamental role of culture in the evangelization of a people.

In the light of the aforementioned state of Christianity in Africa, and in order to make Christianity deep-rooted, there is need for a new church model and direction in African ecclesio-missiocentric theology that will engender genuine evangelization of Africans. The need for an African model of the church is undergird by the fact that human beings are deeply tied to their cultures and cannot be properly evangelized unless the Christian faith becomes incarnated in their cultures. The church in Africa should be able to articulate its own theology for the service of its people.

The theology of inculturation serves not only as the process through which the incarnation of the faith in a culture is actualized but also as a method for authentic evangelization. The model of the church as the extended family, which is characterized by relationality and communality as the essence of being, provides a theological framework for articulating an African ecclesio-missiocentric theology of inculturation for the evangelization of Africa. The new vision of African ecclesiology proposed underscores pluralism in theology and inexorably a liturgy that is distinctively African—an African Rite. The model has sociopolitical, economic, and ecclesiological implications, not only for the church in Africa, but also for the universal church and the cosmic order. The *ecclesio-missiology* envisioned here advocates an acceptance of a plurality of theologies while maintaining the unity of the one, holy, Catholic and apostolic church. At the same time, it provides the platform for evangelization of Igbos, upon which this book is focused.

In articulating an *ecclesio-missiocentric* theology of inculturation, we are conscious of the fact that no single image can encapsulate the complexities of the mysterious nature and character of the church. Similarly, the unity of the church is not dependent on a uniformity or acceptability of the same images/model for the church. Therefore, in order for the faith to be deep-rooted in Africa, it is expedient and necessary to formulate a specifically African image or model for the church. This image (*ecclesio*) will provide the framework—or rather the foundation—for the evangelization (*missio*) of Africa.

Given the vastness of sub-Saharan Africa, our focus will primarily be limited to the Igbos' notion and understanding of family. Scholars who write about the people, culture, and religion of Africans have often fallen into the temptation of overgeneralization. Most often, sub-Saharan Africans are erroneously conceived as a homogenous people with the same culture. Africa is a diverse continent inhabited by all the different races and most languages of the world. There are many differences among the diverse people and cultures of Africa. Nevertheless, there are fundamental similarities among the people of Africa: the concept of family is one of such. For the purpose of clarity, the Nigerian Igbo concept of family, which is similar to that maintained in other African cultures, will underpin our quest for a new direction in African ecclesiology.

ACKNOWLEDGMENT

This work could not have seen the light of the day without the assistance I received from numerous people in the course of my study. My deepest gratitude goes to my family, my first teacher on what it means to belong to a family. I remain ever grateful for your love. My sincere appreciation goes to Drs. John McCarthy, Susan Ross, Richard Costigan, SJ (Loyola University Chicago professors in theology), and Father Christopher Okoro (Ebonyi State University Abakaliki, Nigeria) for their guidance, encouragements, and invaluable help during my studies at Loyola University. I cannot thank you enough. I am also grateful to Rev. Jim Barrett, pastor of St. Margaret Mary Church, Chicago. My sincere thanks go to Frs. Hal Murphy, Ted Ploplis, and Arlene Paolicchi, Jim Hazard, for their encouragements and useful suggestions while this book was at its infancy.

I remain indebted to my friends: Chris Okorie, Joseph Orji, Chux Okochi, Ken Chigbo, Chidi Obasi, Camillus Ugwu, Vivien Echekwubelu, Kieran Nduagbo, Emeka Adibe, Matthew Abba, Edward Inyanwachi, Matt & Margie Lohmeier, Anthony Chukwudi Njoku, Greg Okafor, Ezebuchi Agu, Bernard Okafor, Cajetan Ebuziem, Jerome Onwughalu. You have all been friends indeed. I appreciate your making out time to read the manuscript and for your critical comments and suggestions. I thank also Father Joseph Kabari who graciously accepted to write the Foreword to this book. Your critical suggestions are highly appreciated. There are numerous people I would like to thank whose names are omitted. You are not forgotten.

LIST OF ABBREVIATIONS

AG	Ad Gentes
AFER	Africa Ecclesiastical Review
AMECEA	The Association of Member Episcopal Conference of Eastern Africa
ATR	African Traditional Religions
CBCN	Catholic Bishops Conference of Nigeria
CWO	Catholic Women Organization
ICEL	International Commission on English in the Liturgy
IMBISA	The Inter-Regional Meetings of Bishops of Southern Africa
LG	Lumen Gentium
LXX	Septuagint
NT	New Testament
OT	Old Testament
SCC	Small Christian Communities
SEDOS	Service of Documentation and Study

FOREWORD

It is the observation of many that the Catholic Church in Africa needs to be more Africentric in its self-understanding and presentation than it has been so far. It ought to do this if it is to survive the challenges of a surging African religio-cultural renaissance being fuelled by a growing intellectual sophistication of the African people. Furthermore, even more crucially, it should do so in order to capture the imagination of ordinary folks that lack much education. This is not to say that Christ and his message should cease to be the center of Catholic Christianity. Rather, it is to say that the Gospel needs to be more effectively presented in the languages and thought patterns, the idioms and images, the signs and symbols, of the various African cultures of this vast continent. History shows that the Eastern and Western European traditions of Christianity benefitted from such inculturation over the centuries. Similar inculturation in contemporary Africa, the church leadership and the faithful agree, would certainly help to make the faith more easily appealing and the appropriation of the faith much more assured and stable.

Many an ordinary African still finds some unease with the language and logic of the Roman Catholic evangelizing methodology. This is paradoxical for a church whose sacramental system is much closer to the traditional African religious systems than the biblicism of much of Protestantism. The intellectual elite are worried about the rather culturally imperialistic ethos of the Roman Catholic system. For Africans, the questions are now deeper and much more urgent: they are about African cultures and self-identity and the relevant intellectual foundations thereof. Must Africans remain objects of foreign interpretations and designs of salvation, or should they now come to their own appreciations of the good news? As Pope Paul VI urged, can we now be missionaries to ourselves? Such interrogations now tend to challenge the very philosophies and theologies, the complex of worldviews that underpin the practices of the church. The problem seems to arise from the supposed, but debatable, incompatibility between the traditional African religio-cultural worldviews and the Judeo-Christian ones.

FOREWORD

Many note that in spite of the Second Vatican Council and the consequent gestures and postures of aggiornamento, much has not changed in the African Catholic Church, and that the earlier structures and styles of the Eurocentric missionary church, theological and administrative, laid in the colonial era, are still very much in place. Much has been written about inculturation on the African continent. However, there does not seem to be the theological will to make progress. If anything, there seem to be a conservative interpretation of the Vatican II documents these days, especially in the African world. The changes in Africa have been generally marginal, mostly in the realm of liturgical gestures. Again, while Africans have largely taken over the administration of their local churches, the ethos and the norms of the administration as well as of theological reflections have changed very little. Many of the African ecclesiastical elites, eager to avoid charges of heresy, seem to be much more suspicious of their own traditional African religio-cultural ideas than the Vatican itself.

When the above situation is compared with what has taken place in most of the indigenous African Christian churches, or the churches of the African diaspora, one finds some telling differences with regard to their approaches to the inculturation of the Gospel. In their cases, most now do historically reclaim and reconnect with the contributions of Africans, especially those of classical North and Northeast Africa, (Egypt, Ethiopia, Nubia, etc.) to the early growth and spread of the Christian faith. Their biblical and theological studies do emphasize how genuinely African the Christian faith has been from the beginning, and they highlight the contributions that Africans have made from those early ages. Thus, they are eager to and easily dismiss the false idea (of Moslems and the secular elite) that Christianity is a religion foreign to Africa.

Furthermore, in many of these cases, even more importantly, the challenges of historical and social realities have compelled these Africentric churches to reinterpret and rearticulate the Christian Gospel in signs and symbols that have been dictated by their own experiences of the sacred, their relations to the worlds of nature, to history, culture, and politics; and their needs of liberation, redemption, reconciliation, and the other benefits that Christianity offers. Above all, substantial uses are made of those elements of African traditional ontology, cosmologies, and spiritualities that help them to better appropriate the Christian Gospel in theory and in practice. For instance, in many of them, not only are the worship structures and prayer formulae more truly indigenous, distilled out of their own experiences, and expressed in their own images and idioms, but ancestral devotions is also acknowledged and promoted. Thus, many of their approaches have become more self-consciously Africentric. African cultural agency, creativity, and originality, historical and contemporary, usually marginalized in Eurocentric views, are brought into central focus. Moreover, African religious values are seen as compatible with the Judeo-Christian ones, instead of being demonized. In them, one begins to see the outlines of an African Catholic Christian rite if the

Roman Catholic Church would allow such a possibility. Thus, even in those parts of Africa and the African diaspora where the people did not participate in the classical era of the faith, as they did in North and Northeast Africa, Africans have self-consciously appropriated and rearticulated the Gospel in the language and logic of their contemporary cultures.

It is in the light of the above observations that one begins to appreciate the efforts of the author of this work on the theme of an African (catholic) ecclesiology. The book reflects the new philosophical and theological self-consciousness and self-identity gaining ground among many of the younger clergy of the Christian churches, including some Roman Catholic clergy. The goal of many of these churches is to represent the Christian faith from the perspective of the African trying to answer the question of Jesus: "And who do you say that I am?" Their intention is to develop an image of the church that is truly African and that will better serve the authentic evangelization of the African peoples, especially, in this case, the Igbo people of Nigeria. It is to enable them know and accept Christ and his good news in their own idioms and images, signs, and symbols. This is what the inculturation of the Gospel is all about. This work, then, is an exercise in Gospel inculturation, particularly in the area of ecclesiology.

The author begins with the problem of the received images of the church. He shows that out of the many images present in the scriptures and in the history of the magisterium, the Catholic Church has over time come to emphasize the imperial and the institutional paradigm under the pressures of medieval and modern European historical and political developments. In place of this, he urges the use of the African-Igbo image of the extended family. Such a very African-Igbo basic understanding would be quite compatible with and accommodative of some of the other scriptural conceptions of the church, for example, the church as the people of God, and as communion or fellowship of the faithful. Indeed, the concept of the family of God is also scriptural, as it is found in both the Hebrew and the Christian testaments. African bishops and the Vatican have also accepted this image of the church in Africa as the author of this work acknowledges. However, quite often, the bishops tend to speak of what they call an *adoption* of the family or extended family image for the African church that can be misleading in some sense of the term: *adoption*. The use of the language of adoption here does not mean that the paradigm is in any way foreign to Africa. It simply means the affirmation and application of this concept in the theory and the practices of the church.

Now, the more crucial point is what this image of the church means or should mean for the practical life of the church in Africa. It no doubt brings along with it a fresh theological vision of the church insofar as the imperial, institutional picture is replaced with a more homely one informed by the spirit of communion, of participation, of love, of mutual caring, and of sharing. But before we focus on the more practical dimensions of this ecclesiology, it is worthwhile observing that the African family includes both its living and living-dead (ancestors). Thus, this conception of the church must include the practice of ancestral devotions that is always at the core of the African-Igbo family, nuclear and extended. It means that this paradigm must boldly grapple with the African ontology and cosmologies as these clearly affect African traditional spirituality.

Again, on the more practical front, while conceding the possibility of dysfunctional families, the truth is that such families are the exceptions that prove the rule of what families are really meant for: a place for the generation and defense of life and of the good life. The Catholic moral principle of the common good fits into the African moral conception of the role of the family. For the African, the Igbo, it is possible to claim that the image of the extended family of God is even better than that of the Kingdom of God to the extent that it more naturally fosters the vision of love and of peace, of shared resources and values, of mutual trust and commitment. It is, perhaps, naturally more suggestive of the life of the Trinitarian God (i.e., of loving participation and community than the idea of the Kingdom or Reign of God).

According to this author, this conception of the church could better affect, transform, and advance the evangelization of the Igbos not only in terms of liturgical inculturation with all its African fervor and flavors but also in terms of church organization and leadership. For example, first, it should promote what in Igbo terminology he calls "*ohacracy*," that is, a more participatory style of church governance, than obtains at present. Furthermore, it should make the place and the role of the mothers and the women more visible. The wrong impression has been given that women count for nothing in most African societies and cultures. This is simply not true (or only a partial truth in groups where it occurs, if at all). The image of the church as the family or extended family of God stands the chance of revealing the right place and the rights of women and mothers in the African family and in the family of God. This is particularly so in matters of religion where the men and the women play public and equally respected roles in many African societies, including the Igbo.

Finally, I have to say that this is a courageous and excellent call to the African church to answer the question of Jesus, "Who do you say that I am," in its own cultural idioms and images. The African understanding of the church and its mission has much to do, in particular, with the African grasp of who Jesus was and is, and how, in general, the Trinity relates to the African moralities and spirituality of the common good and community harmony. It is a most timely call to Africans to appropriate the faith and its message of a universal family, consisting of concentric circles of families of God.

Rev. Joseph Kabari, PhD (Catholic Diocese of Port Harcourt, Nigeria).

INTRODUCTION

According to the Second Vatican Council, the church is a mystery.[1] The church's mysterious nature and character stem from its divine constitution. At the same time, the church is a community of believers bound together in God, by faith in Jesus Christ, through the Holy Spirit. The church is "a kind of sacrament or sign of intimate union with God, and of the unity of all mankind. She is also an instrument for the achievement of such union and unity."[2] Though a mystery, the church is contemporaneously located in human history and culture and, therefore, bound by existential realities. In other words, human beings are constituent parts of the mystery of the church and bound together by faith in Jesus Christ. Nevertheless, the fact that the church is human does not mean that human reason can exhaustively comprehend its nature. Therefore, in an effort to gain insight into its mysterious character and nature, the church uses various images and models to illuminate what its nature and mission are to and in the world.

Images/models that encapsulate the nature and character of the church have historical and cultural underpinnings. They are drawn from various aspects of human endeavors: pastoral life, agriculture, building construction, family and married life, law, and institution.[3] These images, among others, include the church as sheepfold, a tract of land to be cultivated, the field of God, the kingdom of God, the edifice of God, an institution, the spotless spouse of the spotless lamb, our mother, the temple, the New Jerusalem, the body of Christ, the mystical communion, a sacrament, a herald, a servant, the people of God, and so on. The images enunciated above evolved over the course of the history and development of the church especially in Mediterranean and Greco-Roman cultures.

---

[1] Vatican II Council, *Lumen Gentium*, ed. Walter M. Abbott, SJ (New York: Guild Press, 1966), # 1.

[2] Ibid.

[3] Ibid., # 6.

INTRODUCTION

The church adopts images and models that resonate with the historical and cultural ambit of the people in which it finds itself, especially in the western world. The adoption of familiar images contributed in no small way toward the successful implantation of the Gospel in the west.

Over the course of history, some images of the church became more dominant than others. These dominant images have not always served as "instruments for the achievement of union and unity in the church."[4] Rather, they seek to foster or impose a uniform ecclesiology among all the churches. This is obvious in the African church where missionaries imposed western images, categories, culture, and ecclesiology. This imposition created a myriad of problems for the African church:

- A failure to adequately make a significant impact on the understanding of the nature and mission of the church to the people of Africa and the Igbos, in particular.
- Reinforcement of neocolonialism.
- Generation of a superficial sense of "conversion."
- Creation of a specific, but important, form of religious dualism, which results in an unholy syncretic symbiosis of Christianity with African Traditional Religions—a Christianity that is interlaced with magical beliefs in spirits, divination, witchcraft, and so forth.
- Repression of traditional way of worship and culture. Many Igbo Christians hop on both legs of traditional and Christian religions quite blatantly. Others have carefully divided their lives into two, restricting one part to Christian religion and the other to African traditional religions.

The attendant effect of these problems is a Christian faith that has yet to permeate the fabric of the people's life and culture. The faith at best remains superficial.

The impact made by missionaries is not doubted. Missionary activities affected the sociopolitical, economic, cultural, and religious lives of the Igbos and Africans in general. On the positive side, missionaries were assiduous in their mission to evangelize and propagate the faith among the Igbos. Their efforts bore fruit as evidenced by the teeming Igbo Christian population. Missionaries successfully obliterated some egregious cultural practices among the people, such as killing of twins, human sacrifice, etc. They also brought western education and healthcare to the Igbos.

Despite the noted and remarkable successes of missionaries, the Christian faith, at best, remains superficial among many Igbos, who still have not allowed the Gospel to play a deeper role in their daily lives. Many Igbos have not completely

---

[4] Vatican II Council, *Lumen Gentium*, #1.

given up the African Traditional Religions (ATR) of their forebears and some other cultural practices that are not congruent with the Christian faith. Their homes are decorated with sacramental objects, like statues of saints, medals, and crucifixes, while magical charms or amulets are hidden from prying eyes in the same home.

The superficiality of the faith has created a quagmire and ambivalence in the practice of the faith. Observing such Christians in the course of their normal lives could easily give the impression that they are carbon copies of their Euro-American counterparts, and that the repressed traditional way was no longer alive. One only needs to see the way the same person handles an important crisis in his/her life to know that conversion and full acceptance of faith in Jesus Christ is tenuous.[5] Most Igbos substantially identify with the Christian religion and, for the most part, live their lives in keeping with its tenets, except in moments of crisis involving them or their close relatives and friends.[6]

An atmosphere of superstition pervades the world of many Igbo Christians. These Christians "worship the Christian God in the day and the god of their ancestors at night."[7] This phenomenon is not peculiar to the Igbos. In fact, in a 2008-2009 survey conducted by Pew Research Center's Forum on Religion and Public Life in nineteen sub-Saharan African nations, roughly a quarter or more of the population in eleven out of the nineteen countries surveyed said they believe in the protective power of juju (charms or amulets), shrines, and other sacred objects.[8] The survey found that belief in the power of such objects is highest in Senegal (75 percent) and lowest in Rwanda (5 percent). In the same survey, many of the highly committed Christians believe that sacrifices to ancestors or spirits can protect them from harm. More than 20 percent in the nineteen countries surveyed say they possess traditional African sacred objects, such as shrines to ancestors, feathers, skins, skull, etc. More than one-third of the people surveyed said they sometimes consult traditional healers when someone in their household is sick.[9]

In hindsight, one can argue that the shallowness of the faith among many of the Igbo Christians stems from wrong missionary methodologies in the evangelization of the Igbos in particular and Africans in general. Appraising the missionary methodology that was operative in Africa, Father Anthony Chukwudi Njoku argues

---

[5] Isichei, P. A. C. and Mccarron, M., "Methods in Evangelization in African Cultures," *The Nigerian Journal of Theology*. no. 4 (1988): 102.

[6] Ibid., 103.

[7] Ibid., 102.

[8] Pew Forum on Religion & Public Life, *Islam and Christianity in Sub-Saharan Africa* (April 15, 2010), 33. For an online version of this survey, go to: http://pewforum.org/uploadedFiles/Topics/Belief_and_Practices/sub-saharan-africa-full-report.pdf.

[9] Ibid.

that missionaries adopted a theology that at best could be called "Echo theology."[10] Thus, after many centuries of missionary evangelization in sub-Saharan Africa, the people have remained passive participants and consumers of western theological knowledge.[11] In their zeal to pass on a "pure" and "untainted" faith, missionaries did not distinguish between westernization and evangelization, and as such, they failed to engage their host cultures in dialogue with the Gospel. Their zeal no doubt clouded their vision from seeing any parallels of Christianity in African cultures.

Because of their keen desire to evangelize the "dark continent" of Africa, missionaries condemned everything African and made the people believe that there was nothing salvageable or worth redeeming in their cultures. African cultures were seen as primitive, barbaric, savage, accursed, and demon-infested. According to Emmanuel Edeh, "Elements in the traditional cultures not found in the foreign cultures of the missionaries, were labeled as devilish and uncivilized . . . such cultures were earmarked for annihilation or replacement with the 'superior,' 'civilized,' and 'saintly' elements of the (missionaries') foreign culture."[12]

In fact, Father Joseph Lutz, a pioneer Catholic missionary in Igboland, summed up the mindset of missionaries to Igboland when he said, "All those who go to Africa as missionaries must be thoroughly penetrated with the thoughts that the Dark Continent is a cursed land, almost entirely in the powers of the devil."[13] The result of this missionary methodology is the superficiality of the Christian faith among many Igbos.

The missionaries' difficulties and failures were compounded by the simultaneous colonization of Africa by western governments, which created a host of other problems such as the perception of missionaries as agents or collaborators of colonial masters. Because Christianity came along with colonialism, missionaries

---

[10] Anthony P. C. Njoku, "Requiem for Echo Theology: Globalization and the End of the Missionary Era," *Bulletin of Ecumenical Theology*, no. 16 (2004): 54-55. Njoku is of the view that Echo Theology was a form of method—a repetition of what theologians in the West thought out and gave as the interpretation of sacred text, constitutions, and conciliar documents of the Church to non-Western churches. The purveyors of this theological method were the early missionaries to Africa. The consequent result of such method was that it made the people passive apprentices, consumers rather than producers of theological knowledge, ill-informed about their roots, branches, and organizational structures and inner dynamics of Christianity. Unfortunately, Njoku laments that this method has continued unabated in the twenty-first century African Church.

[11] Ibid., 53.

[12] Emmanuel M. P. Edeh, *Towards an Igbo Metaphysics* (Chicago: Loyola University Press, 1985), 150.

[13] Holy Ghost Archives, cited by Christopher Ejizu, *Ofo, Ritual Symbols* (Enugu, Nigeria: Snaap Press, 1986), 148.

were viewed with suspicion. Chinua Achebe, in his celebrated *Things Fall Apart*, aptly captures the mood of the people against the missionaries and colonizers in Igboland, when he sadly remarks through one of the characters of the book, Obierika:

> Our own men and sons have joined the ranks of the stranger. They have joined his religion and they help to uphold his government . . . . Does the white man understand our custom about land? How can he when he does not even speak our tongue? But he says our customs are bad; and our own brothers who have taken up his religion also say that our customs are bad . . . the white man is very clever. He came quietly and peaceably with his religion. We were amused at his foolishness and allowed him to stay. Now he has won our brothers, and our clan can no longer act like one. He has put a knife on the things that held us together and we have fallen apart.[14]

The "thing that held us together," which has been severed, as Obierika lamented, is solidarity, or rather, a sense of inter-relatedness that is inherent in Igbo ontology. In other words, the method through which Christianity was brought to Africa often undermined collective solidarity and the sense of interrelatedness that pervade the ontological matrix that held the Igbo precolonial and Christian traditional society together.[15] Moreover, the scandal of Christian division with its attendant fragmented denominations, all vying for the soul of the Igbo, further polarized this sense of communality. It is my contention that the undermining of this ardent sense of communality and belongingness among the Igbos contributed immensely to the problems plaguing Christianity in Igboland today.

As the Igbos and indeed Africans have become missionaries to their people as evidenced with the emergence of indigenous clergy and theologians, the onus of evangelizing and deepening of the faith rests solely on the hands of indigenous missionaries and clergy. It is my belief that a way toward a solid grounding of the faith would require an adoption of a new model (*ecclesia*) of the church that is authentically Christian and African. The model envisioned will articulate a *missio ecclesia* for the church in Africa and particularly among Igbos. My position is predicated on the fact that the New Testament did not adopt one particular model or definition of the church. On the contrary, in the New Testament, we find a

---

[14] Chinua Achebe, *Things Fall Apart* (New York: First Anchor Books edition, 1994), 176. This book accurately paints a vivid picture of the life of the Igbos prior to the coming of European merchants, missionaries, and colonizers.

[15] Emmanuel M. P. Edeh, *Towards an Igbo Metaphysics*, 151.

wide panorama of models/images of the church.[16] Since prevalent images do not resonate with the Igbos and Africans, they have lost their potency and relevance in addressing the traditional and contemporary Igbo people.

Cognizant of the not-so-deep-rooted Christian faith in Africa, the 1994 Synod of Bishops for Africa proposed a new method and vision of the church in Africa. For the synod fathers, "Africans can be more easily enabled to experience and to live the mystery of the church as communion by utilizing to good advantage the African understanding of the family, especially as regards the values of family unity and solidarity."[17] The synod fathers believe that the model of the church as the family of God would engender authentic evangelization of Africans.

Similarly, John Paul II, while giving his approval and support to the new image, says, "Not only did the synod speak of Inculturation, but it also made use of it, taking the church as God's family as its guiding idea for the evangelization of Africa. The synod fathers acknowledged it as an expression of the church's nature particularly appropriate for Africa."[18] The pope goes further to enjoin African theologians "to work out the theology of the church as family with all the riches contained in this concept, showing its complementarities with other images of the Church."[19] This work is, therefore, a response to the papal call for a theological reflection on the African image of the church as an extended family.

In this book, I argue that given the not-so-successful missionary evangelizing methods and strategies for implanting the faith and the colossal success that African Independent and Pentecostal churches are making in Africanizing Christianity, a new vision of *ecclesia* must be articulated if the church must remain relevant to the people. The model of the church as an extended family of God offers us the best possible theological methodology for a new direction in ecclesiology and mission.

The adequacy of the metaphor of the extended family becomes evident when the importance of the family in African cultures is understood. For Africans, the concept of family denotes broader meaning than western concept of family. The family is a network of kinship, inter-relatedness, solidarity, and communalism.

> The kinship system is like a vast network stretching laterally (horizontally) in every direction, to embrace everybody in any given

---

[16] Paul S. Minear, *The Images of the Church in the New Testament* (Philadelphia: The Westminster press, 1975), 25.

[17] Synodus Episcoporum Coetus Specialis Pro Africa, *Instrumentum Laboris: The Church in Africa and her Evangelizing Mission Towards the year 2000* (Vatican: Libreria Editrice, 1993), 25.

[18] John Paul II, *Ecclesia in Africa: Post-Synodal Apostolic Exhortation* (Vatican: Libreria Editrice, 1995), # 63.

[19] Ibid.

local group. It means that each individual is a brother or sister, father or mother, grandmother or grandfather, or cousin or brother in-law, uncle or aunt or something else to everybody else. That means that everybody is related to everybody else . . . the kinship system also extends vertically to include the departed and those yet to be born.[20]

In addition, the extended family is the bedrock of existence and sustenance. Only in terms of the other does an individual become conscious of his/her own being, duties, and responsibilities toward himself and the other.

This book is divided into twelve chapters. Chapter 1 discusses the Igbo people (Ndigbo, *Ibo*) of Southeast Nigeria, who constitute the focal point of this work. Basically, I will give a synopsis of the culture, ontology, and *weltanschauung* (worldview) of Ndigbo. I consider this fundamental because a people's worldview, culture, and social structure are pivotal in a study and understanding of that people. To know a people is to know their culture and worldview.

Chapter 2 will discuss the meaning of the term church, an exposition of the importance and use of images in the church, and a critical hermeneutical review of prevalent images in the church. I will expound the ecclesiology that underpins the use of images and conclude with an identification of factors that militate against their acceptability in the African church. The work of Avery Dulles and magisterial documents will be made use of in this discourse. This chapter presents a theological survey of the literature on the images/models of the church.

Chapter 3 launches us into the discussion of the *extended family as an image for the church*. First, the chapter will articulate the general notion of family from sociological and anthropological perspectives. Second, the chapter will progress into an analysis of the Igbo concept and understanding of extended family. The Igbo notions of *Ezi Na Ulo, Oha, Ikwu n'Ibe*, which form the hinges of the extended family structure and social order, will be expounded in detail. The chapter will also discuss the Igbo theo-ontological notion of "being as belongingness," which is the nucleus of the extended family. Third, the chapter will lay out the theological groundwork of the extended family model by enunciating the scriptural, magisterial, and liturgical foundations of the model. The intent is to ground the image of the extended family in both the theological tradition of Christianity and the Igbo culture.

In chapter 4, I will discuss the theology of inculturation and its relationship to evangelization. The chapter will embark on a historico-theological excursus on the relationship between faith and culture. The goal here is to examine critically the symbiotic relationship between faith and culture (biblical, conciliar, and magisterial perspectives on this question will be explored). I consider this apropos

---

[20] John S. Mbiti, *African Religions and Philosophy*, 2nd ed. (London: Heinemann, 1990), 102.

INTRODUCTION

because the topic of this book could be summed up as the role and function of culture and its relationship to evangelization, or rather propagation of the Christian faith. The chapter also discusses the historico-theological basis of the theology of inculturation and its indispensability in the evangelization of the Igbos and sub-Saharan Africans in general.

Chapter 5 investigates the relation of a theology of inculturation to theological pluralism. In enunciating the theology of inculturation as part of theological pluralism, I will draw from David Tracy's Revisionist method of correlation.[21] It is my hope that for the evangelization of Africans to be effective, it must correlate with Africa's "situation" and cultures. Because the revisionist method of correlation affirms the reality of plurality in theology, this reality should be seen as a value that enriches rather than divides. Therefore, a pluralism of theologies gives us the impetus to "learn incomparably more about reality by disclosing really different ways of viewing both our common humanity and Christianity."[22] In employing the tools of a revisionist method of correlation to postulate a theology of inculturation, a hermeneutical approach to the Gospel through the prism of Igbo culture will be articulated.

Because the extended family model affects the church in a variety of ways, especially in the relationship between churches in various localities, chapter 6 will discuss the leadership structure of the church as the extended family of God. The chapter proposes the adoption of *ohacracy* (communal governance), an integral part of the Igbo extended family system, as the structure best suited for the church. Chapter 7 will focus on the thorny questions of the status and role of women in the church as the extended family of God.

Chapter 8 seeks to understand evangelization (*missio*) through the prism of the theology of inculturation and the emerging new model of the church (*ecclesia*) in Africa and among the Igbos, in particular. This will lead to a discourse (in chapter 9) on sacramental and liturgical inculturation, ritual, symbol, celebration of the Eucharist with African food and drink. The intent here is to demonstrate that local

---

[21] David Tracy, *Blessed Rage for Order: The New Pluralism in Theology* (Chicago: The University of Chicago Press, 1996), 3. Tracy argues that a revisionist method of correlation reinforces the reality of pluralism and the fact that there is no one central theological interpretation of reality or "the situation." Thus, we have to make a commitment to a critical reformulation of both the meanings manifested by our common human experience and the meanings manifested by an interpretation of the central motifs of the Christian tradition. The revisionist critical method of correlation is able to speak within the plural situation without lapsing into one while at the same time remaining loyal to its primary subject referent-God. This method uses the tools of hermeneutics and narration. For a detailed analysis of Tracy's revisionist method of correction, see also his *Analogical Imagination: Christian Theology and the Culture of Pluralism* (New York: Crossroad, 1981).

[22] Ibid.

churches in their rich and complex diversity of theology, liturgy, and local customs could be autonomous and at the same time remain part of the one, holy, apostolic, and Catholic Church.

Chapter 10 lays out a pragmatic course for an authentic deepening of the faith among the Igbos, while maintaining the momentum of Christian evangelical missionary activities. At issue here is the adoption of Small Christian communities as the basic structure of the church as the extended family of God. Chapter 11 continues the discourse in the previous chapters by articulating an Igbo/African Ancestral ecclesiology.

Chapter 12, the last chapter, focuses on a critical assessment and consequential implications of the model of the church as family of God that I have articulated. The approach will be a critical review and evaluation of why this image is not only important for evangelization and deepening of the Christian faith among the Igbos but also its implications for the universal church.

Chapter 1

THE IGBO PEOPLE

The words *Ibo*, *Igbo*, and *Ndigbo* simultaneously refer to the territory, language, and people of southeastern Nigeria, West Africa.[1] While foreigners prefer *Ibo* because of difficulty in pronouncing "gb" in *Igbo*, the people themselves prefer *Ndigbo* or *Igbo* (ig-bō) to designate its people, language, and homeland.[2] While *Igbo* specifically denotes the language and people of Southeast Nigeria, *Ndigbo* on the other hand means the people of Igbo ancestry. In this book, *Igbo* and *Ndigbo* will be used interchangeably in referring to the people, territory, and language of the Igbo. The meaning of each usage will be clear from the context in which it is used.

The Igbos constitute one of the three largest ethnic groups in Nigeria. The United States of America Central Intelligence Agency (CIA) estimates Nigeria's population at about 150 million. Ndigbo number about thirty-five million people, approximately 26 percent of Nigeria's 150 million people.[3] Population densities in the Igbo heartland are very high, ranging on average from 750 to 1,000 per square kilometer. Igbo territory also occupies a continuous stretch of territory of about 25,280 square kilometers. Of the thirty-six states in Nigeria, five states—Abia, Anambra, Ebonyi, Enugu, and Imo—constitute the ancestral homeland of Ndigbo. However, there are significant number of Igbo people living in the Akwa Ibom, Cross River, Delta, and Rivers states. It is worth noting that the Igbos are peripatetic. Hundreds of thousands of Ndigbo live throughout the thirty-six states that make up Nigeria and in myriad nations beyond the borders of Nigeria.

---

[1] Victor C. Uchendu, *The Igbo of Southeast Nigeria* (New York: Holt, Rinehart and Winston, 1965), 3.

[2] Emmanuel M. P. Edeh, *Towards an Igbo Metaphysics* (Chicago: Loyola University Press, 1985), 14.

[3] CIA World fact Book: *Nigeria:* https://www.cia.gov/library/publications/the-world-factbook/geos/ni.html#top (accessed March 22, 2010).

The Igbos, with a population of over thirty-five million are without doubt one of the major ethnic nationalities in sub-Saharan Africa. In the classification of African languages, the Igbo language arguably belongs to the Sudanic linguistic group of the *Kwa* language subfamily of the Niger-Congo family.[4] The Niger-Congo family, which is an offshoot of the Bantu family, covers, to a large degree, the sub-Sahara region of Africa. This accounts for the Igbo sharing several cultural traits and affiliations with the rest of their brothers and sisters in the sub-Saharan region.

Before the advent of colonial administration, the largest political organization among the Igbos was the village group, a federation of villages, or clans averaging about 5,000 persons. Members of these groups shared a common market and meeting place, a common deity, and ancestral cults. These people perceived themselves as descending from a common ancestor or group of ancestors. Authority in the village group was vested in a council of lineage heads, influential and wealthy men and women.

The Igbo Worldview *(Weltanschauung)*

The Igbo worldview is an amalgamation of its cosmology and ontology. The same is equally true of other ethnic groups in the sub-Saharan region. Studies have shown that the Igbo share similar worldviews with the rest of sub-Saharan Africa. Elements of such worldviews include the meaning of life, death, and the hereafter; creation; initiations; values; idioms, and proverbs; a deep sense of religiosity; respect for the sacred; belief in the Supreme Being; ancestor veneration; extended family system; etc. These worldviews pervade the entire spectrum of the region.

John Mbiti, explaining how this similarity came about, asserts, "Studies of African religious beliefs and practices show that there are probably more similarities than differences." Mbiti goes on to explain that:

> Fundamental concepts like the belief in God, existence of the spirits, continuation of human life after death, magic and witchcraft, seem to have been retained when one people may have split or branched off in the course of centuries, the new groups forming "tribes" of their own, which now we can recognize under the broad ethnic and linguistic groupings of African peoples.[5]

---

[4] Dietrich Westermann and M. A. Bryan, *Languages of West Africa: Handbook of African Languages Part II* (London: Oxford University Press, 1952), 89-90.

[5] John S. Mbiti, *African Religions and Philosophy*, 101.

The Igbo worldview holds that in the cosmological order, there is one world divided into two spheres: the world populated by all created beings both animate and inanimate, and the invisible world,[6] the dwelling of the creator, deities, disembodied and malignant spirits, and the ancestors.[7] The invisible world is the future abode of the living after their earthly lives are over. Though there are two spheres (physical/visible and spiritual/invisible) in the world, there is an inseparable continuum between the two spheres by a constant interaction and exchange between the inhabitants of the "two worlds." According to Uchendu, "The world of man and the world of spirits are also interdependent. Between them there is always some form of interdependence, a beneficial reciprocity."[8] This interdependence necessitates some reciprocity, which is made possible through sacrifices on the part of the living and beneficence on the part of the spirits:

> The principle of reciprocity demands that the ancestors be honored and offered regular sacrifice, and be "fed" with some crumbs each time the living take their meal; it also imposes on the ancestors the obligation of prospering the lineage, protecting its members, and standing with them as a unit against the machinations of wicked men and malignant spirits. The same principle requires that all spirits and deities whose help is invoked during a period of crisis and who stand firm throughout it be rewarded with appropriate sacrifice.[9]

The invisible world, just like the visible, is full of activities. The dead continue their lineage system in the invisible world. Sometimes, they reincarnate into the world of human beings. The way a person lived on earth determines his or her state of life in the spirit world. If a person lived an immoral and wicked life here on earth, he or she would not be able to share fellowship with his or her ancestors in the after-life; his or her spirit will become restless, roaming aimlessly in the spirit world without resting in peace. Such spirits become malignant and wreak havoc in the animated world of matter.[10]

Death has an important role in Igbo cosmology. It serves as a gateway into the spirit world and most especially for reuniting people with their ancestors. Death is seen as the dissolution of the flesh and separation of the soul from the body. At death, a person's spirit enters a separate existence, maintaining the life of the

---

[6] This world is real for the Igbos and for other ethnic groups in sub-Sahara Africa. It is characterized by different spheres of activities.

[7] Victor C. Uchendu, *The Igbo of Southeast Nigeria*, 11.

[8] Ibid., 14.

[9] Ibid.

[10] Ibid.

individual in another sphere or form of existence.[11] A death, which occurs at a ripe old age, is considered a good death and a cause for joy, while the death of a youngster is viewed as tragic and attributed to some disruption in the cosmic order.

The Igbo worldview subscribes to belief in a hierarchical order of beings. At the top of the hierarchical order is God (Supreme Being), the ontological source of all beings. Igbo ontology understands God as the self-subsisting being, who is immanent, transcendent, and completely Other. This God is the source of all existence and sustenance to other beings. For the Igbo, God, *Chi-ukwu,* is above every other spirit, good or evil, controlling all things in the invisible and visible world, dispensing rewards and punishments according to merit. Any disruption in the cosmic order such as drought, floods, famines, sudden deaths, unknown disease, etc., for which there is no explanation, is attributed to God.[12]

Many non-African scholars have variously held that African religion is animistic or that Africans have no concept of God before their contacts with European explorers and missionaries. Such positions are blatantly erroneous. Africans and indeed Igbos have a strong belief in the existence of a Supreme Being—Chukwu (*Chi-ukwu)*, a belief that is no different from the Judeo-Christian concept of God. However, *Chi-ukwu* is not the God of the monotheist, who believes that worship should exclusively be reserved to one God, nor is this God understood polytheistically. The Igbo concept of God is not analogous to the God of the pantheist, who believes that God and the universe are one, nor is *Chi-ukwu* trinitarian in nature. Rather, for the Igbos, the belief in the Supreme Being is best expressed in Bolaji Idowu's term as "diffused monotheism." This term concomitantly denotes belief in a supreme God as well as in lesser gods *(chi)*.

The Supreme God is more transcendent than immanent and, as such, delegates certain portions of its animating authority to lesser gods who work as *Chi-ukwu*'s messengers.[13] Because the Supreme Being is transcendent and far removed from human beings, sacrifices are regularly offered to the lesser gods who exert more immediate influence on humans. The Igbos' concurrent belief in the existence of the Supreme Being and other divinities could also be called henotheism[14] or inclusive monotheism.

---

[11] T. U. Nwala, *Igbo Philosophy* (Lagos: Lantern Books, 1985), 144.

[12] George T. Basden, *Among the Ibos of Nigeria* (New York: Barnes & Noble, 1966), 215.

[13] Bolaji E. Idowu, *Olodumare: God in Yoruba Belief* (New York: A & B Publishers, 1994), 204.

[14] *The New Encyclopedia Britannica,* vol. 26, 15th ed. (Chicago: Encyclopedia Britannica Inc., 2005), 547. The term Henotheism was introduced by Max Müller (1823-1900), a philologist and scholar in comparative mythology and religion. However,

Next in the ontological and hierarchical order are the divinities who, as God's messengers, act as intermediaries between God and human beings. Their work varies according to their nature. As was mentioned earlier, some are benevolent, while others are believed to be malevolent. The malevolent spirits are in opposition to the Supreme Being, *Chi-ukwu*. Evil spirits are creatures of God, but they fell out of favor with God. Evil spirits wreak havoc in ways ranging from instigating natural disasters to inflicting sickness and death upon human beings. Some of them were once human beings, but at their moment of death, they become estranged from their ancestors. This constitutes the Igbo equivalent of the Christian eschatological understanding of hell: the estrangement of someone from his or her ancestors upon death. One is said to be in hell if the person becomes unacceptable to the ancestors. The spirit of such a person does not rest but rather roams aimlessly in the spirit world.

After the divinities/spirits are the ancestors who once lived here on earth, but having lived good lives, become divinized at death. The ancestors wield great power and influence in human affairs.[15] They are sometimes referred to as the living-dead. Their spirits are believed to continue to live within their family, and they exert some measure of influence and interference on those who are alive.

Below the ancestors are human beings—*mmadu*. *Mmadu* occupy a central position in Igbo cosmology and ontology. They constitute the point of intersection between the living and the dead; that is, human beings are the bridge between the living and the dead. Human beings equally have the potentiality of being divinized at death, when they enter the realm of the ancestors.

Human life is sacred because it is created by God and cannot be replicated. It is, therefore, of supreme importance. It is the most precious, holiest, and greatest gift of God.[16] To terminate unjustly any human life renders the killer(s) inadmissible into the spirit world unless restitution is made. The sacredness and dignity of life is extrapolated from Igbo sayings like *ndu bu isi*—life is of supreme importance, *ndu ka aku*—life is greater than wealth, *chinwendu*—life belongs to God, etc.

Correlated to the concept of *ndu*—life is the strong belief in reincarnation (*ilo uwa*) among the Igbos. Children are believed to be reincarnations of people who have already passed through this world. A man would point to his daughter and inform you that she is her mother, grandmother, or sister who has come back to life. The same is equally applicable to male children.[17]

---

many later authors prefer to use the term monolatry. Both terms mean belief in the supremacy of a single god without denying the existence of other gods.

[15] Chigekwu G. Ogbuene, *The Concept of Man in Igbo Myths* (New York: Peter Lang, 1999), 114.

[16] Ibid., 97.

[17] George T. Basden, *Among the Ibos of Nigeria,* 60.

Below *mmadu* are animals, plants, minerals, inanimate objects, lands, environment, and so on. Human beings are masters of animals and plants. They are to use them for food and sustenance. Nevertheless, human beings have an obligation to tend and care for these lower beings. Abuse or mistreatment of these lower beings, the land, or the environment is often met with severe punishment. The offender is made to pay restitution and or to repair the damage done.

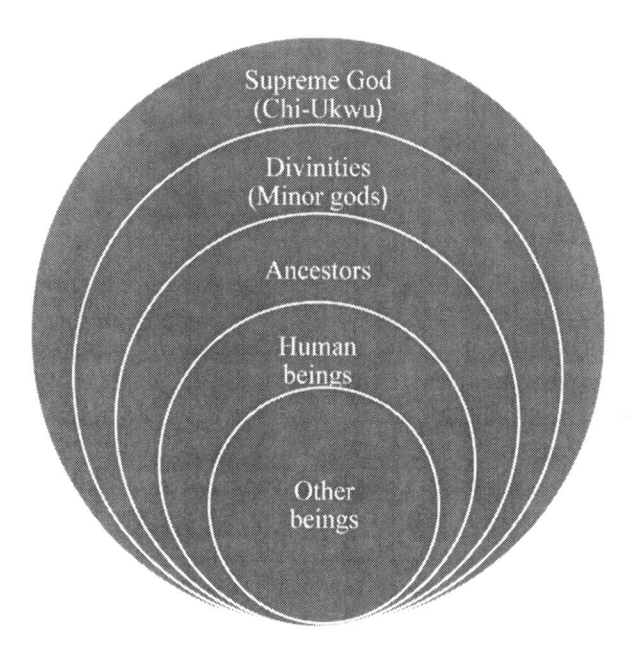

Supreme God (Chi-Ukwu)
Divinities (Minor gods)
Ancestors
Human beings
Other beings

Central to the Igbo ontology is the complex interrelatedness of all human beings. A person is born into a vast network of extended family. The saying "It takes a village to raise a child" rings true in Africa. This philosophy undergirds the vast network of interrelatedness. Everybody is related to everybody in one form or the other. Life is lived communally and in solidarity with others, while individualism is abhorred. As Western ontology defines and understands "being" in the Aristotelian sense of "that which is" or "the thing in itself," or a person in the Boethian notion of "individual substance of a rational nature," Igbo ontology defines and understands the human person in terms of relationships and belongingness.

Chigekwu Ogbuene, an Igbo scholar, succinctly captures the crux of the Igbo concept of existence and relationality when he contends that, "The Igbos do not conceive of man [human beings] as a being existing by itself and apart from its ontological relationship with other beings."[18] In other words, "to be" for

---

[18] Chigekwu Ogbuene, *The Concept of Man in Igbo Myths*, 114.

the Igbos "is to belong." *Igwe bu ike,* "I am because we are." Every human being owes his or her existence to the community. To exist means to be in communion and relationship with the other. An individual takes his or her existence from the otherness of others, or rather, from the extended family. While western ontology emphasizes a "turn to the self," Igbo ontology lays emphasis on a "turn to the otherness" in the ontological understanding of the human person.

John Mbiti sheds light on the common notion of ontology among sub-Saharan Africans when he says:

> Only in terms of other people does the individual become conscious of his own being, his duties, privileges and responsibilities toward himself and toward others. When he suffers, he does not suffer alone but with the corporate group; when he rejoices, he rejoices not alone but with his kinsmen, his neighbors and his relatives, when dead or living, when he gets married, he is not alone neither does the wife "belong" to him alone so also the children belong to the corporate body of the kinsmen . . . whatever happens to the whole group happens to the individual. The individual can only say: I am, because we are: and since we are therefore I am.[19]

Underlying the unity and interaction of beings is participation and solidarity, which takes place on different degrees and levels. A person exists insofar as he/she relates to other persons. Communalism, or the Swahili term *ubuntu*, becomes the essence of existence.

A recap of the Igbo worldview could be outlined thus:

- Igbos believe in a complex spider-web-like universe in which all beings are linked together.
- There is a continuous interaction of all beings visible and invisible.
- These interactions could lead to positive or negative results.
- The Igbo also hold tenaciously to the existence of God, described in western terminology as the prime mover or the uncaused cause.
- The Supreme Being or God does not exist in isolation from other gods.
- The Supreme Being is more transcendent than immanent; however, God's immanence is extrapolated from the activities and functions of the other pantheons.
- The Igbo world is hierarchically structured, but this structure does not undermine the egalitarian nature of human beings who are at the center of the intricate web of the universe.

---

[19] John S. Mbiti, *African Religions and Philosophy,* 106.

This cosmo-ontology pervades the world of the Igbo people and their philosophy of life. Some western scholars brand this philosophy as primitive, uncritical, and often located in the realm of mythology. Nevertheless, this philosophy and worldview continue to exert considerable influence on the life of the Igbo people. The modern Igbo person is inextricably influenced by this cosmo-ontology.

The Igbos are not the only group in Africa with this worldview. Indeed, other ethnic groups in sub-Saharan Africa share similar cosmo-ontological worldview. The world is conceived as being a whole with God at the summit, the ancestors and benevolent spirits ranking next, the malevolent spirits and the strong of this world, and at the bottom, humans as terrestrial beings.[20]

Igbo Concept of Family

In the introductory section, we noted that Ndigbo share common fundamental concepts and beliefs with the rest of the people of sub-Saharan Africa. The concept of family is a classic example. As John Mbiti rightly points out, for sub-Saharan Africans, the family has a much wider circle of members than the word suggests in Europe or North America.[21] Family and kinship could extend to or cover the whole clan or village, the totality of people, living and dead who acknowledge a common ancestor as the source of their being.[22] Mbiti notes that the kinship system is like a vast network stretching horizontally in every direction, to embrace everybody in any given local group. What this means, he says, is that everybody is related to everybody else.[23]

For the Igbos, the family is understood within the framework of the extended family system. The family includes not just parents and children, but also grandparents, uncles, aunts, brothers, and sisters who may have their own children, as well as domestic helpers. The Igbo family maintains some connectedness and continuity with their dead relatives, who are referred to as the living-dead.

These dead relatives in Igbo understanding are alive not just in the memories of their loved ones, but they also continue to live on in the "other world." These living-dead are the ancestors who wield some measure of influence and control in the lives of their living relatives. Because of the influence of the living-dead and the belief that these ancestors are not actually dead, oblation and libation are

---

[20] François K. Lumbala, *Celebrating Jesus Christ in Africa* (New York: Orbis Books, 1998), 43.

[21] John S. Mbiti, *African Religions and Philosophy*, 102.

[22] Victor C. Uchendu, *The Extended Family in Igbo Civilization*: Ahiajoku Lecture Series, http://www.ahiajoku.igbonet.com/1995/ (accessed September 6, 2005).

[23] John S. Mbiti, *African Religions and Philosophy*, 102.

offered to deceased family members at certain times of the year for a variety of reasons:

> The food and libation so offered are tokens of the fellowship, communion, remembrance, respect and hospitality being extended to those who are the immediate pillars or roots of the family. People say that they see departed members of their family coming and appearing to them. When they do, the living-dead enquire concerning the affairs of the human family, or warn against danger, rebuke the living for not carrying out particular instructions.[24]

Interestingly, the Igbo notion of the family also includes the unborn that are yet to be conceived. The unborn inspire hope as the future generation of the family.[25] To ensure the continuity of the family's lineage, sacrifices are offered to attract unborn souls/spirits. Parents are anxious to ensure that their adult children find husbands and wives who will bear children in order to maintain the family lineage. A great premium is placed on the ability to have children, and failure to do so is tantamount to the obliteration of the family. Hence, a man or woman, regardless of his or her social ranking, who does not procreate is considered an *efulefu*: a waste to the family and the society. Unmarried persons, except in special cases, are objects of scorn and disdain. To be childless is one of the greatest calamities that could befall any Igbo person.[26]

Marriage is at the heart of the Igbo notion of the extended family and considered as one of the most important events in the life of any individual. It is through marriage that the survival of the family and society is ensured. "Without marriage, there would be no genealogy. Marriage creates . . . kinship matrices."[27] Furthermore, the connection between in-laws (ogo) that marriage creates enables a wide range of kinship on both sides of the ogo relationship. Hence, through marriage, communal and kinship ties are extended. It is no wonder, then, that marriage is a communal affair.

Emmanuel Edeh is right when he observes that the principle that dictates the choice of a marriage partner is based on the Igbo notion of life and existence. "The Igbos," Edeh says, "have a very high regard for life. Life is not a personal business, which can be tampered with. Life and existence are not properties that belong wholly and entirely to individuals."[28] Thus, for the Igbo, the union of man

---

[24] Ibid., 104-105.

[25] Emmanuel Chukwu, *Ezi-Na-Ulo: The Extended Family of God*, 54.

[26] George T. Basden, *Among the Ibos of Nigeria* (New York: Barnes & Noble, 1966), 68.

[27] Victor C. Uchendu, *Ezi-na-ulo: The Extended Family in Igbo Civilization*. Ahiajoku Lecture Series, http://www.ahiajoku.igbonet.com/1995/ (accessed September 6, 2005).

[28] Emmanuel M. P. Edeh, *Towards an Igbo Metaphysics*, 57.

and woman in matrimony is not just between two individuals but also between their families and the community.

Since marriage is at the heart of family and kinship relationship, the community plays an active role in ensuring its success. The whole community is involved during the process of marriage of young people and also plays a significant role in mediating marital disputes and cases of divorce when they arise.

Most often, the preferred form of marriage is polygamy. Emmanuel Chukwu's argument[29] that the African notion of family is mistakenly shown to be polygamous is untenable and incorrect. On the contrary, polygamy was normative in traditional African and Igbo societies. George Basden is right when he argues that:

> Polygamy . . . is inseparably bound up with the family and social life of the Ibos and, without exception, touches the lives of every man and woman in the country. Polygamy is favoured and fostered equally by men and women; in some respects, the latter are the chief supporters of the system . . . the ambition of every Ibo man is to become a polygamist, and he adds to the number of his wives as circumstances permit. This is an indication of social standing and, to some extent, a sign of affluence; in any case, they are counted as sound investments.[30]

With modernization and the emergence of professionals in society, polygamy is quickly becoming obsolete. However, there are still pockets of polygamous families among the Igbos. Acquisition of material wealth and the influence of Christianity have made polygamy the exception to the norm, but society does not frown at its practice.

Marriage among the Igbo is exogamous, though there are few cases of endogamous marriages.[31] Exogamous marriage widens social links and creates an intricate and complex web of relationships between families. Overall, exogamous marriage fosters the extended family structure. "Igbo exogamy is not only based on biological principles. It also has a social foundation. It is the kinship principle in its social and biological sense that is generally applied . . . besides being a factor

---

[29] Emmanuel Chukwu argues in his doctoral dissertation that it is a misrepresentation and wrong to argue that marriages in traditional African societies and particularly among the Igbos are always polygamous. He insists that before the colonization of Africa, polygamous marriage was not and is never the norm, but rather the exception. He maintains that the confusion between monogamy and polygamy in the African context stems from the temptation on the part of foreign scholars to identify polygamy with African community consciousness. See his *Ezi-Na-Ulo: The Extended Family of God*, 46.

[30] George T. Basden, *Among the Ibos of Nigeria*, 97. See also Victor C. Uchendu, *The Igbo of Southeast Nigeria*, 49.

[31] Victor C. Uchendu, *The Igbo of Southeast Nigeria*, 49.

modifying the centrifugal forces of Igbo separatism, exogamy protects premarital ethics."[32]

The Igbo notion of family is best nuanced in such Igbo concepts like *Ezi-na-ulo, Ikwu na Ibe, Umunna/Umunne, Oha,* etc. These concepts will be examined shortly to further explain the Igbo notion of family and how their beliefs can advance my argument for its acceptability as an image for the church in Africa, particularly among the Igbos.

Ezi-na-Ulo

The Igbo concept of family is best understood within the *ezi-na-ulo* conceptual framework. *Ezi-na-ulo* literally means the outside, surrounding (*ezi*), and *(na)* house or household (*ulo*). *Ezi-na-ulo* bears much similarity to the Greek notion of *oikos* (house). Just as *oikos* includes not only human beings, but property, and could therefore mean family or household,[33] *ezi-na-ulo* embodies the Igbo consciousness of family, which is coterminous with the extended family system. *Ezi-na-ulo* is constituted by various nuclear families, all of which lay claim to a common ancestor.

A renowned Igbo ethnographer, Victor Chikezie Uchendu, offers an insightful elucidation of the Igbo notion of *ezi-na-ulo* when he argues that:

> *ezi n'ulo* is more than a homestead. It is a cultural phenomenon of great complexity. A basic special unit in Igbo social organization . . . . *Ezi n'ulo* is not just a bundle of material cultural traits; it is a people—people united by a bond of kin network interlocking functions and reciprocities. We term this network of people *ezi n'ulo*, an extended family.[34]

Uchendu goes further to argue that the Igbo notion of extended family, understood within the context of *ezi-na-ulo*, "is a social system lacking a fixed number of specifiable positions . . . but consisting of two or more familiar positions of which one or more resulting dyads is not a nuclear dyad."[35] Uchendu, in essence, is arguing that the extended family is marked by persistent patterns of social relationships which prevail from generation to generation.

In summation, Uchendu outlines the basic distinguishing characteristics of *ezi-na-ulo*—the extended family:

---

[32] Ibid., 54.
[33] Sarah B. Pomeroy, *Families in Classical and Hellenistic Greece*, 20.
[34] Victor C. Uchendu, *Ezi-na-ulo: The Extended Family in Igbo Civilization,* Ahiajoku Lecture Series, http://www.ahiajoku.igbonet.com/1995/ (accessed September 6, 2005).
[35] Ibid.

- The extended family includes a wide range of affinial and blood relatives.
- Some of the relatives are close-knit and interact in the day-to-day affairs of the extended family; others live far apart but interact with their extended families especially in times of celebrations and family crises.
- In the African situation, while the husband/wife relation (nuclear family) is gaining in importance, it is seldom the hub of the extended family system.
- The father/son or mother's brother/sister's son relationships are the traditional emphases in Igbo culture with consequences for the radical adjustment of the nuclear families in the system, which face conflicting loyalties.
- Members of the extended family have many rights with respect to one another, and at any given time, these reciprocal rights may be active or dormant.
- Members of the extended family exercise moral sanctions and control over one another.
- Ideally, the interests of the extended family affect the behavior of the nuclear components in the system.
- Members of the extended family can trace their common ancestry to several generations and offer communal sacrifices to the gods.[36]

In the Igbo extended family system, the family structure is mostly cognatic; that is, a person's descent is strictly limited either in the father or mother's line. In cases of patrilineal descent, the family structure emphasizes the role of the father or male head of the family, while matrilineal descent highlights the role of the mother or female head of the family.[37]

Some Igbo societies like Afikpo, Edda, Abam, Bende, etc. have double descent kinship. In this kind of kinship system, a person enjoys simultaneous matrilineal and patrilineal descent, but his or her affiliation is unambiguously matrilineal.[38] At the same time, a person in the double descent structure has obligations toward each of the kin groups to which he or she belongs.

---

[36] Ibid.

[37] Emmanuel Chukwu, *Ezi-na-ulo*, 41.

[38] Victor C. Uchendu, *Ezi-na-ulo: The Extended Family in Igbo Civilization*.

Umunna/umunne

Umunna is a derived from two words *umu*—children and *nna*—father. Prima facie, *umunna* literally means children of the same father. However, a closer study of *umunna* reveals that it transcends its literal meaning. Depending on the context in which the term is used, *umunna* could actually refer to children who belong to the same father or to a complex interrelationship of people who share common ancestors or lineage. Conversely, the corollary of *umunna*, *umunne*, literally means children of the same mother.

Just like *umunna*, *umunne* has two layers of meaning: while it can be used to reference a person's siblings (nuclear family), it could also be used in the same extended manner of *umunna*—extended family. When used in the same sense as *umunna*, *umunne* refers to relations in the mother's lineage,[39] or to a complex inter-relationship of people who share common ancestors or lineage. However, these two terms are used interchangeably to denote the same group of people.[40] The context in which each is used clarifies its meaning. Igbo communities that are patrilineal emphasize *umunna*, while *umunne* is emphasized by matrilineal Igbo societies.

Umunna/umunne is widely used among the Igbo to denote kindred and inter-relatedness. It is impossible to think of an Igbo person without an *umunna*. An Igbo without an *umunna*, Uchendu argues, "is an Igbo without citizenship both in the world of human beings and in the world of the ancestors."[41] This emphasizes the importance of the community over individualism.

The belief in common ancestors as the source of their being underpins participation in the *umunna/umunne* family structure. There is no limit to the size of *umunna/umunne*. The number of nuclear families that constitute an *umunna* and the population of an *umunna* vary; some run up to a hundred, while others consist of markedly less.[42] Membership in *umunna* is permanent unless one is ostracized from the community for breaking certain taboos, such as killing one's kin, incest, etc.

In a traditional Igbo community, communality or belongingness predicates the concept of *umunna*. Everybody within a given locality is a brother/sister or father/mother and tends to relate as such. The Igbos find solidarity in relating to their *umunna*. Consequently, the Igbos recall the spirit of *umunna* whenever they find themselves outside of the natural *umunna*, by forming another community. The Igbos do this by first identifying with those who speak the same language

---

[39] John E. E. Njoku, *The Igbos of Nigeria: Ancient Rites, Changes and Survival* (New York: The Edwin Mellen Press, 1990), 28.

[40] Peter Osuchukwu, *The Spirit of Umunna*, 34.

[41] Victor C. Uchendu, *The Igbo of Southeast Nigeria*, 12.

[42] Peter Osuchukwu, *The Spirit of Umunna*, 35.

as them, even if they do not belong to the same community. "Wherever the Igbos are found, this spirit is always exhibited. They gather and form a non-blood or non-ancestor-related *umunna*. In this case, language plays an important role. Language binds them together, just as the Word of God binds Christians."[43]

The *umunna*, extended family, includes people who share a past, present, and future together. "The African conception of communality, particularly as manifested among the Igbo of West Africa, consists of a spiritual unity that binds people together, thus creating a communal bond that is unbreakable by distance or death."[44] This sharing can happen even in the absence of a constant direct face-to-face encounter or with people who do not have immediate biological connections. The community extends itself beyond those whom we remember or with whom we are conscious of being connected.[45]

Ikwu-na-ibe

Correlated with the Igbo concept of *umunna/umunne* is the concept of *ikwu-na-ibe*. *Ikwu n'Ibe* is another concept that is related to the understanding of the extended family structure. *Ikwu* means kin, while *ibe* denotes one's neighbor.[46] *Ikwu* is one's family and all of his or her relations on both the father and mother's side. In other words, a person's *ikwu* are his or her uncles, aunts, cousins, nephews, nieces, grandparents and their relations, etc. Sometimes, one's *ikwu* stretches to include the entire village.

On the other hand, *ibe* denotes one's neighbors who derivatively are counted loosely as part of the extended family. The neighbors being referred to in this instance do not necessarily mean those who live around your household but are not related to you. Neighbor in this context can also refer to people of other communities and villages. The Igbo create affinity with their *ibe* through marriages or by *igba ndu* (covenant). *Igba ndu* literally means joining lives together. *Igba ndu* creates "blood brotherhood" with people who do not share a common ancestor.[47] It is designed to "build trust" especially among enemies, and establish some affinity with different communities.

Ikwu n'Ibe creates some sort of protection for individuals. When an individual is ostracized from his or her *ezi-na-ulo*, *ikwu na ibe* provides a safe haven or

---

[43] Ibid., 40.

[44] Okechukwu A. Ogbonnaya, *On Communitarian Divinity* (New York: Paragon House, 1994), 4.

[45] Ibid.

[46] Ibid., 56.

[47] Victor C. Uchendu, Ezi-*na-ulo: The Extended Family in Igbo Civilization*, http://www.ahiajoku.igbonet.com/1995/ (date accessed September 6, 2005).

refuge for him or her. For example, if a person inadvertently kills his/her kinsman or woman, he is banished from his community for a certain period of time. The murderer's place of refuge would be his *ikwu*.[48] If the murder was premeditated, one's *ikwu* cannot offer refuge to murderer.

The preceding description of the Igbo concept of family and kinship shows how flexible the system is. The Igbo notion of family can otherwise be said to be open-ended. On one hand, it delineates membership of the family. On the other hand, membership is stretched to the extent that it includes those who are remotely related and or consanguinely unrelated.

Oha

Correlated to the Igbo *ezi-na-ulo* and *umunna* is the Igbo notion of *oha*. *Oha* is the community and also the basis for authority and governance in the Igbo family system. The Igbo world is based on egalitarian and republican ideologies. The neologism *ohacracy* is the form of governance and authority that is operative in the Igbo extended family system. The term *ohacracy* is derived from the Igbo stem *oha*, meaning community or assembly, and *cracy* from the Greek verb *krateein*, to rule or organize. Thus, *ohacracy* means leadership by the community members.[49] *Ohacracy*, therefore, is the form of governance in which the community determines the praxis of the sociopolitical life of the people, while taking into account basic individual and group peculiarities.[50]

Ohacracy is not exactly the same as western democracy. Unlike western-style democracy by which the people govern indirectly through their elected representatives, *ohacracy* is direct and participatory. The *oha* constitutes the assembly and has the power of governance; in this way, every citizen participates in issues that concern the community. In other words, the *oha* is the sovereign body of *ezi n'ulo* or *umunna* that decides the affairs of the community, as a

---

[48] Chinua Achebe, *Things Fall Apart*, 124, 130. Okonkwo inadvertently shot and killed his townsman. This killing constituted a desecration of the land. The punishment for such act is banishment from the community for a period of seven years. The only option available for Okonkwo was to seek refuge among his *ikwu* mother's kin in a different community. Among the Igbo, inadvertent murder is known as female ọchu while willful murder is called male ọchu. Premeditated murder attracts perpetual banishment from the community including the murderer's *ikwu*.

[49] Pantaleon Iroegbu, *African Vicious Triangle a plea for Ohacracy: The socio-political leeway* http://www.etes.ucl.ac.be/Publicatons/DOCH/DOCH/DOCH%2039%20(Iroegbu).pdf (accessed January 29, 2006).

[50] Ibid.

whole.[51] In essence, *ohacracy* is a form of governance that is premised on the maxim that "whatever concerns all must be discussed by all." Every individual in the community is as important as any other.

Oftentimes, Igbos say *oha nwe madu*—the community owns the individual. The efficacy of *oha* is often buttressed in the Igbo word *ohakwe*, which means if the community allows or accepts *oha kara si*. *Ohacracy*, therefore, determines the *modus operandi* and *modus vivendi* of the sociopolitical life of the Igbo. It is a consultative and collaborative leadership structure. All forms of dictatorship or dominion by a group are ruled out. The assembly of the *oha* is presided over by elders of the community. *Ohacracy* gives impetus to the Igbo ontology of being that is rooted in belongingness. In another chapter, we shall discuss the implications of *ohacracy* in the extended family image of the church.

Thus far, we have enunciated the ideal notion of the Igbo understanding of family. De facto, this ideal is far from being realized. The danger of the extended family being abused is grave and real. There is the tendency in human beings to discriminate and exclude those who are not related to them. The danger of *clannishism* is ever present. However, the adoption of the extended family metaphor as an image for the church, I believe, would help to purify, or rather Christianize it and remove elements that tend to discriminate and cause recriminations.

A Brief Account of the Beginning of Christianity among the Igbos

The history of Christianity among the Igbos goes back to the arrival of European merchants in Igboland around the fifteenth century. European trade in the city of Onitsha, found in Lower Niger, dates back to 1434 with the arrival of Portuguese traders in Igbo territory. The Portuguese were the major trading partners with the Igbos until the eighteenth century. The arrival of Dutch and British traders in the eighteenth century broke the Portuguese monopoly in the Lower Niger Coast.

The Lower Niger Coast, Onitsha, served as the point of contact with Igbo traders who functioned as intermediaries in the infamous slave trade. However, with the abolition of the slave trade, a new vista opened. The Royal Niger Company (RNC), owned by British traders operating at Onitsha, shifted their trade from slaves to raw materials like palm products, timber, elephant tusks, and spices for European industries.[52] This change in resources meant that European traders were no longer confined to the coastal areas. As such, they were able to enter into the hinterlands of the Igbo territory. In the course of trading, the British government

---

[51] M. Ozoemenam, *Ohacracy as a System of Government in Igbo Culture area of Nigeria*. Cited in Peter Osuchukwu, *The Spirit of Umunna and the Development*, 52.

[52] Victor C. Uchendu, *The Igbo of Southeast Nigeria*, 4.

colonized the Igbo territory. These traders paved the way for missionary activity in Igboland.

With the colonization of the Igbos, British missionaries were invited and encouraged to evangelize and conquer the restless souls of the Igbos. In 1857, Bishop Samuel Crowther successfully established the Church Missionary Society (Anglican) at Onitsha.[53] Bishop Crowther saw Onitsha as the high road to the heart of the Igbo nation and, as such, worthy of being the springboard for starting the evangelization of the Igbos.[54] The successful establishment of the Anglican mission was followed in 1885 with the establishment of a Roman Catholic mission in the same region. With the arrival of Fr. Joseph Emile Lutz, a French Holy Ghost priest, and his companions and the subsequent establishment of the Roman Catholic Church, the battle for the evangelization of the Igbo people intensified.[55]

The history of Christianity in Igboland cannot be complete without mentioning the efforts and contribution of Obi Anazonwu, the king of Onitsha. Anazonwu warmly welcomed Catholic missionaries, just as he did their Protestant counterparts. The king gave the Catholic missionaries unfettered rights to exercise their religion without any hindrance.[56] Onitsha became the main gateway to evangelizing other Igbo communities and towns. It is interesting to note that the plot of land on which the Catholic missionaries built their first church and which later became the epicenter for missionary evangelization was given to the Catholic Church by Bishop Crowther, an Anglican missionary. In giving the land to the Catholic Church, the bishop said, "I acquired this land for God's cause, take it."[57]

The spiritual odyssey of the Catholic Church in Eastern Nigeria began with the erection of the first place of worship in Onitsha, called Holy Trinity Church. Emboldened from the successful establishment of the church at Onitsha, the missionaries at once sought to penetrate the hinterland.[58] From Onitsha, Christian missionary activities expanded to different towns and villages in Igboland. Notable early missionaries to Igboland represented the following denominations: Anglican, Roman Catholic, Presbyterian, and Methodist.

---

[53] Ibid.

[54] Celestine A. Obi, "Background to the Planting of Catholic Christianity in the Lower Niger," *A Hundred Years of the Catholic Church in Eastern Nigeria 1885-1985*, eds., Celestine A. Obi et al. (Onitsha: Africana-FEP Publishers, 1985), 13. This book offers a comprehensive history of Catholic Christianity in Eastern Nigeria; we do not wish to rehash all the details here.

[55] Ibid., 14.

[56] Ibid., 19.

[57] Elizabeth Isichei, *A History of Christianity in Africa: From Antiquity to the Present* (Grand Rapids, Michigan: William B. Eerdmans Publishing Company, 1995), 93.

[58] Ibid., 25.

The growth of Christianity among Ndigbo has been phenomenal. In a 2009 survey conducted by the Pew Forum on Religion & Public Life in Nigeria, nearly all of those who identified themselves as Igbo say they are Christians. It is estimated that about 96 percent of Igbos consider themselves as Christians.[59]

Igbos arguably have the highest Catholic population and the highest number of religious men and women, priests, and bishops among the various ethnic groups (Hausa/Fulani, Yoruba, Efik, Ijaw, Tiv, Ibibio, Nupe, etc.) of Nigeria. Out of the fifty-one Catholic dioceses in Nigeria (at the time of writing), thirteen dioceses—Aba, Abakaliki, Ahiara, Awgu, Awka, Enugu, Nnewi, Nsukka, Okigwe, Onitsha, Orlu, Owerri and Umuahia—are located in Igboland.[60] They also boast of many major seminaries and institutes for the formation of the clergy, men and women religious. These institutes include Bigard Memorial Seminary, Enugu; Seat of Wisdom Major Seminary, Owerri; Spiritan International School of Theology, Attakwu; Spiritan School of Philosophy, Isienu; Blessed Tansi Major Seminary, Onitsha; Claretian Institute of Philosophy, Nekede, Owerri, Pope John II Seminary Okpuno, Awka; etc.

Despite the evidence suggesting that the Catholic Church in Igboland has made tremendous progress, the influence of the Gospel on the Igbo worldview and culture to a great degree remains shallow. Many Igbo people are neither obedient children of their traditional society and cosmo-ontology (which they refuse to relinquish), nor are they willing to wholly accept what the westernized form of Christianity offers them. This quagmire leads us into a critical reexamination of missionary methodology and the postulation of a new model of the church (*ecclesia*) that takes cognizance of the Igbo worldview as a vehicle for evangelization (*missio*) and a deepening of the Christian faith.

---

[59] Pew Forum on Religion & Public Life, *Islam and Christianity in Sub-Saharan Africa*, 38.

[60] Catholic Bishops Conference of Nigeria, http://www.cbcn.org (accessed December 10, 2010).

Chapter 2

IMAGES OF THE CHURCH

The Meaning of Church

The word "church" evokes varied meanings to people depending on the range of application. Sometimes it is used to denote a building, a place of worship, or a congregation of people who share common faith and beliefs. Hence, we often hear people say Catholic Church, Anglican church, Presbyterian church, or the church at such and such a place.

The etymology of the word *church* goes back to the Anglo-Saxon word *cirice, circe* (modern German *kirche*). In contrast to the Germanic languages, the Romance languages kept a direct connection with the New Testament rendition of Greek, εκκλεσια, Latin *ecclesia*, Spanish *iglesia*, French *eglise*, and Italian *chiesa*.[1] Hans Küng contends that the origin of the word "church" was the Byzantine Greek form χυριαχη, which means "belonging to the Lord," or in its full form "belonging to the house of the Lord."[2] However, there are instances where *ekklesia* is also used to denote an ordinary meeting or assembly of a people without a religious purpose.[3] A similar Greek term *synagogue*, the Hebrew equivalent of *edah*, came to be used for an assembly of people of Israel without any religious significance. The assembly could include those who have socioeconomic ties or those who share the same concern about the purpose and meaning of life. This assembly of people could even be an unruly gentile mob.[4] According to Eric Jay, long before the emergence of Christianity, *ekklesia* was used to denote an assembly of the

---

[1] Hans Küng, *The Church* (New York: Sheed and Ward, 1967), 82-83.

[2] Ibid.

[3] Howland T. Sanks, *Salt, Leaven and Light, the Community Called Church* (New York: Crossroad Publishing Company, 1997), 44.

[4] Kevin Giles, *What on Earth is the Church? A Biblical and Theological Inquiry* (London: SPCK, 1995), 7.

whole body of citizens who met to elect magistrates, confirm political decisions, or hear appeals arising from judicial decisions.[5] *Ekklesia* also referred to Greek city councils, gathering of Jewish people as a whole, or an individual Jewish congregation. Hence, church (*ekklesia*) and synagogue (*synagoge*) were originally synonyms.[6]

The Septuagint (LXX) used the term *ekklesia* as the Greek equivalent of the Hebrew word *qahal*, meaning the entire community of the children of Israel, as the covenant people of God who have gathered together for religious purposes.

The term *ekklesia* is also used by the LXX specifically to refer to the gathering of the people at the foot of the Mount Sinai to receive the Torah that God gave Moses (Deut. 9:10; 10:4; 18:16; 31:30).[7] Eric Jay, elucidating this theory declares, "*Ekklesia* is used as the Greek (LXX) version of the Old Testament to translate *qahal YHWH /ekklesia kupiou* (εκκλεσια κυπιου) to mean the gathered people of God, a people called into being by God, who from time to time are gathered together for such solemn religious occasions as the receiving of the law."[8] In this case, the term refers to a community of believers in Jesus. Subsequently, the term church came to be identified with people who, whether actually physically gathered together for worship or not, are bound to the same faith in Jesus Christ (Acts 19:32, 39, 40).[9]

The Gospel of Matthew is the only one that uses the term εκκλεσια, "church," to refer to a group of people either in the making or already established. After Peter had made the great Christological confession, "You are the Messiah, the Son of the living God" (Matt. 16:16), Jesus said to him:

> Blessed are you, Simon son of Jonah. For flesh and blood has not revealed this to you, but my heavenly Father. And so I say to you, you are Peter, and upon this rock I will build my Church . . . I will give you the keys to the kingdom of heaven. Whatever you bind on earth shall be bound in heaven; and whatever you loose on earth shall be loosed in heaven. (Matt. 16:17-19).[10]

---

[5] Eric G. Jay, *The Church: Its Changing Image Through the Twenty Century*, Vol.1 (Atlanta: John Knox Press, 1980), 5.

[6] Michael L. White, *From Jesus to Christianity* (New York: HarperCollins Publishers, 2004), 120.

[7] Kevin Giles, *What on Earth Is the Church?* 7.

[8] Eric G. Jay, *The Church: Its Changing Image*, 6.

[9] Kevin Giles, *What on Earth Is the Church?* 23.

[10] All biblical citations are from *The New American Bible*.

In the above passage, Jesus speaks of the church not in the present, but in the future. Jesus then instructs Peter to build up the church εκκλεσια.[11]

Because of this mandate, Peter played a prominent role in the post-resurrection church as indicated by the early chapters of the book of the Acts of the Apostles.[12] One can therefore argue that by assigning Peter the task of founding a group of followers, Jesus created a distinct community of believers, to which we can ascribe the appellation εκκλεσια "church." The disciples who constitute the membership of this community accepted the salvation Jesus offered and shared in his life and ministry.[13] After his resurrection, Jesus enjoined his disciples to go and make disciples of all nations, baptizing them in the name of the Father, and of the Son, and of the Holy Spirit and teaching them to observe all that he has commanded (Matt. 28:19-20; Mark 16: 15).

The second occurrence of the term *ekklesia* in the Gospel of Matthew is in Jesus' discourse on the need to reconcile with one's brother or sister who sinned against him or her before one can bring one's gift to the altar. If all attempts to reconcile with your brother fail, you are obliged to report him to the church (Matt. 18:15-17). One can argue that Jesus was speaking of conflict resolution in an ecclesial community. However, this discourse appears to be situated in the context of an already established community of believers in Jesus Christ. The church can be told what has taken place and speak to the offender.[14] For Matthew, this church is made of true and false disciples until the final day when the Lord will separate the wheat from the weeds (Matt. 7:24-30). Saint Augustine called this composition *corpus mixtum*.[15] The *corpus mixtum* could also be understood as the entirety of humanity constituting the church. True believers will be separated from false or nonbelievers on the Last Day.

In the Acts of the Apostles and Pauline epistles, we find a more nuanced understanding of εκκλεσια. However, it is used in a variety of ways. With the birth of the post-Easter church on Pentecost, "the community of believers devoted themselves to the teaching of the apostles and to communal life" (Acts 2:42ff). It is in Acts 5:11 that we encounter the use of the term *church* in reference to the community of believers. However, there are some instances in which the author of the Acts of the Apostles (19:32, 39, 41) uses the term in a secular sense in speaking of an unbelieving mob who have unlawfully assembled.[16] The author of Acts of the

---

[11] Hans Küng, *The Church*. 73.
[12] Kevin Giles, *What on Earth Is the Church?* 41.
[13] Ibid., 47.
[14] Ibid., 54.
[15] Ibid., 61.
[16] Ibid., 83.

IMAGES OF THE CHURCH

Apostles equally uses *ekklesia* (20:28) to refer explicitly to the universality of the church, without geographical boundaries.[17]

Opinions are varied as to what precisely Paul meant in his usage of the term εκκλεσια. An examination of Paul's usage reveals two layers of understandings: on the one hand, *ekklesia* refers to the local Christian church.[18] On the other hand, *ekklesia* connotes the universal church, composed of various local churches whose members are "saints" and chosen by God (1 Cor. 1:2). It is pertinent to note that the meaning of each usage must be deciphered from the context. For example, in his epistle to the church at Ephesus, Paul speaks of the church of God as being constituted by the local community, which the elders, as guardians of the flock, are to feed. At the same time, Paul adds that Christ shed his blood for his εκκλεσια. In this sense, the reference is to the universal church (Eph. 5ff; 1 Cor. 6:4; 14:5, 12).

Because of Paul's use of *ekklesia* to denote both a particular and universal church, we can speak in terms like the church in Rome, in Nigeria, in America, etc. to mean particular churches in these localities. We can also speak of the universal church, comprising the totality of all particular local churches. "When addressing a specific group of Christians, Paul can locate them geographically and theologically. Thus he writes to the church of God that is in Corinth . . . in Christ Jesus (1 Cor. 1:2), to the church of the Thessalonians in God the Father and in the Lord Jesus Christ (1 Thess. 1:1ff)."[19]

What then is the church? The reality called church is very difficult to encapsulate in a single definition. A definition in Aristolelian and Thomistic senses of genus and species will obscure the nature and character of the church. A brief excursus into the development and meaning of εκκλεσια in the different eras of the church will help us understand the meaning of the term "church."

As I have noted, the term *ekklesia* has undergone various usages over the course of history: from a secular assembly of ordinary citizens to a sacred assembly of people who profess belief in Jesus Christ. This sacred assembly of believers, Karl Rahner says:

> was founded in the first place by the fact that Jesus is the person whom the believers professed to be the absolute saviour and to be God's historically irreversible and historically tangible offer of himself and by the fact that he would not be who he is if the offer of himself which

---

[17] Ibid., 86.

[18] Edmund Hill, "Church," *The New Dictionary of Theology*, ed. Joseph Komonchak et al. (Wilmington: Michael Glazier, 1987), 187.

[19] Kevin Giles, *What on Earth is the Church?* 115.

God made in him did not continue to remain present in the world in an historically tangible profession of faith in Jesus.[20]

Hence, the term *ekklesia*, church, used in a religious context, can refer either to a particular assembly of believers or the universal assembly of believers in Jesus Christ. In each of these cases, whether referring to particular churches/assemblies or the universal church, Jesus is ever present and real to the gathered people.

The early Christians and the patristic era understood the term εκκλεσια or more particularly the extended εκκλεσια του θέου—the church of God—as a community of God's people, the new Israel of God, gathered in the name of Jesus Christ, the new Moses.[21] This ecclesiology can be appreciated against the backdrop of the early church's struggles with persecution, in the self-understanding of its mission to the Greco-Roman world, and in the light of controversies and heretical teachings that were prevalent in their time. Interestingly, the fathers of the church used New Testament images to underscore the meaning and nature of the church. For example, Cyril of Jerusalem saw the church as a spiritual society that God called into existence to replace the Jewish people.[22] St. John of Chrysostom saw the church as the bride whom Christ has won for himself at the price of his own blood.[23]

At this juncture, we are going to make a considerable leap from the early church era to the modern understanding of the meaning, nature, and mission of the church. We make the leap not because there was no detailed ecclesiology during the intervening period. The period in question is not germane to this work. Suffice it to point out that there was a great deal of theological discourse in the intervening period, which greatly impacted our contemporary understanding of the nature and mission of the church. During this intervening period, emphasis was placed on the church as the divinely authorized social and juridical means of communicating Christ's salvation to human beings.[24] Consequently, the church at this period became a "highly structured organization centered on the papacy, for which increasingly the claims of primacy and supremacy were made."[25] In

---

[20] Karl Rahner, *Foundations of Christian Faith: An Introduction to the Idea of Christianity*, trans. William V. Dych (New York: Crossroad, 1978), 329-330.

[21] Ibid., 239.

[22] John N. D. Kelly, *Early Christian Doctrines*, Revised edition (New York: HarperCollins Publishers, 1978), 401.

[23] Ibid., 408.

[24] Dennis M. Doyle and F. X. Lawlor, "Church, II: Theology of," *New Catholic Encyclopedia*, 2nd ed., vol. 3, eds. Berard L. Marthaler et al (Washington: Gale Group, 2003), 588.

[25] Eric G. Jay, *The Church: Its Changing Image*, 97.

addition, the Augustinian ecclesiology of the church as the mystical body of Christ dominated the intervening period.[26]

In the sixteenth century, the celebrated theologian Robert Bellarmine (1542-1621) offered a definition of the church as: "The community of men brought together by the profession of the same Christian faith and conjoined in the communion of the same sacraments, under the government of the legitimate pastor and especially the one Vicar of Christ on earth, the Roman pontiff." [27] For a long period, Bellarmine's definition of the church held sway and influenced the church's ecclesiology and mission.

Bellarmine's definition of the church has faced a number of criticisms. For example, his definition constricts the church's nature and mission. His definition excludes many people from membership of the church. As Dulles rightly notes, Bellarmine's definition excludes pagans, Moslems, Jews, heretics, catechumens, and Christians who do not recognize the pope as the visible head of the church. Thus, only faithful Roman Catholics and churches in communion with the papacy are members of the true church.[28]

The First Vatican Council's (1869-1870) strict juridical and hierarchical view of the church was replaced by the Second Vatican Council's (1962-1965) new understanding of *ekklesia*. While avoiding a juridical definition of the church, the council sought to emphasize the supernatural character of the church when it referred to the church as a mystery.[29] In defining the church as a mystery, the council thus assents to the divine constitution of the church. *Lumen Gentium* asserts:

> The Father . . . planned to assemble in the holy Church all those who would believe in Christ. Already from the beginning of the world the foreshadowing of the Church took place. She was prepared for in a remarkable way throughout the history of the people of Israel and by means of the Old Covenant. Established in the present era of time, the Church was made manifest by the outpouring of the Spirit.[30]

---

[26] Ibid., 102.

[27] Cited in Avery Dulles, *Models of the Church*, Expanded edition (New York: Doubleday, 2002), 8.

[28] Ibid.. It is worth noting that the document *Dominus Iesus* issued by the Congregation for the Doctrine of the Faith in 2000 echoes Bellarmine's points when it contends that there exists a single Church of Christ, which subsists in the Catholic Church, governed by the successor of Peter and by the bishops in communion with him. Joseph Cardinal Ratzinger, *Dominus Iesus* (Boston: Pauline Books and Media, 2000), # 17.

[29] *Lumen Gentium*, # 1.

[30] Ibid. #5.

The council further states, "The mystery of the holy church is manifest in her very foundation, for the Lord Jesus inaugurated her by preaching the good news, that is, the coming of God's kingdom, which, for centuries, had been promised in the Scriptures."[31] At the same time, the church is a community of believers bound together in God by one faith in Jesus Christ through the Holy Spirit. The church is "a kind of sacrament or sign of intimate union with God, and of the unity of all mankind. She is also an instrument for the achievement of such union and unity."[32]

It is precisely because the reality of the term church eludes a single definition that Vatican II referred to the church as mystery. However, there is no consensus among theologians as to what is implied by Vatican II's definition of the church as "mystery." Dulles understands mysteries as realities of which we cannot speak directly. Therefore, to speak about the church one must, as Dulles says, "Draw on analogies afforded by our experience of the world . . . . By attending to the analogies and utilizing them as models, we can indirectly grow in our understanding of the Church."[33] Dulles further argues that the use of the term mystery to designate the church implies that it "is not fully intelligible to the finite mind of man, and that the reason for this lack of intelligibility is not the poverty but the richness of the Church itself."[34]

On one hand, Archbishop Bruno Forte, a member of the International Theological Commission, argues that the church is a mystery, because "it is not reducible to sociological categories, because it bears within itself the signs of the amazing encounter between the world of the Spirit and the world of humankind."[35] Archbishop Forte's argument clearly indicates that although the church is a mystery, it is contemporaneously located in human history and culture and, therefore, bound by the realities of space and time.

On the other hand, the theologian Kevin Giles argues that the church "is not above history, devoid of sociological form, or without 'tares' mixed with wheat, but with the passing of time, these aspects of the Church in the world became more accentuated and at times seemed almost to obscure the theological definition of the church as the body of Christ."[36] In other words, human beings are constituent parts of the mystery of the church, bound together by one faith in Jesus Christ. The church, Giles further notes, "is a community of believers, who, as individuals, carry their faith with them as persons, and who, whether in actual physical assembly for

---

[31] Ibid.
[32] Ibid.
[33] Avery Dulles, *Models of the Church*, 2.
[34] Ibid., 10.
[35] Bruno Forte, *The Church: Icon of the Trinity* (Boston: St. Paul, 1991), 64.
[36] Kevin Giles, *What on Earth is the Church?* 194.

the Eucharist or not, are viewed as forming a unity through the identity of their religious beliefs and aspirations of conduct."[37]

It is important to point out that the mysterious character and nature of the church does not mean that nothing more can be said on the topic. The understanding of the church as a mystery means that "it is a reality indeed imbued with the hidden presence of God. It lies therefore, within the very nature of the church to be always open to new and ever greater exploration."[38] We can always gain new insights through further exploration. The church is a living institution, always evolving and reforming itself. It leaves room for Christians of every age to gain their own understanding of the church's meaning, nature, and mission within the ambient of their history and culture.

For Joseph Komonchak, the key issue with regard to the mysterious nature of the church is where, in whom, and how the mystery of the church is realized.[39] In answering these questions, Komonchak contends that Vatican II in effect adopted various images. Quoting Giuseppe Colombo, Komonchak argues that the notion of mystery requires both reference to Christ and the effort to identify its social and historical referents.[40] The International Theological Commission in its report published before the Synod of Bishops in 1985 accentuated this notion when it says: "The character of 'mystery' designates the Church insofar as it derives from the Trinity; the character of 'historical subject' belongs to the Church insofar as it acts in history and contributes to its direction."[41]

The church is also described as a paradox. According to the French theologian Henri de Lubac, the church is composed of both visible and invisible elements. It is temporal and spiritual, divine and human, saints and sinners; it is both an object of faith and sociological inquiry.[42] Hence, the church is not only a mystery but a paradox. De Lubac surmises that the Gospel is replete with paradoxes; for example, the church is said to be holy, yet it is full of sinners. De Lubac, nevertheless, concedes that the nature of the church as mystery offers more theological grounding than its paradoxical nature: "The Church is a mystery for all time out of man's grasp because, qualitatively, it is totally removed from all other

---

[37] Ibid.

[38] Yves Congar and D. O'Hanlon, eds., *Council Speeches of Vatican II* (New York: Paulist Press, 1964), 26.

[39] Joseph Komonchak, "The Synod of 1985 and the Notion of the Church," *Chicago Studies*, vol. 26, (1987): 337.

[40] Ibid.

[41] Ibid., 337-338.

[42] Henri de Lubac, *The Church: Paradox and Mystery*, trans. James R. Dunne (New York: Alba House, 1969), 4.

objects of man's knowledge that might be mentioned. And yet, at the same time, it concerns us, touches us, acts in us, and reveals us to ourselves."[43]

The understanding of the church as a mystery reminds us that the church is not purely a human contrivance but has divine foundation. Since the divine cannot be circumscribed, the church must be open to new ideas and insights. The question of "a made-to-fit-all" or a uniform understanding of church runs contrary to its very nature. This understanding informs my quest to postulate an African model that would further accentuate the mysterious nature of the church and Africans' unique understanding of *ekklesia* in the twenty-first century.

Use of Images in Understanding the Meaning of the Term Church

As indicated earlier, no single definition can adequately express or encapsulate the reality of what we call the church. Recognition of the limitedness of a single or an all-embracing definition led the Vatican II Council into defining the church as a mystery. Because the church is a mystery, the ensemble of its nature, depths, and character eludes the human mind. However, with the use of images or models, some insights can be gained as to the meaning of the nature, character, and mission of the church. "Any reality that is inherently a mystery will demand for its perception the awakening of the imagination. So will any reality whose existence is a sign, however ambiguous, of the operation of invisible demonic or divine forces."[44] Therefore, the church in its efforts to further its self-understanding employs several images to make its nature, mission, and character comprehensible.

Images serve a variety of functions in language and theology. First, images serve as rhetorical tools designed to help people describe and convey an impression concerning something that is either known or unknown. In other words, images are like analogies or metaphors, which constitute an efficient way of communicating social values, political attitudes, religious beliefs, etc.[45] Second, images help us perceive a given reality in symbolic terms, especially when the nature of this reality is not easily apprehended by the mind.

Images also function as symbols. An image becomes a symbol if it moves from being a merely logical comparison to awakening feeling or affectivity. In this vein, Bernard Lonergan holds that a symbol is "an image of a real or imaginary object

---

[43] Ibid., 4.

[44] Paul S. Minear, *Images of the Church in the New Testament*, 22.

[45] Marie E. Lassen, "The Roman Family: Ideal and Metaphor," *Constructing Early Christian Families: Family and Social Reality and Metaphor*, Moxnes Halvor, ed. (London: Routledge, 1997), 103.

that evokes a feeling or is evoked by a feeling."[46] A symbol may also function as a model, especially if it helps explain further the meaning of something that is not fully intelligible. Reflecting on the interplay between image and model, Dulles opines that when an image is employed reflectively and critically to deepen one's theoretical understanding of a reality it becomes a model.[47] Theologically, images and models project, integrate and conceptualize our varied insights and understanding of the mystery of the church.[48] In view of the interplay between images and models, I am going to use the two terms interchangeably to denote one and the same reality.

Different ages emphasize different aspects of the church in their quest to understand the nature and mission of the church. "In every age a particular view of the Church is expressed by the Church in practice, and given conceptual form, *post hoc* or *ante hoc*, by the theologians of the age."[49] A cursory look at the history of the church substantiates this view. For example, the early Christians used metaphorical language in articulating the fundamental Christian concepts and beliefs. They adopted metaphors stemming from different strata of life such as: pilgrimage, slavery, and warfare.[50] The early Christians often called themselves "the saints" (Acts 9:13, 32, 41, 26:10), the "community of God," "body of Christ," etc.[51] Second-century apologists, with the exception of Justin, rarely used the term *ekklesia*. Their preoccupation was centered on the one God and the central place Christ occupies in the mystery of salvation. It was only with the later fathers that attention began to be focused on the church.[52]

As the church suffered persecution by and opposition from the secular state, its image shifted. The church was called various names: militants, wayfarers, elect, pilgrims, etc. During the reign of Emperor Constantine in the fourth century, when the church became stable and free from persecution in the Greco-Roman world, there was also a shift in the self-image the church projected to the world. The church became an institution.

It is pertinent to underscore the fact that the different understandings of the nature and character of the church by a particular age do not indicate that the church is always in a state of flux. There is, as Hans Küng correctly notes, "a constant factor in the various changing historical images of the Church, something which survives however much the history of mankind, of the Church and of theology may

---

[46] Bernard Lonergan, *Method in Theology* (Toronto: University of Toronto Press, 1979), 64.
[47] Avery Dulles, *Models of the Church*, 15.
[48] Peter Osuchukwu, *The Spirit of Umunna*, 112.
[49] Hans Küng, *The Church*, 4.
[50] Marie E. Lassen, *The Roman Family*, 103.
[51] Karl Rahner, *Foundations of Christian Faith*, 336.
[52] Hans Küng, *The Church*, 6.

vary." This constant factor, Küng says, is revealed in change; its identity exists only in variability, its continuity only in changing circumstances, its permanence only in the varying outward appearances.[53]

Hermeneutical Review of Images of the Church

Paul Minear, in his *Images of the Church in the New Testament*, identifies nearly one hundred images of the church in the New Testament.[54] Over the centuries, some of these images have gained more currency and dominance than other images. In this section, I am going to examine a few of the predominant images. The factor that informs my selection of these images is that they provide the framework of the church's ecclesiology and missiology.

The Church as the People of God

Vatican II Council's dogmatic Constitution on the Church (*Lumen Gentium*) devoted its second chapter to the image of the church as the *People of God*. This image is distinctively biblical with deep roots in the Old Testament. The Old Testament refers to Israel as the עם יהוה (*am Yahweh*). The Septuagint (LXX) translates *Am Yahweh* as *laos theou*, to denote the people of God, not in the sense of population or mass of people, but in the sense of nation or national community.[55] An exegesis of *Am* or *laos* shows that it is used in the Old Testament in a restrictive sense to refer specifically to the people of Israel in their relationship with God as his chosen people.[56] In his promise to deliver Israel from bondage, God said to the people of Israel, "I am the Lord. I will free you from the forced labor of the Egyptians and will deliver you from their slavery. I will rescue you by my outstretched arm and with mighty acts of judgment. I will take you as my own people, and you shall have me as your God" (Exod. 6: 6-7).

---

[53] Ibid.

[54] Paul Minear, *Images of the Church*, 66. These images among others include The Salt of the Earth (Matt.5:13), A Letter from Christ (2 Cor. 3:2-3), Fish and Fish Net (Luke 5:1-11), The Boat (Matt. 8:23-27), The Ark (Matt. 24:36-42, 2 Peter 2:4-10), Unleavened Bread (Matt. 16:6, 1 Cor.5:7), Branches of the Vine (John 15), The Fig Tree (Luke13:6-9), God's Planting and God's Building (1 Cor. 3:9), Building on a Rock (Matt. 16:18-19), Bride of Christ (2 Cor. 11:1f), The Wedding Feast (Rev. 19:9, Mark 2:19, Matt. 22:1-10), The People of God (1 Peter 2:9-10), A Holy Nation (1 Pet. 2:9), and so forth.

[55] Hans Küng, *The Church*, 116.

[56] Ibid.

IMAGES OF THE CHURCH

The special position of Israel is reiterated after Israel's deliverance from Egypt when God said to Moses, "Thus shall you say to the house of Jacob (Israel); tell the Israelites: You have seen for yourselves how I treated the Egyptians and how I bore you upon eagle wings and brought you here to myself. Therefore, if you hearken to my voice and keep my covenant, you shall be my special possession, dearer to me than all other people, though all the earth is mine. You shall be to me a kingdom of priests, a holy nation" (Exod. 19:3-6 see also Lev. 26:12).

The perception of the Israelites as the people of God, it could be argued, establishes the foundational framework of Judaism and the history of Israel as a nation. Israel's faith, Küng contends, is summed up thus: "Yahweh is the God of Israel and Israel is the people of Yahweh. This is true from the moment when Israel was led out of Egypt by God's merciful call and came to see itself as a national and religious unity."[57]

The New Testament understanding of Israel's choice as the people of God can be better appreciated and understood within the context of Christianity's salvation history. Christian salvation history began when God chose Israel as God's people. From them a savior was born, and a new people of God came into being.

In the New Testament, we find a fundamental shift from the use of λάόσ *(laos)* "people" exclusively for the Israelites to a fellowship of Jews and gentiles who are bound together through common faith in Christ Jesus. New Testament authors appropriated the title *People of God* to refer to believers in Christ irrespective of their nationality.[58]

The Jerusalem Council (Acts 15) supports the idea that non-Jews were also considered People of God. In his summation during the council, Paul avers, "Symeon has described how God first concerned himself with acquiring from among the Gentiles a people for his name" (Acts 15:14). The implication of this is that the People of God are now constituted not by being a descendant of Abraham or by circumcision but by being a member of the community of those who have been redeemed and for whom there is no further obstacle in their relationship to God.[59] Thus, membership in the People of God was no longer by circumcision as required by the covenant God enacted with Abraham but by faith and baptism in Christ.

The author of the *First Epistle of Peter* applies the prerogatives of ancient Israel to the Christian community in the church. "But you are a 'chosen race' *(genos eklekton)*, a royal priesthood, a holy nation *(ethnos hagion)*, a people of his own so that you may announce the praises of him who called you out of darkness into his wonderful light. Once you were 'no people' but now you are God's people" (1 Pet. 2:9-10; cf. Rom. 9:25-26).

---

[57] Hans Küng, *The Church*, 116.
[58] Kevin Giles, *What on Earth is the Church?* 11.
[59] Peter Osuchukwu, *The Spirit of Umunna*, 98.

THE CHURCH AS THE EXTENDED FAMILY OF GOD

Some fathers of the church equally emphasized the image of the church as the People of God. Melito of Sardis (c. AD 180), in his *Homily on the Pasch*, describes how the church is the realization of the new People of God, thus displacing Israel:

> As it is in corruptible images, so it is in incorruptible; as it is in the earthly, so it is in the heavenly. For the Lord's salvation and truth have been prefigured in the people, and the teachings of the Gospel have been proclaimed in the Law. The people were the outline of the plan, and the Law a draft of the parable, but the Gospel is the Law explained and fulfilled, and the Church is the receptacle of truth. The model, then, was of value before the reality, and the prefigured was splendid before its fulfillment. That is to say, the people was [sic] important before the Church emerged, and the Law was remarkable before the Gospel shed its light. But when the Church was built, and the Gospel preached, the figure was emptied of its meaning, after it had been translated into truth, and Law was likewise emptied, after it was translated into the Gospel. Just as the figure becomes redundant when it transmits its image to reality, and the prefigure is made void when it is illuminated by explanation, so also the Law reached its term when the Gospel came to light, and the people went into oblivion when the Church came into existence.[60]

Origen (185-254?), another father of the church, expressed similar views on how the church is the new People of God: "You, therefore, O people of Israel, who are 'the portion of God' who were made 'the lot of His inheritance,' 'shall not have' it says, 'other gods besides me' (Exod. 20:3) . . . but do not think that these words are spoken only to that 'Israel' which is according to the flesh . . . these words are addressed much more to you who were made Israel spiritually by living for God, who were circumcised, not in the flesh, but in heart. For although we are Gentiles in the flesh, we are Israel in spirit."[61]

It is worth noting that many of the fathers interpreted the image of the new people of God narrowly, to the point of excoriating the Jews who were the original people of God. The Old Israel was viewed as lawless and even accused of deicide—murdering the Son of God.[62]

---

[60] Melito of Sardis, *Homily on the Pasch*. Cited in Thomas Halton, *The Church: Messages of the Fathers of the Church* (Wilmington: Michael Glazier, 1985), 63-64.

[61] Ibid., 69.

[62] Ibid., 65. Melito of Sardis is regarded as the first person to accuse Jews of committing deicide for killing Jesus. See his *Homily on the Pasch*.

The fathers of Vatican II adopted the Old and New Testament imagery of the People of God to further accentuate the ecclesiology of the mystery of the church. The council fathers taught that there is a spiritual bond linking the people of the New Covenant (church) with Abraham's stock (Israel).[63] According to the council, the Church of Christ acknowledges that the beginnings of her faith and her election are already found among the patriarch, Moses, and the prophets. The church professes that all who believe in Christ, Abraham's sons and daughters according to faith (cf. Gal. 3:7), are included in the same patriarch's call and, likewise, that the salvation of the church was mystically foreshadowed by the chosen people's exodus from the land of bondage.[64] Vatican II council teaches:

> The Church, therefore, cannot forget that it received the revelation of the Old Testament through the people with whom God in his inexpressible mercy deigned to establish the Ancient Covenant. Nor can it forget that it draws sustenance from the root of that good olive tree onto which have been grafted the wild olive branches of the Gentiles. Besides, the Church recalls too that from the Jewish people sprang the apostles, its foundation stones and pillars, as well as most of the early disciples who proclaimed Christ to the world.[65]

From the affirmation of its roots in Judaism, the council fathers went on to teach that the church, which constitutes the new people of God, "subsists" in the Catholic Church, which is governed by the successor of Peter and by the bishops.[66] This new People of God also share in Christ's prophetic, priestly, and kingly offices.[67] In teaching that the Church of Christ "subsists in" the Catholic Church, Vatican II makes a fundamental shift in Catholic ecclesiology. Prior to Vatican II, the Roman Catholic Church had taught that the Church of Christ is "in" the Catholic Church.

The use of the phrase "subsists in" was a watershed in ecumenism. It marked a remarkable shift from the original identification of the Church of Christ with the Roman Catholic Church. Nevertheless, the precise meaning of what "subsists in" means is still a subject of debate in Catholic ecclesiology. Contributing to the debate of what "subsists in" means, Dulles remarks that the meaning is presumably that the Church of Christ is truly present in its essential completeness in the Catholic Church, but that there is some discrepancy, so that "the Roman Catholic Church, as a sociological entity, remains under an obligation to become more perfectly

---

[63] Vatican II, *Nostra Aetate*, # 4.
[64] Ibid.
[65] Ibid.
[66] *Lumen Gentium*, # 8.
[67] Ibid., # 12.

one."[68] Similarly, Daniel Donovan argues that prior to Vatican II, the tendency among Catholics since the Reformation was to think of themselves as the one true church and to deny any ecclesial significance to Protestant communities.[69] However, the shift in Catholic ecclesiology led to the affirmation that the Church of Christ "is" not the same as the Roman Catholic Church but rather "subsists in" it. It equally opened a new vista for ecumenical dialogue with other ecclesial communities.

The hermeneutical analysis of the image of the church as the *People of God* reveals its Jewish foundation. The new People of God are those who, in the same sense as Israel, were called by God and are constituted by a common faith in Christ. God invites all to become members, but as human beings endowed with free will, we can either reject or accept the invitation. Membership of this new People of God is by choice. It is not a question of our being a chosen People of God but of our being a choosing people. In this case, we make a choice to be either members of the choosing people or otherwise.

The image of the People of God raises a number of questions and limitations. First, the church uses the same Old Testament imagery to describe both the historical, ethnic, and religious Jewish entity and the new people (Christians) who profess faith in Jesus. To some critics, the image conjures the image of an amorphous crowd or, at best, refers to the laity alone in the church. However, as Walter Kasper argues, the image of the church as the *People of God* does not refer to the laity alone as distinct from the clergy. The image constitutes an organic structure of the church, the people gathered around their bishop and attached to their shepherd.[70]

The identification of a particular group of people as the *People of God* is tantamount to excluding some people as not belonging to the church. Minear is right when he says, "To identify a particular society as the people of God is immediately to set it over and against all other people. This people and it alone has been constituted in a special way by God's action."[71] If a particular group of people is regarded as the people of God, what would the rest of the people be called? Obviously, all peoples—Moslems, Jews, Christians, Hindus, Buddhists, Animists, etc.—are people of God because one God created them. The image, therefore, does not adequately mirror the totality of God's people nor does it promote ecumenism and unity of the human race with whom God entered into a covenant (Gen. 8-9). Besides, the image of the church as the *People of God* arrogates Israel's identity to Christians.

---

[68] Avery Dulles, *Models of the Church*, 118.

[69] Daniel Donovan, *The Church as Idea and Fact* (Wilmington, Delaware: Michael Glazier, 1988), 78.

[70] Walter Kasper, *Theology and Church* (London: SCM Press, 1989), 162.

[71] Paul Minear, *Images of the Church*, 68.

The Church as a Communion

Johann Mohler[72] is regarded as playing a central role in the development of the image of the *Church as a Communion*. Mohler revived this image in the nineteenth century in reaction to the hierarchical institutional model of the church.[73] Other theologians who contributed to the development of this image include Yves Congar, Henri de Lubac, Karl Rahner, and Jerome Hamer. The image of church as a communion appropriates other biblical images like Body of Christ, People of God, etc., to accentuate and illuminate further the mysterious character of the church. The image also played a pivotal role in the ecclesiology of the Vatican II Council and the Extraordinary Synod of Bishops of 1985.

Derived from the Greek κόιηόηιά *(koinonia)*, meaning "participation" or "share," and Latin *communio*, the church as communion is one of the prevalent images in Catholic ecclesiology. But precisely what this concept means has been a subject of debate. The debate has led to a consequent development of the concept in many directions. Basically, this image emphasizes that the church is a fellowship between human beings and God.[74] Its centrifugal point, therefore, is toward a communion that revolves around the relationships between the three persons of the Trinity, human beings, communion of Saints, the relationship between bishops dispersed throughout the world, and the dynamic interplay between the universal church and particular churches.[75] It can also mean a sharing of gifts or a mutual exchange of gifts within the Church of Christ. It can equally mean a sense of solidarity or collaboration among particular churches as envisaged in the Pauline epistles (see I Cor. 10:6ff).

One of the advocates of Communion ecclesiology, Jerome Hamer, rejects Bellarmine's definition of the church because of its juridical and institutional undertones. Harmer argues that the mystical body of Christ is "a communion which is at once inward and external, an inner communion of spiritual life signified and engendered by an external communion in profession of the faith, discipline and

---

[72] Johann Adam Mohler (1796-1838), *Unity in the Church*, trans. Peter C. Erb (Washington D.C.: The Catholic University of America Press, 1996), 194-196 [German original: Mainz, 1825]. Mohler lays out his perspectives on the unity of the Church and communion ecclesiology. Mohler wrote against the backdrop of the medieval understanding of the Church in juridical and institutional senses. Mohler strongly believed that the Church as a living organism should have diverse elements; hence, he argued against the imposition of a rigid uniformity in the Church.

[73] Avery Dulles, *Models of the Church*, 42.

[74] Dennis M. Doyle, *Communion Ecclesiology* (New York: Orbis Books, 2000), 13.

[75] Ibid., 12.

the sacramental life."[76] Hamer, in essence, is saying that the church is not just an assembly of human beings, but over and above this, the church is a fellowship between God, saints, angels (invisible), and human beings (visible).[77] Hamer rejects the idea of treating the church as a merely human or rather a sociological reality. He maintains that the image of the church as a communion brings to the fore the mystical and transcendental elements of the church.[78]

Some advocates of communion ecclesiology contend that the communion image will lead to a recovery of the early Christians' understanding of the church, in which each particular church/patriarchate was in communion with other churches. Anne Carr is of the view that "there was no single 'early church' but rather a plurality of churches/communities. All were one in their confession of faith in Christ, but each had its own particular form and distinctive self-understanding."[79] Each Christian community had its liturgy, rules, and regulations. There was no uniform ecclesiology and liturgy operative at the time. Churches in particular regions formed patriarchates and were autonomous. Each patriarchate saw itself as *unus inter pares* with other patriarchates. They nevertheless turned to one another for support and advice when the need arose.

Hermann Pottmeyer argues that the early church fathers understood the universal church to be a community of, or a communion of, churches (*communio ecclesiarum*). The fathers, he says, "saw each individual church not simply as a part of the universal church, but as itself truly church." As such, each church was "a member of the communion of churches that manifests itself in the communion of the bishops with each other and with the pope, that is, in the college of bishops."[80] This communion was the source of collegiality of bishops with the bishop of Rome. For Pottmeyer, therefore, the underlying hallmark of *Communio* is that it "signifies a community of people who share with one another . . . a *common* faith, and therefore a *common* hope and (ideally) a *common* charity."[81]

Proponents of this stream of thoughts argue that as a fellowship of believers, the image of the church as a *Communio* promotes diversity of theology, liturgy, and mission. They also hold that communion ecclesiology should lead to the decentralization of papal authority and its power of governance over the universal

---

[76] Jerome Harmer, *The Church Is a Communion* (New York: Sheed & Ward, 1964), 93.

[77] Ibid., 159.

[78] Dennis M. Doyle, *Communion Ecclesiology*, 15.

[79] Anne E. Carr, *Transforming Grace* (New York: The Continuum Publishing Co., 1998), 195.

[80] Hermann J. Pottmeyer, *Towards a Papacy in Communion: Perspectives from Vatican Councils I & II*, trans. Matthew J. O'Connell (New York: Crossroad Pub. Co., 1998), 118.

[81] Ibid., 119.

church. This position informs their call for a return to the early church model of communion ecclesiology. Pottmeyer argues that such a change would:

> Move beyond centralization to a restoration of the communion of churches within the unity of the universal church." This communion, Pottmeyer went on to say, has a threefold meaning: "*soteriological*—the communion of the redeemed with God through Jesus Christ in the Holy Spirit; *sacramental—theological*-the communion of the body of Christ, the church, through sharing in word and sacrament, and, in particular, through sharing in the Eucharistic body of Christ; and *ecclesiological*—the communion of the churches and the communion of the faithful.[82]

The Vatican II Council expressed a multifaceted vision of "communion." On one hand, while avoiding a juridical definition of the church, the council emphasized the mystical communion of the people of God, bound together by love. To be a member of the church is to share in the love of the Trinity.[83] Explaining the nature of the mystical communion of the people of God, the council states, "It follows that among all the nations of earth there is but one People of God, which takes its citizens from every race, making them citizens of a kingdom that is of a heavenly and not of an earthly nature. For all the faithful scattered throughout the world are in communion with each other in the Holy Spirit, so that 'he who occupies the See of Rome knows the people of India are his members.'"[84] The council goes further to teach:

> By divine Providence it has come about that various churches established in diverse places by the apostles and their successors have in the course of time coalesced into several groups, organically united, which, preserving the unity of faith and the unique divine constitution of the universal Church, enjoy their own discipline, their own liturgical usage, and their own theological and spiritual heritage. Some of these churches, notably the ancient patriarchal churches, as parent-stocks of the faith, so to speak, have begotten others as daughter churches. With these they are connected down to our own time by a close bond of charity in their sacramental life and in their mutual respect for rights and duties. This variety of local churches with one common aspiration is particularly splendid evidence of the catholicity of the undivided Church.[85]

---

[82] Ibid.
[83] Dennis M. Doyle, *Communion Ecclesiology*, 74.
[84] *Lumen Gentium*, #13.
[85] Ibid., #23.

On the other hand, while espousing the communion that exists between individual bishops and the pope, the council held that bishops who govern these particular churches are not simply vicars of the pope. "Bishops," the council says, "have succeeded to the place of the apostles as shepherds of the church, and that he who hears them, hears Christ."[86] Nevertheless, the council taught that the exercise of the office of the bishop can only be done within the ambience of a hierarchical communion with the universal head of the church—the pope.[87] Therefore, for Vatican II, on one hand, particular churches exist in communion, and, on the other hand, the essential element of full incorporation into the church is the bond of ecclesiastical government exercised in collegial communion.[88]

At any rate, the church as *Communio* is not coterminous with exercise of authority in the church. The ecclesiology of the church as a *Communio* cannot be reduced to purely organizational or structural or, rather, to questions of power and authority. The ecclesiology of Communion ought to serve as a foundation for order, unity and diversity in the church. Besides the visible communion that exists between the different members of the particular churches, the mystical communion or bond is not just a sociological or anthropological reality. The church as *Communio* transcends the visible world. The church as a *Communio* embodies not only those who are still living but also those who have gone before us and have been marked with the sign of faith—the saints.[89]

The image of the church as a communion has major implications for communion ecclesiology and missiology. If *Communio* is strictly understood to mean a fellowship of churches, the image holds a great appeal to ecumenical dialogue and diversity that ought to exist within a unity.

The image is well grounded in patristic tradition and offers a model for church structures and interrelationship, particularly between the universal church and local churches. The image could also serve as a point of departure (*terminus a quo*) for ecumenical dialogue between different churches. Nevertheless, there are obstacles that need to be surmounted.

Although Vatican II's teaching that other ecclesial bodies and churches may contain elements of salvation[90] marked a fundamental shift from previous ecclesiologies, the council's teaching, nevertheless, creates a hydra-headed difficulty for ecumenical dialogue. The problem is further exacerbated by the narrow interpretation of *Communio* in the document *Dominus Iesus*, issued by the Sacred Congregation for the Doctrine of the Faith in 2000. The document, among

---

[86] Ibid., # 20.

[87] Ibid., # 21-23.

[88] Ibid., # 13.

[89] Ibid., # 50. The council devoted the whole of chapter 7 to discussing the mystical communion that exists between the living and dead (saints) members of the church.

[90] *Lumen Gentium*, # 8.

other things, declared that many Christian denominations are not churches in the proper sense. In the words of the document:

> There exists a single Church of Christ, which subsists in the Catholic Church, governed by the Successor of Peter and by the Bishops in communion with him. The Churches, which while not existing in perfect communion with the Catholic Church remain united to her by means of the closest bonds, that is, by apostolic succession and a valid Eucharist, are true particular Churches. On the other hand, ecclesial communities, which have not preserved the valid Episcopate and the genuine and integral substance of the Eucharistic mystery, are not Churches in the proper sense; however, those who are baptized in these communities are, by Baptism, incorporated in Christ and thus are in a certain communion, albeit imperfect, with the Church.[91]

One is left to wonder how these ecclesial bodies, which are not regarded as churches, can enter into authentic ecumenical dialogue with the Catholic Church. *Dominus Iesus* is a step backward in the Christian ecumenism envisaged by Vatican II Council.

Despite Vatican II's emphasis on communion and participation, there has been an unprecedented increase in the ecclesiastical bureaucracy and centralization of power and authority in the church, which has arguably stifled the essence of communion ecclesiology. Joseph Komonchak is right when he remarks that the traditional episcopal structures of governance have been supplemented by the authority of various kinds of "professionals" in the Vatican.[92]

The Church as the Bride of Christ

The Second Vatican Council adopted the image of the *Church as the Bride of Christ* in discussing the nature of the mystery of the church. The council, quoting the book of Revelation, refers to the church as "the spotless spouse of the spotless Lamb."[93] The Bride of Christ imagery is analogously derived from the Old Testament reference of Israel as the "bride" or "wife" of God. Old Testament prophets like Hosea, Jeremiah, Ezekiel, and Isaiah, while describing the type of relationship that exists between Yahweh and the people of Israel, sometimes used spousal imagery. An example of one of the passages that illustrates the spousal parallel the prophets drew upon in their perception of God's relationship with Israel was when Isaiah

---

[91] Joseph Cardinal Ratzinger, *Dominus Iesus*, #17.
[92] Joseph Komonchak, *The Synod of 1985*, 336.
[93] *Lumen Gentium*, # 6.

specifically called God the husband of Israel: "Fear not, you shall not be put to shame; you need not blush, for you shall not be disgraced. The shame of your youth you shall forget, the reproach of your widowhood no longer remember. For he who has become your husband is your Maker; his name is the Lord of host; Your redeemer is the Holy One of Israel, called God of all the earth" (Isa. 54: 4-5). Other references of Israel as the bride/wife of God include Jeremiah 2:2-3; 3ff; Hosea 2:19; Isaiah 54:1-8, 10; 62:4-5; Ezekiel 16:23f; and Malachi 2:14.

The New Testament uses the bridal image to explain the nature of the church, which has become the new People of God. The author of the Gospel of Mark referred to Jesus, the head of his church, as the bridegroom, and insofar as he is with his bride (church) and guests, they cannot be subjected to fasting (Mark 2-19).

In Pauline epistles, we find a more explicit and detailed use of the image of marital relationship to the church. It is important to note here that the usage of this imagery is varied in the Pauline epistles. One clear use of this image in an ecclesiological sense is found in his second epistle to the Corinthians. Exhorting the Corinthian church, Paul wrote: "For I am jealous of you with the jealousy of God; since I have betrothed you to one husband to present you as a chaste virgin to Christ" (2 Cor. 11:2). Paul referred to the local church of Corinth as the bride of Christ and urged them to remain faithful. They were not to be seduced into "adultery" by accepting "another Jesus," "another spirit," or "another Gospel." Such disloyalty to her betrothed, Minear argued, "is tantamount to the temptation to which Eve succumbed. Behind this pattern of thought is the picture of Jesus, the husband."[94]

Paul in his epistle to the Ephesians compared the relation of the church to Christ with the ideal relation that should exist between a husband and wife. Paul urged wives to be submissive to their husbands. Husbands in return are to love their wives as Christ loved his bride, the church (Eph. 5:21-33). Paul sees the union of Christ and his church as a model for the union of a Christian husband and his wife.

Paul, by using the analogy of husband and wife, underscored the profound and intimate unity between Christ and the Christian community *ekklesia,* the church. "Christ so loved his Church that he gave his life for her. In the same manner, husbands should love their wives and be ready to give their lives for their brides."[95] Nevertheless, the relationship between Christ and the church and husband and wife constitutes, as Paul maintains, a *sacramentum magnum,* a great mystery.

John Paul II invokes the bride image as befitting not only for the church but also for women. While congratulating women on their great achievements in life, the pope reiterates the image of the church as the bride of Christ:

---

[94] Paul Minear, *Images of the Church,* 55.
[95] Kevin Giles, *What on Earth is the Church?* 144.

> This *image of spousal love,* together with the figure of the divine Bridegroom—a very clear image in the texts of the Prophets—finds crowning confirmation in the Letter to the Ephesians (5:23-32). *Christ* is greeted as the bridegroom by John the Baptist (cf. *Jn* 3:27-29). Indeed Christ applies to himself this comparison drawn from the Prophets (cf. *Mk* 2:19-20). The Apostle Paul, who is a bearer of the Old Testament heritage, writes to the Corinthians: "I feel a divine jealousy for you, for I betrothed you to Christ to present you as a pure bride to her one husband" (2 Cor. 11:2). But the fullest expression of the truth about Christ the Redeemer's love, according to the analogy of spousal love in marriage, is found in the Letter to the Ephesians: *"Christ loved the Church and gave himself up for her"* (5:25), thereby fully confirming the fact that the Church is the bride of Christ.[96]

The bridal image of the church, of all other images, is the most criticized. Critics argue that this image has served as a legitimizing tool for denying women their rights in the church. This image has helped to develop a patriarchal ideal. Since the husband is the "head" of the wife, a wife then must be submissive to her husband. This obviously creates sundry problems among married people. As Susan A. Ross says, "For too long the Christian churches have supported a hierarchical theology of marriage that has presumed the superiority of men over women and, in effect, has given men permission to abuse their wives and children. This theology has the additional disadvantage of freezing gender roles."[97] Consequently, the bridal model of the church does not promote the equality of all children of God.

Critics of the bridal model of the church, among other things, surmise that this model is responsible for gender inequality in the church. The bridal imagery has also been used to deny women ordination in the Catholic Church. The image inexorably continues to promote the all-male priesthood. The argument that only men can be icons of Christ and that priests act in *persona Christi* (in the person of Christ) raises a critical question of whether women are incapable of imaging the divine simply because they are women. Shirley William, a Catholic and former senior minister in the British Labor government, articulates this quagmire very clearly when she sadly notes that for too long, women have been stereotyped in

---

[96] John Paul II, Apostolic Letter, *Mulieris Dignitatem: On the Dignity and Vocation of Women on the Occasion of the Marian Year* (Boston: Pauline Books & Media, 1988), # 23.

[97] Susan A. Ross, "God's Embodiment and Women," *Freeing Theology: The Essentials of Theology in Feminist Perspective,* ed. Catherine M. LaCugna (San Francisco: HarperCollins Publisher, 1993), 202.

the church as saintly mothers or wicked temptresses.[98] William goes further to lament that "women's individual humanity has gone unrecognized. For too long the exploitation of women, their disproportionate suffering as victims of poverty, violence and sexual abuse, have been ignored by the Church. And even now, the pope does not consider women ontologically fit for the priesthood."[99]

The bride image of the church does not foster the kind of ecclesiology that would promote authentic propagation of the Gospel in Africa. Moreover, given the patriarchal nature of the African society and the unenviable track record of maltreatment of women, the image would rather exacerbate the oppression of women, becoming a ready tool for suppressing women's voices in the church and in the society.

The Church as Institution

The *Church as an Institution* is another dominant image that exerts tremendous influence in the ecclesiology of the church in all its ramifications. The image of the church as an institution has its offshoot from the understanding of the church as a community of believers gathered together under a visible head. According to Vatican II, the church has two forms: visible (men and women) and invisible (saints, angels, Trinity). The visible church, constituted and organized in the world as a society, subsists in the Catholic Church, which is governed by the successor of Peter and by the bishops in union with that successor.[100]

In recognizing the church as a society of believers, this image highlights the structure of government and its formal element in society. The image seeks to understand the nature of the church in terms of its visible structures, rights, and powers of governance.[101]

The development of the Institutional image dates back to the early period of the church. With the expulsion of the disciples from synagogues and Jewish communities, the early Christian communities separated from the Jewish society. They set up parallel organizational structures and organized themselves as a distinct society. Their allegiance was to God rather than to human beings (Acts 5:29).

It was with the fathers of the church that a formal and institutional structure began to emerge. St. Ignatius of Antioch (cf. 117), describing the central role of the bishop in the life of the church, wrote in his epistle to the church in Symrna:

---

[98] John Cornwell, *The Pontiff in Winter: Triumph and Conflict in the Reign of John Paul II* (New York: Double Day, 2004), 134.

[99] Ibid.

[100] *Lumen Gentium*, #8.

[101] Avery Dulles, *Models of the Church*, 27.

> See that ye all follow the bishop, even as Jesus Christ does the Father, and the presbytery as ye would the apostles; and reverence the deacons, as being the institution of God. Let no man do anything connected with the Church without the bishop. Let that be deemed a proper Eucharist, which is [administered] either by the bishop, or by one to whom he has entrusted it. Wherever the bishop shall appear, there let the multitude [of the people] also be (*ubi episcopus, ibi ecclesia*); even as, wherever Jesus Christ is, there is the Catholic Church. It is not lawful without the bishop either to baptize or to celebrate a love-feast; but whatsoever he shall approve of, that is also pleasing to God, so that everything that is done may be secure and valid. [102]

Correlated with Ignatius's argument on the central position of the bishop in the church is Cyprian of Carthage's summation that bishops constitute the visible sign of unity in the church. According to Cyprian, "The large body of bishops is joined by the bond of mutual concord and the chain of unity . . . it must be understood that the bishop is in the Church and the Church in the bishop and he is not in the Church who is not with the bishop."[103]

It is pertinent to note that the early church's form of institutional structure and governance was different from the present day structure. In the beginning, the institutional structures were rudimentary and loose.[104] By the middle of first century, different churches that were in existence (e.g., Pauline, Petrine, Johannine, etc.) appear to have been institutionally structured with the adoption of such offices as *episkopos* (an overseer or superintendent of the community), *presbyteroi (*elders), and *diakonoi* (servants). These offices, though secular in character, constituted the leadership of the church.[105]

From the patristic period to Vatican I, the institutional model of the church held sway. Various councils and popes promoted and entrenched an institutionalized church. For example, by the middle ages, there were developments in laws and reforms especially by Pope Gregory VII, which led to a more juridical and institutional understanding of the church. However, Vatican Council I (1869-1870) clearly defined the nature and scope of the institutional image of the church. The council, in its dogmatic constitution, clearly asserts that the church is a perfect

---

[102] Ignatius of Antioch, *The Epistle to the Symrnaeans VIII. 2.* http://www.newadvent.org/fathers/0109.htm (accessed, July 11, 2009). Emphasis mine.

[103] Cyprian of Carthage. *Epistle Lxviii. 8* http://www.newadvent.org/fathers/0506.htm (accessed July 11, 2009).

[104] Avery Dulles, *A Church to Believe in: Discipleship and the Dynamics of Freedom* (New York: Crossroad, 1987), 31.

[105] Edmund Hill, "Church," *The New Dictionary of Theology,* 191.

society primarily because the Lord Jesus Christ founded it. In its schema on the church, the council said:

> The Church has all the marks of a true society. Christ did not leave this society undefined and without a set form. Rather, he himself gave its existence, and his will determined the form of its existence and gave it its constitution. The Church is not part nor member of any other society and is not mingled in any way with any other society. It is so perfect in itself that it is distinct from all human societies and stands far above them.[106]

The schema went further to state that the church is not a community of equals in which all the faithful have the same rights. Rather, the church is a society of unequals because of its hierarchical constitution.[107]

The Second Vatican Council's *Lumen Gentium* takes up the issue of the hierarchical structure of the institutional church. While not breaking from the Vatican I Council's stance, *Lumen Gentium* affirms the hierarchical structure of the church. For Vatican II, "The Lord Jesus Christ instituted a variety of ministries in his Church for the sole purpose of nurturing the constant growth of the People of God."[108] The council goes on to state that the task of carrying out this responsibility lies with the bishops, who are successors of the apostles. By their episcopal consecration, bishops are conferred with the authority to teach, sanctify, and govern the church. However, these offices can only be exercised in hierarchical communion with the head and members of the college of bishops.[109]

There is no doubt that for the church to carry out its mission effectively, it needs some form of authority and structure. It will be difficult, if not impossible, for the church to perform its mission without some stable organizational features. It could not unite people and nations into a well-knit community of conviction, commitment, and hope and could not minister effectively to the needs of humankind, unless it has responsible officers and properly approved procedures.[110]

---

[106] The *Primum Schema De Fide Catholica* (*First Draft of the Constitution on the Church*). Cited by Avery Dulles. *Models of the Church*, 29. Vatican I Council did not conclusively discuss the schema because of political upheaval at the time. The council was hurriedly adjourned. Vatican II Council took up this issue in its dogmatic constitution on the Church, *Lumen Gentium*.

[107] Ibid., 31.

[108] *Lumen Gentium*, #18.

[109] Ibid., #21, 22.

[110] Avery Dulles, *Models of the Church*, 27.

Dulles, lending his support to the institutional model of the church, argues that institution does not imply institutionalism. He draws a distinction between institutionalism and the institutional structure of the church. For him, the church should not be understood in terms of institutionalism—a system in which the institutional element is treated as primary. This, he says, is a deformation of the true nature of the church. Dulles, nevertheless, believes that the church has fallen into institutionalism.[111] However, the *Lumen Gentium* attempted to mitigate the institutionalism of the church when it defined the church as not just a visible society but also as a mystery and situated the hierarchy of authority in terms of service/ministry and not dominion.

The image of the church as an institution is fraught with many problems, which make it difficult to advance an ecclesiology that enhances the nature, mission, and the mysterious character of the church. The institutional image presents the church as a pyramid rather than a communion or community of believers. The institutional model promotes a certain triumphalism with its attendant clericalism and centralized power structure. Anne Carr was right when she said, "The image stresses authority as command, not service, and obedience as submission or conformity, not Christian freedom."[112] Carr goes on to offer a scathing criticism of the hierarchical image when she avows:

> This is a patriarchal model of the church in which the focus on authority and obedience is one of coercive power that suggests distrust of the members who are envisioned more as children than as responsible adults . . . . This hierarchical, patriarchal, clerical and military model of the church is simply in conflict with the gospel models of mystery, mystical communion, and mission.[113]

Notwithstanding the fact that the *Lumen Gentium* correctly noted that bishops are not vicars of the pope but of Christ and, as such, have the right to teach, sanctify, and lead the people of God, many feel that bishops do function more like vicars of the pope, and their ministries are limited by the powerful Roman curia and the pope. Local bishops have to wait for instructions from Rome before they can act on some local situations. A case in point is the sexual abuse scandal that rocked the American church in 2002. Priests who were accused and found guilty of sexual abuse were shuttled from parish to parish as their bishops waited for Rome to laicize or sanction them. Commenting on this, John Cornwell said, "Bishops did not fail (to act) because they were weak and venal men; they failed because of generations of increasing enfeeblement of their office by Rome,

---

[111] Ibid., 37.
[112] Anne E. Carr, *Transforming Grace*, 199.
[113] Ibid.

further undermined by a pope who acted as both universal and local pastor."[114] If the church is less centralized and if local communities have a voice in the governance of the church, some of these scandals could probably have been nipped in the bud.

Cardinal Franz König shared similar thoughts in his critical comments on the state of the universal church when he argued for the decentralization of the church authority. Cardinal König reasons that, "The Roman Curia remains a powerful force tending in the opposite direction, toward centralism." In fact, he says, "*De facto* and not *de jure,* intentionally or unintentionally, the curial authorities working in conjunction with the pope have appropriated the task of the episcopal college. It is they who now carry out almost all of them."[115]

The church in Africa and indeed in Nigeria is not free from the centralization of authority of the pope and the Roman Curia. For instance, local African bishops have to get permission from Rome before they can inculturate any aspect of the local culture into the liturgy. Approval is also required for any liturgical text translated into the vernacular. It is curious that this *recognitio* has to be obtained from the Curia, which knows little or nothing of the culture and language of the people in question.

The image of the church as an institution obfuscates the role and position of the laity who are not members of the hierarchy. Vatican II taught that the laity, by virtue of their baptism, share in the priestly, kingly, and prophetic mission of Christ, but it remains to be seen how they can exercise these offices in a hierarchical church, where the power of governance is restricted to the bishops and priests. Thus, the image of the church as an institution and the de facto application of clericalism in the church reduces the laity as Dulles rightly noted "to a condition of passivity, and . . . make(s) their apostolate a mere appendage of the apostolate of the hierarchy—a view endorsed by Pius XI and Pius XII in their description of 'Catholic action.'"[116]

There appears to be an internal conflict in the *Lumen Gentium*'s images of the church as the People of God and as Institution when it says that the People of God are hierarchically constituted.[117] First, the image of the People of God in the *Lumen Gentium* creates classes—the clergy on the one side and the laity on the other. Second, the image of the People of God bestows authority and power of governance exclusively on the clergy, though Vatican II called this authority and power "service." Third, the image creates clericalism and inequality in membership of the church. Fourth, the hierarchical constitution of the people

---

[114] John Cornwell, *The Pontiff in Winter,* 236.

[115] Franz König, "My Vision for the Church of the Future," *Tablet* 253 (March 27, 1999), 424.

[116] Avery Dulles, *Models of the Church,* 35-36.

[117] *Lumen Gentium,* #18.

of God is at odds with the Old and New Testaments' use of the image. The word *laos,* "people," as used in the two testaments, does not show a distinction of classes within the community as the *Lumen Gentium.* On the contrary, *laos* indicates rather the fellowship of all in a single community. The distinction it implies is "between the whole people of God and the 'non people,' the 'world,' the heathens."[118]

Finally, despite the reforms initiated by Vatican II Council, the organizational (leadership) structure of the church remains Tridentine—the clergy (hierarchy) on one side and the laity on the other side who remain excluded from leadership positions in the church. Again, among the prevalent images that we have examined, the image of the church as an institution dominates all other images. Much of the ecclesiology and missiology of the church are predicated on this model

---

[118] Hans Küng, *The Church,* 127-128.

Chapter 3

THE QUEST FOR AN AFRICAN MODEL OF THE CHURCH

The review of the selected images of the church in the previous chapter shows their historical and cultural circumscription. The church was able to take deep roots in the west because it adapted models that were congruent with western cultures. These models contributed immensely toward a solid understanding of the church, which resulted in the successful implantation of the Gospel in the west. However, when it came to the evangelization of sub-Sahara Africa, no African image or metaphor was adopted to explicate the nature of the mysterious character of the church. African cultures were adjudged incapable of being purveyors of the mystery of the church and the Gospel.

Missionaries to Africa imposed western images that were alien to the people. The consequences are the present crises of faith in Africa and the perception of Christianity as a foreign imposition. Paul Minear could not have stated it more correctly when he writes that, "We must note that those images which are most central to a true self-understanding are also the most misleading when used in a milieu alien to their native one. It is dangerous to detach one image from its initial rootage in one vocabulary and worldview and to give it rootage in another. We can easily accomplish this transplanting without producing any decisive change in the community's perception of its intrinsic nature."[1]

Minear's views inform our quest to propose an African image (ecclesiology) that will address the shortfalls of the missionary methodology that was operative in the evangelization of the Igbos. To redress this anomaly, we are moved *mutatis mutandis*, to construct a local ecclesiology for the church in Igboland. We are motivated by the need to continue the mission of the church—evangelization and deepening of the faith among the Igbos and Africans.

Since local churches have the elements necessary for sanctification, it seems antithetical to impose a uniform ecclesiology, and to the idea of unity in diversity,

---

[1] Paul S. Minear, *Images of the Church*, 25.

which Vatican II promoted. The ancient maxim, "In essentials unity, in nonessentials diversity, in all things charity," should be the guiding principle. Thus, to insist on ecclesial unity without accepting diversity of ecclesiologies, risks collapsing all churches into forced and unhealthy ecclesial uniformity.

The Gospel exists always in inculturated forms. It is counterproductive to impose upon people images that are alien to them. Precisely because of this imposition, we seek to postulate an ecclesiology that would help the people of Africa, in general, and the Igbos of Southeast Nigeria in their understanding of the church. Apparently, a more encompassing image of the church, such as the *extended family image*, will provide the framework for African ecclesiology that will lead to a genuine evangelization of the people.

Pope Paul VI rightly notes that, "The nature of the church as a mystery is open to new and ever greater exploration."[2] Thus, models/images that the church adopts to communicate its mysterious character should not be restricted to a particular culture. Consequently, the mystery of the church allows us to search for images that are appropriate for the understanding of its nature and mission to Africans.

The Family

The term "family" is derived from the Latin word *familia* meaning a household under one head that is regarded as a unit.[3] In this vein, Rosemary Ruether holds that *familia* means something very different from the English world *family*. For Ruether, *familia* refers to persons and things under the sovereign control of the male head of household or *paterfamilias*.[4] At any rate, *familia* is at the root of the concept of family.

Sociologists have offered differing definitions of family. While some definitions are narrow, others are broad. George Murdock describes the family as "a social group characterized by common residence, economic cooperation and reproduction, including adults of both sexes, at least one of whom maintains a socially approved sexual relationship, and one or more children, own or adopted, of the sexually cohabiting adults."[5] Given the reality of the moment, Murdock's definition is no longer tenable. In the first instance, his definition fails to take

---

[2] Yves Congar, and D. O'Hanlon, eds., *Council Speeches of Vatican II* (New York: Paulist Press, 1964), 26.

[3] Elizabeth J. Jewell, and Frank Abate, eds., *The New Oxford American Dictionary* (New York: Oxford University Press, 2001), 611.

[4] Rosemary R. Ruether, *Christianity and the Making of the Modern Family* (Boston: Beacon Press, 2000), 13-14.

[5] George Peter Murdock, *Social Structure* (New York: Macmillan, 1949), 1.

cognizance of the fact that not all cohabiting couples have children.[6] Second, Murdock's presumption that families must be formed by heterosexual marriage and include two parents is equally disputable in light of the current reinterpretation of family, which includes single parent families, same-sex families, and so forth. Third, in view of the current mobility of people, family members do not necessarily have to live in the same household. Besides, families are often formed not only by marriage but also through economic, social, ideological, and religious bonds.

For the Catholic Church, the family is not just a sociological construct or the fruit of a particular historical and economic situation. On the contrary, the church holds that the family "is the *original cell of social life* . . . the natural society in which husband and wife are called to give themselves in love and in the gift of life."[7] The crux of this definition is that it sees family in terms of its functionality—fecundity within the context of marriage. It does not say anything about other members of the family and/or other forms of families.

In our contemporary era, the notion of family is loosely applied to different forms of social, political, religious, and economic groups. On account of this, it is impossible to define "family" solely in terms of marital bond of a husband and wife with their children living in one household or even, in biological terms, the union of man and woman. Thus, family is not defined only by biological relationships but also by affiliation or association with a group.

In my view family is a theo-ontological and social institution. In other words, family can be constituted by the union of man and woman in marriage with the fruits (child/ren) of their conjugal union, their relations both living and dead, as well as their livestock and domesticated animals. A group of people who share common ideals, faith, beliefs, ties, and bonds also can constitute the family. This understanding is not limited to heterosexual unions; it leaves open the modus of bonding or ties. These groups can be formed to meet economic, social, political, or religious needs. Finally, this definition does not limit the family to a household of individuals living together; it extends to include all people who share a common bond. Hence, the church could equally be understood as a family.

The family constitutes the fundamental structure of human society. It is necessary for the rearing of children, basic survival, and development of the human race. Of course, there can be no society without families constituting it. Society is a composite or an aggregate of various family units. Aristotle reiterates this when he argues that the family is prior to and more fundamental than the *polis*. For him, a strong foundation of the family is essential to a strong society.[8]

---

[6] Lee D. Millar Bidwell, and Brenda J. Vander Mey, *Sociology of the Family: Investigating Family Issues* (Boston: Allyn & Bacon, 2000), 7.

[7] *Catechism of the Catholic Church* (Liguori, MO: Liguori publications, 1994), # 2207.

[8] Aristotle, *Nicomeachian Ethics*, 1162 A17-19. Cited in Sarah B. Pomeroy, *Families in Classical and Hellenistic Greece: Representations and Realities* (New York:

Similarly, John Paul II argues that the family is the first cell of human society. "The family has vital and organic links with society, since it is its foundation and nourishes it continually through its role of service to life: it is from the family that citizens come to birth and it is within the family that they find first schooling on the social virtues, the animating principles for the existence and development of the society itself."[9]

This overview of definitions on the general notion of family reveals some salient points on the nature and meaning of family, which are vital to the image of the church as an extended family. First, the family is a natural institution, constituted by marriage of man and woman and any offspring they may have. Family also includes same-sex couples[10] and single parent families. Second, the family is a sociological reality in that society is a composite of various family units and households. Third, the family is a communion of individuals with common interests such as religious institutions, social clubs, etc. Fourth, the family is not restricted to blood relations, legal or formal marriage, adoption of children, or even procreation. Members of a family may not always live together.[11] Unity or oneness underpins the basic characteristic of the family. Just as the Igbos say *otu oke osisi anaghi eme ohia*—one big tree cannot constitute a forest; an individual cannot constitute a family.[12]

Traditionally, there are two kinds of family units: nuclear and extended families. All other forms of families fall within these two typologies. Different nations and cultures have variant understanding of what the family is and place emphasis on one form or the other. Just as the concept of family varies from culture to culture, the extended family connotes a variety of meanings and categorizations. For example, it may mean an expansion of the nuclear family or, rather, a household that includes kith and kin in addition to the members of the nuclear family. In this case, the extended family means all living, consanguine kin that are closely knit together. In such an extended family structure, each member can always trace

---

Oxford University Press, 1998), 36-37.

[9] John Paul II, *Apostolic Exhortation: Familiaris Consortio, On the Role of the Christian Family in the Modern World* (Boston: Daughters of St. Paul Press, 1981), # 42.

[10] This assertion remains contentious and unacceptable to many conservatives, traditional societies, and churches. However, it is worth noting that despite scathing attacks from civil and religious bodies, same-sex marriages, and families have been legitimized in some countries such as Belgium, Canada, the Netherlands, Spain, South Africa, Sweden, some states in the United States of America, and so forth.

[11] Elaine Leeder, *The Family in Global Perspective: A Gendered Journey* (Thousand Oaks, California: Sage Publications, 2004), 24.

[12] Emmanuel Chukwu, *Ezi-Na-Ulo: The Extended Family of God Towards an Ecological Theology of Creation* (Sacrae Theologiae Doctor Dissertation, Katholieke Universiteit Leuven, 2002), 39.

his or her lineage either patrilineally or matrilineally. More often than not, the extended family includes parents, siblings, grandparents, uncles, aunts, cousins, nephews, nieces, etc.[13] The extended family also includes distant kin who may live far away from each other.

The interpersonal relationships of members of the extended family can be very deep, to the extent that each individual is seen a brother or sister, father or mother, grandmother or grandfather, or cousin to one another.[14] In some cultures, the extended family includes the entire clan or village. In this case, everyone is in one way or the other related to everyone else. In-laws are also part of this extended family structure.

The extended family is most common in cultures where ties between male and female kin are important for socioeconomic reasons. The extended family system is common in many developing nations. Conversely, Western culture, with its individualistic and affluent lifestyle, identifies more with the nuclear family. One of the reasons for this dichotomy is that the extended family structure is more pronounced in regions in which economic conditions make it difficult for the individual to achieve self-sufficiency.

Typically, in an extended family structure, a group of male and female kin live together, sharing their resources. These include agricultural lands, livestock, and ritual property, such as sacred objects, sacred sites, and worship of common deity. These characteristics of the extended family are common in African societies and among the Australian Aborigines. An important feature of the extended family system is that it offers aid to individuals in areas where government essential services are not adequate or unavailable. One leans on his or her extended family for support, sustenance, and survival.

The Extended Family as a Model for the Church

During the Special Assembly for Africa of the Synod of Bishops held in Rome in 1994, the synod fathers called for adoption of inculturation theology as a paradigm for genuine evangelization of the African continent. The image of the church as an extended family of God[15] was repeatedly echoed by the synod fathers as being ad rem for ecclesio-missiology on the continent. The call became necessary because of the lack of any African ecclesiology and the inadequacy of missionary

---

[13] John S. Mbiti, *African Religions and Philosophy*, 2nd ed. (London: Heinemann Educational Publishing Company, 1997), 102.

[14] Ibid., 103.

[15] For the purpose of clarity, these terms, the church as the extended family of God and the church as the family of God, are used interchangeably in this book to denote the same reality.

methodology in Africa. The synod fathers contend that "it is felt that Africans can be more easily enabled to experience and to live the mystery of the church as communion by utilizing to good advantage the African understanding of the family, especially as regards the values of family unity and solidarity."[16] Benezet Bujo, an African theologian, shares similar views when he argues that the understanding of the church by Africans will rely on a correct understanding of the African sense of community and family.[17]

John Paul II, acknowledging the necessity and fundamental role of the extended family model for the African church in its task for genuine evangelization, said:

> Not only did the synod speak of inculturation, but it also made use of it, taking the Church as God's family as its guiding idea for the evangelization of Africa. The synod fathers acknowledged it as an expression of the Church's nature particularly appropriate for Africa. This image emphasizes care for others, solidarity, warmth in human relationships, acceptance, dialogue and trust. The new evangelization will thus aim at building up the church as family.[18]

John Paul II, however, cautioned that "this image must avoid all ethnocentrism and excessive particularism." The pope insists that the image must "instead encourage reconciliation and true communion between different ethnic groups, favouring solidarity and the sharing of personnel and resources among the particular churches, without undue ethnic considerations."[19] The pope goes on to charge theologians in Africa with the task of working out the theology of the church as family, while showing its complementarity with other images of the church.[20]

The Igbo extended family, which I examined previously, has all the characteristics of fulfilling the yearnings of Africa's quest for an ecclesiology that is grounded in its cultural matrix. The African concept of family and communality, particularly as manifested among the Igbos, consists of a spiritual unity that binds

---

[16] Synodus Episcoporum Coetus Specialis Pro Africa. *Instrumentum Laboris: The Church in Africa and her Evangelizing Mission Towards the year 2000* (Vatican: Libreria Editrice, 1993), #25, (henceforth *Instrumentum Laboris*).

[17] Benezet Bujo, "On the Road Toward an African Ecclesiology: Reflections on the Synod." *The African Synod: Documents, Reflections, Perspectives*, ed. Browne Maura (New York: Orbis Books, 1996), 140.

[18] John Paul II, *Post-Synodal Apostolic Exhortation: Ecclesia in Africa* (Vatican: Libreria Editrice, 1995), #63.

[19] Ibid., 6.

[20] Ibid.

people together; this leads to a communal bond that is unbreakable even by distance or death.[21]

The Igbo concept of family is both sociologically and spiritually similar to the meaning of *ekklesia*. A profound sense of *sensus communium* pervades the entire spectrum of the African worldview. John Paul II rightly reiterates this when he contends that in African cultures and traditions, the role of the family is everywhere held to be fundamental. African cultures have an acute sense of solidarity and community life, which expresses the indispensability of the extended family.[22]

The critical question then is how can the Igbo notion of the extended family serve as an image of the church? The Igbo concept of family is grounded on communalism, relationality, and universal brotherhood/sisterhood anchored in a common ancestor; hence, it covers the widest possible range of kinship and inter-relatedness. The extended family does not necessarily emphasize consanguine relationships but rather the fact that each member sees himself or herself as belonging to one common ancestor. As Igbos continue to trace their individual genealogical lineage, they believe they will ultimately come to a common proto-ancestor who is the origin of their family. Emmanuel Chukwu is right when he observes that the identification of a blood relationship among all the Igbos strives for the ultimate formation of a universal brotherhood or sisterhood. "This," he goes on to say, "shows the Igbo bondedness or unity in the conception of human beings."[23] This common origin of all human beings is the *locus standi* and foundation of the extended family as the model of the church. This is also what the concepts of *Ezi-na-ulo* and *umunna/umunne* embody for Ndigbo. *Umunna* and its corollary *umunne* engender being as belongingness and communalism in the one extended family of God.

The Igbo fundamental ontology of being as belongingness and a deep sense of community undergird its interrelatedness with their fellow human beings. This ontological understanding of being equally shapes the Igbo notion of family. "To be human," as Mbiti notes, "is to belong to the whole community, and to do so involves participating in the beliefs, ceremonies, rituals and festivals of the community."[24] Consequently, one can argue that those who belong to *ezi-na-ulo* family-community of *umunna/umunne* have the same ancestor and are members of one extended family. For Emmanuel Chukwu, "the extended family is the real family among the Igbos; and, because it points to all directions, it is also the community in the Igbo worldview. This accounts for why we adopt it to argue in favor of the common origin

---

[21] Okechuwku A. Ogbonnaya, *On Communitarian Divinity,* 4.

[22] John Paul II, *Ecclesia in Africa,* # 43.

[23] Emmanuel Chukwu, *Ezi-na-ulo,* 53.

[24] John S. Mbiti, *African Religions and Philosophy,* 2.

of all creatures."[25] By virtue of this common origin, all human beings belong to the cosmic community and ultimately to the same family of God. Mercy Oduyoye, a Ghanaian theologian, shares similar views when she aptly observes:

> Africans recognize life as life-in-community. We can truly know ourselves if we remain true to our community, past and present. The concept of individual success or failure is secondary. The ethnic groups, the village, the locality, are crucial in one's estimation of oneself. Our nature as beings-in-relation is a two-way relation: with God and with our fellow human beings.[26]

It is important to stress that the Igbo cosmo-ontological concepts of community and the extended family are not restricted to those bound together by blood. The community is not just an aggregate of individuals who find themselves bound by consanguine, geographical, or political boundaries; rather, the community is an open-ended reality that embraces people who may live hundreds of miles apart. The community does not annihilate or subsume an individual's identity and freedom. Each individual in the *ezi-na-ulo* family maintains his or her individuality. As Chinua Achebe rightly observes:

> For whereas many cultures are content to demonstrate the value and importance of each man and woman by reference to the common fatherhood of God, the Igbo postulate an unprecedented uniqueness for the individual by making him or her the sole creation and purpose of a unique god-agent, *chi*. No two persons, not even blood brothers, are created and accompanied by the same *chi*.[27]

However, while individuals are essential in and of themselves for the continuity of the community, the community is ontologically superior to individuals. The "person-in-community" is a very important reality in Igbo society. A person is primarily a member of the community and secondarily an individual who relates with others.[28]

---

[25] Emmanuel Chukwu, *Ezi-na-ulo,* 352.

[26] Mercy Amba Oduyoye, "The Value of African Religious Beliefs and Practices for Christian Theology," *African Theology En Route*, eds. Kofi Appiah-Kubi, and Sergio Torres (New York: Orbis Books, 1979), 110-111.

[27] Chinua Achebe, *Hopes and Impediments: Selected Essays* (New York: Anchor Books, 1990), 57-58.

[28] Joseph Healy, and Donald Sybertz, *Towards an African Narrative Theology* (New York: Orbis Books, 1996), 106.

Biblical Foundation of the Family as a Model for the Church

The notion of extended family as an image for the church is not alien to the history of ecclesiology. The metaphor of family has been used biblically, theologically and liturgically to describe the church. However, the precise meaning, nature, and scope of the church as a family have not been developed.

Since scripture and tradition are the two foundations of Christian faith and theology, it necessarily follows that any theological treatise must first begin with and be grounded in them. It is in light of this that we are going to consider the scriptural and traditional bases of the extended family as an image of the church. It has to be noted that the examples upon which I draw in this section predominately speak about family in general terms. In those instances, it is to be assumed that the references to the family are of the extended family.

Old Testament

The concept of family in ancient biblical Israel was fluid and open. The Hebrew terms בית (*bêt*), *bayith*, and *mišpāhâ* (house) are used both in a narrow and broad sense to designate a single household unit (family), wider circle of consanguinity (Gen. 24:38), the clan, tribe, or the ethnic group and nation (Amos 3:1-2).[29] In a narrower sense, *bayith* could mean a nuclear family, that is, a man (*ābh*), his wife (*'ishshāh*), his children including adopted ones (*banim ubhanoth*), his dependent relatives, and his servants and guests. In a broader sense, *bayith* denotes a tribe or the descendants of a person. In this sense, the tribe or descendants are often called the "house of" as in the "House of David" or the "House of Israel."[30] Again, household units that were smaller than a tribe, but larger than a single family, were called *bayith*: for example, *beth 'aharon*, house of Aaron (Ps. 115:10, 12). In addition, the concentric usage of *bêt* suggests the role of the basic family in shaping the larger community.

Theologically, the Hebrew concept of family provided one of the most commonly used analogies for the relationship between Israel and God. Hence, in the Hebrew Bible, we find instances of the people of Israel being referred to as the House of Israel (*bêt Yisra'el*) בית ישראל (2 Sam. 12:18; 1 Kings 12:21; Jer. 11:10; Isa. 8:14; Ezek. 2:3; 8:6, 10-11; 24:1-3). The "House of Israel" could be interpreted

---

[29] David F. Wright, "Family," *The Oxford Companion to the Bible*, eds. Bruce M. Metzger, and Michael D. Coogan (New York: Oxford University Press, 1993), 223.

[30] Hoffner, "בית (bayith)," *Theological Dictionary of the Old Testament*, vol. 11. revised edition, eds. Johannes G. Botterweck, and Helmer Ringgren, trans. Willis T. John (Grand Rapids, Michigan, William B. Eerdmans Publishing Company, 1974), 113.

to mean Israel as one united family or nation. Old Testament prophets used this form of address when they spoke to the people of Israel. For example, Ezekiel used בית ישראל (*bêt Yisra'el*) 182 times as an address to the people of Israel.[31]

The Old Testament use of *bêt* or *bayith* in the broader sense of the term to refer to a clan, tribe, or the nation of Israel is a deliberate one. The term emphasizes Israel's position as the people of God. Halvor Moxnes contends that "kinship and nation were the same and the claim to descend from Abraham was a focal point for Jewish identity."[32]

The foundation of Israel as a nation rests solely on the fact that God chose and enacted a covenant with Isreal's common ancestor, Abraham. As a result, *bêt, bayith Yisra'el* encapsulates the unity of Israel, both as a nation and as the People of God. Israel's kinship ties with God form the basis of their shared spiritual bond.

On the other hand, *mišpāhâ*, also translated as family, only refers to the modern day connotation of an extended family. However, Carol Meyers argues that neither family nor clan best denotes the meaning of *mišpāhâ*. She notes that *mišpāhâ* designates a group of, at least, partly related family units that settled in a given area, which can be understood as the nucleus of an agricultural village. Hence, not all members would have been related by blood, though many would have been, but all would have been committed to the same territory and to shared economic and military efforts.[33]

The concept of the House of Israel as the one family of God gained momentum with the covenant, which Moses mediated between God and the people of Israel on Mount Sinai. The covenant enunciated the terms by which Israel became the people of God.

> You have seen for yourselves how I treated the Egyptians and how I bore you up on eagle's wings and brought you here to myself. Therefore, if you hearken to my voice and keep my covenant, you shall be my special possession, dearer to me than all other people, though all the earth is mine. You shall be to me a kingdom of priests, a holy nation (Exod. 19:4-6).

The import of the Sinaitic covenant was that it served as the basis of Israel's identity as a chosen people. In other words, Israel saw itself as one united household of God under the prism of the covenant. The Sinaitic covenant produced a new

---

[31] Ibid., 114.

[32] Halvor Moxnes, "What is Family? Problems in constructing early Christian families," *Constructing Early Christian Families: Family as Social Reality and Metaphor,* ed. Halvor Moxnes (London: Routledge, 1997), 27.

[33] Carol Meyers, "The Family in Early Israel," *Families of Ancient Israel,* eds. Leo Perdue, et al (Louisville: Westminster, John Knox, 1997), 13.

people, bound together into a homogeneous religious and political community. Moreover, the ratification of the covenant wrought by the offering of holocausts and sacrifice further sealed the relationship between the people and God. This covenant turned the House of Israel into a theocentric community.

In light of the meaning of *bayith*, one can conclude that Jewish religious tradition was interwoven into the fabric of its family life. Evidence of this is deduced from the fact that Jewish festivals were simultaneously communal and family-oriented. These festivals and religious ceremonies bound Jews both to their own families and to the larger community of fellow Jews with whom they shared such ethnic and familial ties. The family became, as it were, the conduit and principal place for the transmission of Judaism.[34]

It is pertinent to note here that there is no clearly defined distinction between the concepts of *bayith and mišpāhâ* in the Old Testament usage of the terms. House and family, as we noted earlier, are sometimes used interchangeably. Most importantly, neither of the terms represents anything as limited or exclusive as our contemporary nuclear family.[35] The Old Testament understanding of the family more often than not was very inclusive. The family included not only those related by consanguinity, but also sojourners, hired servants, etc.

As Israel sought to live as a covenanted household of God in its world of competing deities and nations, its self-understanding as a community and people of God was critical to its survival and maintaining the right relationship with God. God revealed Godself to Israel as the God of Abraham, Isaac, and Jacob. Conversely, Israel addresses God as the God of their fathers Abraham, Isaac, and Jacob (Exod. 3:6), thereby affirming their interrelatedness and unity.

New Testament

The metaphor of family played a central role in the understanding of the church by the first Christians. For example, the images of "God as Father," "Jesus as Son," "children of God," "brothers and sisters," etc., became a means of transmitting Christian theology as well as constructing a church with family characteristics.[36] New Testament authors frequently used the Greek term *oikos*, meaning house, to address believers as family. It is not surprising then that the early Christians called

---

[34] John M. G. Barclay, "The Family as the Bearer of Religion in Judaism and Early Christianity," *Constructing Early Christian Families: Family as Social Reality and Metaphor*, ed. Halvor Moxnes (London: Routledge, 1997), 72.

[35] Brian W. Grant, *The Social Structure of Christian Families* (St. Louis, Missouri: Chalice Press, 2000), 12.

[36] Marie E. Lassen, "The Roman Family: Ideal and Metaphor," *Constructing Early Christian Families: Families and Social Reality and Metaphor*, 103.

themselves *oiko tou theou*, which translates to household of God (Eph. 2:19; 1 Tim. 3:15; 1 Pet. 4:17). The rationale that underpins the usage of *oikos* could be attributed to the fact that initially the early Christians met in domestic private buildings and were led by householders including women, and husbands and wives as joint leaders (Acts 2:46; Rom. 16:3-5; 1 Cor. 16:15, 19).

The early Christians' understanding of the church as the household of God, οἴκος τοῦ θεοῦ, was marked by continuity and discontinuity with Judaism. When the Christians were expelled by their families and from synagogue worship for belonging to the "new sect," they bonded together and became a new family. Admission into this family was marked by conversion and baptism in the name of Jesus Christ. Hence, Christians began to see themselves as the family of God in Jesus Christ.

A parallel can be drawn between the Old Testament use of *bayith* and the New Testament use of *oikos*. The two concepts have a direct bearing on and reference to a group of people who are called or set apart for a special purpose. In the case of Old Testament, *bayith* refers to Israel as the family or chosen people of God, while in the New Testament, *oikos* refers to the new Israel of God in Christ.

Some factors help explain the choice of the family image for the church among the early Christians. First, the family was an important social unit in the Greco-Roman and Jewish cultures. Family occupied a prominent place in these cultures, so it was natural that the new community of God would use this powerful metaphor to refer to themselves. Second, in working out an ecclesiology and theology that was different yet similar to Judaism, the early Christians adopted this powerful image—to show that those who belong to the church are part of the new Israel. It is no wonder that Paul called the church the household of God (1 Tim. 3:15), or part of God's household (Eph. 2:19-22).

The description of the church via kinship and family imagery abounds in Pauline and Petrine epistles. Paul used kinship terms like father/mother, sons, children, and sister/brother to describe the relationships of Christians with one another and with God.[37] However, Paul's use of kinship imagery is varied. For example, in one instance, Paul called himself the father of the community, but in the same epistle, he addressed the community as sisters and brothers (1 Cor. 4:6ff; 4:14ff; 1 Thess. 2:1, 14; 2:11; Rom. 14; 1 Cor. 6:8). Other instances in which kinship metaphors are used in referring to the Christian community can be found in 1 Timothy 5:4, 8, 9-16; Philemon 15-16; and 1 Peter 2:9, 18; 3:7. These passages are replete with metaphors drawn from family life like childhood, adoption, the father/son relationship, and inheritance.[38]

---

[37] Aasgaard Reidar, "Brotherhood in Plutarch and Paul: Its Role and Character," *Constructing Early Christian Families: Family as Social Reality and Metaphor*, 176.

[38] David F. Wright, *Family*, 224.

THE CHURCH AS THE EXTENDED FAMILY OF GOD

It is pertinent to note that family structure in the Hebrew Scripture and New Testament church (was patterned upon the family in classical Hellenistic and Roman cultures) are highly patriarchal. The sovereignty of wives, children, slaves, and all other dependent persons in the family lay in the hands of male head of the household.[39]

A number of questions have arisen regarding the meaning and normativity of family as an adequate image for the church. One such question asks whether relying on the family model necessarily means relying on the patriarchy.[40] This question stems from the fact that the family structure in most cultures is patriarchal. Critics, especially feminists, argue that because patriarchy does not promote equality of women and men but rather makes women subservient to men and engenders the oppression of women, family imagery cannot project a positive image of the church. Besides, some theologians have argued that there is an "antifamily" stream in Christianity with roots in the Gospel.

Rosemary Ruether, while admitting the centrality of the family to ethnic identity and social maintenance both in the Greco-Roman and Jewish worlds, strongly argues that the historical Jesus in fact appears quite often to have endorsed views that might be characterized as "antifamily."[41] Citing several passages from the synoptic gospels to support this "antifamily" stream, Ruether maintains that the antifamily patterns of the gospels are marked by tensions between Jesus and his own family and hometown folks.[42] Ruether goes further to contend that the synoptic gospels present the Jesus movement as a gathering of mostly marginal men and women who have left their families and occupations to form a countercultural community. This community, seen as a new eschatological family, negates the natural family.[43] Ruether mentions some of these antifamily passages: "When a would-be disciple protests that he must first bury his father, Jesus tells him curtly, 'Follow me and leave the dead to bury the dead" (Matt. 8:21-22). For Ruether, this instance disregards the traditional family responsibilities to the dead father in Jewish culture.[44]

Another passage that Ruether cites as part of the antifamily sentiment in the New Testament is Jesus' insistence that no one is worthy to be a disciple who

---

[39] Serene Jones, *Feminist Theory and Christian Theology: Cartographies of Grace* (Minneapolis: Fortress Press, 2000), 78.

[40] The patriarchal structure of the family in the Hellenistic and Roman worlds influenced the first Christians' understanding of the Church as the family. It is worth noting that the patriarchal structure could constitute an obstacle, especially among feminists, toward the acceptance of the model of the church as the family of God. We shall address this critical issue in another chapter, proffering ways of overcoming patriarchism in the Church.

[41] Rosemary R. Ruether, *Christianity and the Making of the Modern Family*, 3.

[42] Ibid., 28.

[43] Ibid., 25.

[44] Ibid.

prefers his/her family to him. "If anyone comes to me and does not hate his own father and mother and wife and children and brothers and sisters . . . he cannot be my disciple" (Luke 14:26). There is no question that the saying about hating one's own family members was stunning to the ears of the first disciples as it is to ours. During the time of Jesus, people did not conceive of themselves as individuals but derived their identity as it is in African ontology from their family, clan, community, and religious group. It would be unimaginable to cut oneself off from family; this would be tantamount to losing one's life itself.[45] One is then left to wonder if Jesus rejected his family and urged his would be followers to do the same.

A critical interpretation of the so-called "antifamily" pericopes in the Gospel will yield a different result. We will do a brief hermeneutics of some of such periscopes: "Then his mother and his brothers came to him but were unable to join him because of the crowd. Jesus was told, 'Your mother and your brothers are standing outside and they wish to see you.' He said to them in reply, 'My mother and my brothers are those who hear the word of God and act on it'" (Luke 8:19-21). If we juxtapose this pericope with another passage where Jesus' mother Mary hears the word of God and keeps it (Luke 1:45) with the leaders of the people who did not when John spoke God's word to them (Luke 3:2), it is clear that Luke emphasizes faith, obedience, and fidelity to the Word of God (Luke 8:11) as the basis for membership in God's people.[46] In that case, the story of Jesus' family seeking him becomes not a tale of rejection but a straightforward affirmation for all who seek Jesus: "This is the people that consist of those who 'hear the word of God and do it.'"[47] This does not suggest hostility on the part of Jesus toward his natural family. It is possible that Jesus is presenting his family as a model for others. Mary heard the Word of God and treasured it in her heart. Jesus might as well have said: if you want to be my disciple, you must be like my mother who heard the Word of God and kept it.

It is worth noting another periscope, which Ruether and other proponents of the biblical "antifamily" stance adduce concerns Jesus' statement that he has come not to bring peace but division: "Do not think that I have come to bring peace upon earth. I have come to bring not peace but the sword. For I have come to set a man against his father, a daughter against her mother . . . one's enemies will be those of his household" (Matt. 10:34-36). For antifamily proponents, Jesus declares his intent to bring division through the rejection of family with these words. Antifamily proponents would be correct here if this passage is given a literal interpretation. However, it seems that the intention of

---

[45] Barbara E. Reid, "Calculating the Cost," *America: The National Catholic Weekly* (Aug. 30-Sept. 6, 2010), 30.

[46] Luke T. Johnson, *Sacra Pagina: The Gospel of Luke*, vol. 3, ed. Daniel J. Harrington, SJ (Collegeville, Minnesota: A Michael Glazier Book, 1991), 134-135.

[47] Ibid.

this statement is that those who accept his message of peace and reconciliation will constitute the new eschatological family of God, which Jesus came to inaugurate. Nevertheless, one does not necessarily have to abandon one's natural family for the eschatological family.

Furthermore, in the gospels, Jesus introduces the idea that a family will be formed through baptism and the acceptance of his teachings. Jesus says, "My mother and my brothers are those who hear the word of God and act on it" (Luke 8:21 cf. Mark 3:35). Jesus here suggests that "family" is more than one's biological relatives. For Barbara Reid, "What Jesus asks, however, is that a disciple be willing to embrace as kin others who are not related by blood. Disciples must act as brother and sister toward those who are different, whether by physical ability or any other status."[48] In other words, consanguinity does not define or determine membership in Jesus' eschatological family. Similarly, the Igbo concept of *ezi-na-ulo* or *umunna*, which forms the nexus for accentuating the notion of the church as the family of God, is not defined or determined per se by consanguinity.

The following summarizes the New Testament's overarching reasons for using kinship and family imagery in referring to the church. The terms express (1) the fundamental and intimate allegiances and commitments to the new community of believers; (2) discontinuity with Judaism; (3) transference of allegiance and belief to another community and society; (4) an ecclesiology that is in continuity with Greco-Roman and Jewish cultures; and (5) a model that the family of Jesus is not constituted by physical or consanguine relationship, but by obedience to the Word of God.

Magisterial Foundation

The family model of the church also has a magisterial foundation, which can be seen through the careful examination of a few magisterial documentations. We shall limit ourselves to an examination of Vatican II Council and a few recent magisterial teachings.

Vatican II

In enunciating the mysterious nature of the church, the Second Vatican Council's dogmatic constitution on the church, *Lumen Gentium*, articulated several images. The council asserts that "in the Old Testament the revelation of the kingdom was conveyed by figures of speech, and in the same manner the inner nature of the church can be known through various images." The council goes on to say, "These

---

[48] Barbara Reid, *Calculating the Cost*, 30.

images are drawn from various spheres of human life and even from family and married life."[49] Alluding to the image of the church in the Pauline epistles, the council teaches, "This edifice is adorned by various names: the house of God (1 Tim. 3:15) in which dwells His family, the household of God in the Spirit" (Eph. 2:18-22).[50] Here the council calls the church God's family and/or household.

Vatican II, after calling the church the family of God, goes on to emphasize its fundamental role in evangelization: "The family is the domestic church. In it (domestic church), parents should, by their word and example, be the first preachers of the faith to their children. They should encourage them in the vocation which is proper to each of them, fostering with special care any religious vocation."[51] The council calls upon Christian couples to manifest the unity that exists between Christ and his church in their families.

The council, by calling the family *domestica ecclesia*, sought to move from an excessively institutional or hierarchical church to the recovery of the early model of the church as a family. The council also sought to highlight the importance of the family as the bedrock of society and the church. The council equally recognized the dignity of marriage by declaring that families could be seen as domestic churches. For the council, the family is also a kind of school of deeper humanity and the foundation of the society because, "In it the various generations come together and help one another to grow wiser and to harmonize personal rights with the other requirements of social life."[52] As such, the family equally constitutes a sacramental entity, which then signifies and shares in the divine love of Christ.[53] Members of the church, by virtue of their intimate relationships with one another, ought to help each other to attain holiness.

John Paul II

Pope John Paul II used the phrase "domestic church" several times in his apostolic exhortation, *On the Christian Family, Familiaris Consortio* to describe the family. In one instance, the pope says:

> The Christian family is also called to experience a new and original communion which confirms and perfects natural and human communion . . . . The Christian family constitutes a specific revelation

---

[49] *Lumen Gentium*, # 6.
[50] Ibid.
[51] Ibid.
[52] *Gaudium et Spes*, #52.
[53] Gregory J. Konerman, "The Family as Domestic Church," *Church Divinity* (1990-1991), 60.

and realization of ecclesial communion, and for this reason too it can and should be called the "domestic Church" (*Ecclesia domestica*).[54]

The pope believes that it is through the conjugal bond that a family, and by extension, the *ecclesia domestica*, is founded. "In matrimony and in the family a complex of interpersonal relationships is set up—married life, fatherhood and motherhood, filiations and fraternity—through which each human person is introduced into the 'human family' and into the 'family of God,' which is the Church."[55]

John Paul II argues that because the family is the domestic church, it also has the mandate to proclaim the Gospel and evangelize its members. "The Christian family, in fact, is the first community called to announce the Gospel to the human person during growth and to bring him or her, through a progressive education and catechesis, to full human and Christian maturity."[56] John Paul II further teaches:

> The Christian family also builds up the Kingdom of God in history through the everyday realities that concern and distinguish its state of life. It is thus in the love between husband and wife and between the members of the family-a love lived out in all its extraordinary riches of the values and demands . . . that the Christian family's participation in the prophetic, priestly and kingly mission of Jesus Christ and of His Church finds expression and realization.[57]

For the pope, therefore, the Christian family's true vocation and concern are the transformation of the earth and the renewal of the world, of creation, and of all humanity; this is equally the concern and mission of the church. The mission of the family, which is also the mission of the church, flows outward in "a civilization of love" for humanity.[58] The civilization of love, as the pope maintains, calls all to provide food, drink, and clothing to those in need; visit the sick and imprisoned; and welcome the needy (Matt. 25:34-36).[59]

John Paul II relied heavily on the nuptial metaphor between a man and woman in his understanding of family. For the pope, the conjugal communion between husbands and wives constitutes the foundation on which is built the broader communion of family, of parents and children, of brothers and sisters with each

---

[54] John Paul II, *Familaris Consortio*, #21, 49.
[55] Ibid., # 15.
[56] Ibid., # 2.
[57] Ibid., # 49.
[58] John Paul II, *Letter to Families* (Boston: Daughters of St. Paul, 1994), # 13.
[59] Ibid.

other, and of relatives and other members of the household.[60] From this nuptial bond, the pope draws parallels between God and humans, and clergy and lay people.[61]

The nuptial metaphor, limited to the male-female relationship has drawn scathing criticism from feminist theologians, who argue that such a model creates inequality and has been used to perpetrate violence and oppression against women. I will revisit this issue in chapter 7. Suffice it to reiterate here that the Igbo concept of family goes beyond the relationship between husband and wife. The Igbo concept of the family is broad; the family includes not only the living but also departed relatives and unborn members.[62]

Ecclesia in Africa

Ecclesia in Africa, the product of the special assembly of the Synod of Bishops for Africa held in Rome in 1994, provides us with an authoritative magisterial foundation for the appropriation of the image of church as the family of God. The working document of the synod, *Instrumentum Laboris*, the *Message* of the Special Assembly for Africa of the Synod of Bishops and the final document *Ecclesia in Africa*, issued by John Paul II, discussed extensively the importance of the family as a model/image befitting the church in Africa.

According to the *Instrumentum Laboris*, the model/image of the church as the family of God aptly correlates with the African understanding of family and the church as family.

> Among the biblical images of the Church enumerated in the Dogmatic Constitution on the Church, *Lumen Gentium*, that of the Church as the House of God (cf. Eph. 2:19-22) is particularly relevant for Africa. Paul VI called the family a 'domestic Church' and considers that 'there should be found in every Christian family the various aspects of the entire Church. Furthermore, the family, like the Church, ought to be a place where the gospel is transmitted and from which the gospel radiates. In a family which is conscious of this mission, all the members evangelize and are evangelized.' In many answers to the *Lineamenta*,

---

[60] Ibid., # 21, 42.

[61] Ibid., # 73. The pope sees the bishop as the father of the "diocesan family." Priests and deacons, the pope says, must equally act toward families as fathers, brothers, pastors, and teachers. The implication of this is that the church (laity) is the bride, while the clergy is the groom (spiritual husbands and fathers).

[62] John S. Mbiti, *African Religion and Philosophy*, 104-105.

there is a strong emphasis on the notion of the Church as the Family of God among human beings.[63]

While acknowledging that for a variety of reasons the renewed ecclesiology of Vatican II has not yet made a sufficient impact on the churches in Africa, the Special Assembly for Africa of the Synod of Bishops insisted that a new model of the church, in which every Christian can find his or her place, is not only necessary but also expedient. This view is bolstered by the fact that, at present, many Africans still experience the church as an alien imposition by missionaries.[64]

The relator general of the synod, Hyacinth Cardinal Thiandoum, archbishop of Dakar, Senegal, while presenting the summary of interventions at the end of the first week of the plenary sessions of the synod, encapsulated the mind of the synod fathers when he said:

> What is very evident from the interventions of the synod fathers is the concern for an evangelization that is inculturated, so that an inculturated Church may be born. The model of this Church is the Church as *communion,* expressed admirably in the African context, as the Church, the Family of God. It is around this central idea that the proclamation of the gospel in Africa and Madagascar is to be lived and structured.[65]

In line with the *Instrumentum Laboris,* the bishops of the Synod adopted the family metaphor as the model for the church in Africa. The *Message of the Synod of Bishops* unreservedly supports the quest for an African ecclesiology that is rooted in the model of the extended family. According to the *Message,* "the extended family is the sacred place where all the riches of our tradition converge, as such it is, the task of Christian families to bring to the heart of this extended family a witness which transforms from the inside our visions of the world, beginning from the spirit of the Beatitudes, without forgetting the various tasks that are ours in society."[66]

Correlating the new African model of the church as the family of God to creation, the *Message of the Synod* says:

---

[63] Synodus Episcoporum: *Coetus Specialis Pro Africa: The Church in Africa and Her Evangelizing Mission Towards the Year 2000, Instrumentum Laboris* (Vatican: Libreria Editrice, 1993), 25.

[64] Ibid.

[65] Hyacinth Cardinal Thiandoum, *Relatio Post Disceptationem* #3. Cited in Joseph O. Faniran, "Journeying Together into the 21st Century," *AFER,* vol. 37, 1 (Feb. 1995), 39.

[66] Message of the Synod, # 27, *The African Synod: Documents, Reflections, Perspectives,* 78.

> The Synod has highlighted that *You are the Family of God*. It is for the Church-as-Family that the Father has taken the initiative in the creation of Adam. It is the Church-as-Family which Christ, the New Adam and Heir to the nations, founded by the gift of his body and blood. It is the Church-as-Family which manifests to the world the Spirit which the Son sent from the Father so that there should be communion among all.[67]

Pope John Paul II affirms that the model of the church as God's family is *ad rem* for the church in Africa. The pope urged that the model should be the locus for evangelization of Africa within the framework of inculturation. "Not only did the Synod speak of inculturation, but it also made use of it, taking the church as God's family as its guiding idea for the evangelization of Africa. The Synod Fathers acknowledged it as an expression of the church's nature particularly appropriate for Africa."[68] The pope goes on to encapsulate the *raison d'etre* and the theological underpinning of the choice of the church as a family of God: "This image emphasizes care for others, solidarity, dialogue and trust. The new evangelization will thus aim at building up the church as family."[69]

Liturgical/Sacramental Foundation

The image of the church as the extended family of God can also be extrapolated from liturgical and sacramental celebrations of the church. For example, the church teaches that in the sacrament of Baptism, we become incorporated into Christ and are formed into one family. Baptism not only initiates us into the dignity of God's people, but we also become a new creation through water and the Holy Spirit. "In the sacrament of Christian initiation (baptism) . . . we receive the Spirit of filial adoption and are part of the entire people of God."[70]

In the sacrament of the Eucharist, there are explicit and ample references to the church as the family of God. A few of these references will be mentioned here. In both liturgical and sacramental celebrations, Christians are often described as "children of God," "members of God's family," or "People of God." In the liturgical celebrations and prayers of the church, in addition to the numerous addresses to God in kinship terms like "Almighty Father," or simply "Father," "God our Father," etc., there are several instances in which the church prays as the family of God. For

---

[67] Ibid., #24.

[68] John Paul II, *Ecclesia in Africa,* # 63.

[69] Ibid.

[70] ICEL, *The Rites of the Catholic Church*, vol. 1, Study edition (New York: Pueblo Publishing Co., 1990), 3. See also Vatican II Council, *Sacrosanctum Concilium* # 6, *Ad Gentes,* # 14.

example, in the solemn blessing or prayer over the people before the end of Mass on the solemnity of Baptism of the Lord, the priest says, "Lord, send your light upon your family. May they continue to enjoy your favor and devote themselves to doing good."[71] Notice that the people (church) in this prayer are addressed as the family of God.

Recounting the redemptive mystery of Christ's passion, death, and resurrection, the *Collect* of Monday in the octave of Easter recounts how God increases the number of members of the church: "Father, you give your church constant growth by adding new members to your family. Help us put into action in our lives the baptism we have received with faith."[72] This prayer praises God for those who have been reborn by baptism and have become members of the church—family of God.

The prayer over the gifts on the Friday of the second week of Easter refers to the church as God's family: "Lord, accept these gifts from your family. May we hold fast to the life you have given us and come to the eternal gifts you promise."[73] Also, the opening Eucharistic prayer for the Fifth Sunday in Ordinary time beseeches God to watch over God's family gathered in prayers: "In faith and love we ask you, Father, to watch over your family gathered here. In your mercy and loving kindness no thought of ours is left unguarded, no tear unheeded, no joy unnoticed. Through the prayer of Jesus may the blessings promised to the poor in spirit lead us to the treasures of your heavenly kingdom."[74]

The *Preface for the Weekdays III* reiterates the fact that the church is the family of God. The church prays thus: "Through your beloved Son you created our human family. Through him you restored us to your likeness."[75] In this prayer, there is a shift from referring to the church as the family of God to a more inclusive human family. The whole human race is acknowledged here as one family of God, which has been created through the Logos, Jesus the Son of God.

The understanding of the human race, as well as the church, as the family is clearly brought out in the *Preface of Marriage I:* "You have designed the chaste love of husband and wife for the increase both of the human family and of your own family (church) born in baptism."[76] Similarly, in the Eucharistic Prayer III, the church equally prays as one family thus: "Father, hear the prayers of the family you have gathered here before you. In mercy and love unite all your children wherever

---

[71] ICEL, *The Sacramentary* (New York: Catholic Book Publishing Company, 1985), 73.
[72] Ibid., 212.
[73] Ibid., 224.
[74] Ibid., 284.
[75] Ibid., 451.
[76] Ibid., 517.

they may be. Welcome into your kingdom our departed brothers and sister, and all who have left this world in your friendship."[77]

A review of the biblical, magisterial, and liturgical/sacramental foundations of the church as the family of God shows that, in principle, the church has *semper idem* seen itself as the one family of God. The church is not a gathering of an amorphous or rowdy crowd but an assembly of people of all races, nations, languages, and cultures who are constituted into a new family of God in Jesus Christ and sanctified by the Holy Spirit.

Although biblical, magisterial, and liturgical sources point to the fact that the church is God's family, the model has not been given the attention that it deserves in Catholic ecclesiology. Its implications for the church have not been explored, nor has the model played any role in promoting and advancing the ecclesiology and mission of the church.

---

[77] Ibid., 554.

Chapter 4

THE THEOLOGY OF INCULTURATION

Since the model of the church as the extended family of God for Africa is predicated on the theology of inculturation, an understanding of the meaning and history of inculturation is critical to connect this model with African ecclesio-missiology. The theology of inculturation not only serves as the theological framework for a deeper appreciation of this model, it also paves the way for an Africentric ecclesiology and missiology.

Inculturation is a relatively new term in theology,[1] but, de facto, its application in the church is as old as Christianity. Inculturation is a theological method that is fundamental to the deep rooting and implantation of the Gospel in any culture. It seeks at the same time to resolve conflict between the Gospel and its encounter with non-Western cultures. Father Oliver Onwubiko, a Nigerian theologian and missiologist, aptly articulates this when he observes that inculturation is "a new vision of an old problem in the Church or a new approach to a solution of the Church and cultures it encounters."[2] Onwubiko's observation stems from the fact

---

[1] John Paul II calls inculturation a neologism in his *Apostolic Exhortation*, *Catechesi Tradendae,* # 53. There is no agreement among theologians as to when and who first used term. Father Ary Roest Crollius, a missiologist contends that it is not impossible that the earliest use of the term was in 1962. Crollius credits P. B. Segura as the first to use the term. See his *What Is So New about Inculturation?* (Rome: Editrice Pontificia Universita Gregoriana, 1997), 27. On the other hand, David Bosch in his *Transforming Mission,* 447, and Aylward Shorter in his *Toward a Theology of Inculturation,* 10, credit Joseph Masson as the first to use the term *Catholicisme inculture* in a 1962 article in which he refers to the urgent need for a Catholicism that is inculturated in a variety of forms. Today the term is widely used in missiological circles.

[2] Oliver A. Onwubiko, *Theory and Practice of Inculturation: An African Perspective* (Enugu, Nigeria: Snaap Publishing Company, 1992), 1.

that the first Christians grappled with questions of the relationship between faith and culture (of the gentiles) and the place of culture in evangelization.

Inculturation gained acceptance among theologians and church leaders from developing countries in the later part of the twentieth century. Ary Roest Crollius, SJ, describes inculturation as a "concept situated in the borderlands between anthropological sciences [culture] and theology, and heavy with implications from both these areas of knowledge."[3] Because the concept of inculturation is relatively new to theology, there is need to explore its evolution, meaning and functionality in the church's self-understanding of its nature and mission. Before I go into this discourse, I will briefly explore similar but different concepts associated with inculturation. Such concepts include culture, enculturation, acculturation, contextualization, and adaptation, a term that the Vatican II Council adopted in its reforms of the Roman liturgy, particularly regarding the celebration of the Eucharist in local languages.

Culture

Since the theology of inculturation involves the inception and the interaction of faith and culture, it is necessary to provide a definition of culture. The word culture has its roots in the Latin word *cultus*, a term having to do originally with the cultivation of the soil, care and tending of crops or animals.[4] When applied anthropologically, culture is the cultivation of human behavior in the society. Human beings cultivate the character of their lives through groups and by living in communities, states, nations, regions, and so forth. In this sense, culture is a modus vivendi, a way of life of a particular group of people or of society.

Edward B. Taylor sees culture as "that complex whole which includes knowledge, belief, art, morals, law, custom and any other capabilities and habits acquired by man [human being] as a member of society."[5] In other words, culture is the ensemble of a people's way of life, which distinguishes them from other human groups or societies.

Culture is a human contrivance in the sense that it is derived from human conventions and constructs that are cognitively acquired as a member of society. By the same token, culture embodies the learned aspect as opposed to the inherited

---

[3] Ary Roest Crollius. *What is So New about Inculturation?* (Rome: Pontifical Gregorian University, 1984), 1-2. Emphasis mine.

[4] Kathryn Tanner, *Theories of Culture: A New Agenda for Theology* (Minneapolis: Fortress Press, 1997), 3.

[5] Edward B. Taylor, *Primitive Culture,* 1891. Cited in Aylward Shorter, *Toward a theology of Inculturation*, 4. Emphasis mine.

aspect.[6] Culture is not just about human behavior but also about ideas, mental constructs, symbols, stories, myths, attitudes toward life, etc.[7] In essence, culture is a vehicle for transmitting meanings embodied in symbols and a phenomenon of human activity.

An essential characteristic of culture is that it is dynamic, always evolving and adapting to innovations and discoveries. What used to be normative, for example, a hundred years ago, could be considered obsolete and outlandish in present society. Another essential characteristic of culture is that it varies from society to society. While the concept is universal in the sense that all people have cultures, it does not follow that all people have the same culture, though there are certain elements that cut across societies. Hence, the classicist assumption that there is only one civilized culture is untenable. Again, although human beings construct and shape culture, they are at the same time shaped and formed by their cultures.[8]

From this brief analysis of culture, it is obvious that culture includes social, religious, behavioral, and cognitive aspects of human beings. Culture is a product of human creative ingenuity that distinguishes groups and societies from each other. It also shapes how people interpret fundamental aspects of their lives. At the same time, culture maintains some form of permanence and uniqueness. It necessarily follows that religion is a human activity, and as a human act, it is equally affected by culture. Therefore, culture is crucial to the church's mission of evangelization and, thus, an integral component of the theology of inculturation.

Enculturation

Enculturation[9] is a sociological concept used analogously to describe the theological notion of inculturation.[10] As a sociological term, it denotes "the process by which an individual becomes inserted into his or her culture."[11] Put in another way, enculturation is the socialization of an individual into his or her culture. Sociologists use the term socialization to refer to an education of an individual by society until one achieves competence in one's own culture.[12] This process could happen through formal education or in an informal way by association and inter-subjectivity.

---

[6] Ibid.
[7] Aylward Shorter, *Toward a theology of Inculturation*, 4.
[8] Kathryn Tanner, *Theories of Culture*, 28.
[9] David Bosch, *Transforming Mission*, 447. Bosch credits Pierre Charles as the first to introduce the concept from cultural anthropological circles into missiology.
[10] Aylward Shorter, *Toward a Theology of Inculturation*, 5.
[11] Ibid.
[12] Peter Schineller, *A Handbook on Inculturation* (New York: Paulist Press, 1990), 22.

An important attribute of enculturation is that it is an ongoing process. As long as a person is alive, he or she continues to gather cultural information, even subconsciously, from images, symbols, rituals, customs, norms, etc. To a greater extent, the individual teaches himself or herself, through the process of adaptive learning, the rules and norms that are valued by society. Again, Shorter offers an insight into how this occurs when he notes that the images or symbols of a culture are in themselves didactic; they teach the individual to construct his or her own categories and even to transcend them in the very act of constructing them.[13]

The difference between enculturation and inculturation lies in the fact that while enculturation inserts an individual into his or her own culture, inculturation inserts the Christian faith into a culture where it did not previously exist. Inculturation is a theological method, which adopts the tools of cultural anthropology. Enculturation, as a sociological concept, deals primarily with human behavior and socialization. It is more of a socio-anthropological concept than a theological method. Nevertheless, inculturation sometimes adopts enculturation's method of socialization of the faith into a culture. A classic example is the total Christianization of Europe and the Europeanization of Christianity that occurred during the middle ages.

Acculturation

Acculturation is closely related to the theological concept of inculturation. It is often confused with and sometimes used interchangeably with inculturation. However, it is worth noting that the two terms are not one and the same. Although acculturation differs from inculturation, it is a sine qua non for inculturation. While acculturation is a cultural anthropological concept denoting the interaction of two cultures and the changes that result,[14] inculturation, as we mentioned earlier, is a theological concept. For instance, acculturation would occur when an individual migrates to a different country. The process of that individual's integration in the host culture is called acculturation.

Since human beings have cognitive and rational capacities, they are able to adapt to particular cultural traditions; hence, in the process of acculturation, the individual reflectively assimilates some aspects of the new culture the individual finds him or herself and, at the same time, retains some of his or her own culture. The result of acculturation can be discerned post factum at the conscious level. However, many of the conflicts acculturation engenders are worked out at the subconscious level.[15] Acculturation elicits some changes in ideas and behaviors.

---

[13] Aylward Shorter, *Toward a Theology of Inculturation*, 5.
[14] Ary Roest Crollius, *What Is So New about Inculturation?* 4.
[15] Aylward Shorter, *Toward a Theology of Inculturation*, 7.

It also demands a critical openness, mutual respect, and receptivity toward other cultures.

Adaptation

The recognition of cultural pluralism by the church marked a watershed in the emergence of the theology of inculturation. Pope Pius XII, arguably, made this recognition official in his address to the Pontifical Mission Aid Societies in 1944.[16] This recognition, without doubt, led to the adoption of the concept of adaptation in theology by Vatican II.

Adaptation is understood as "the extrinsic adaptation of the one Catholic faith in order to render it acceptable to different groups of people."[17] For Father Anscar Chupungco, president and professor of Liturgical History at the Pontifical Liturgical Institute in Rome, adaptation is characterized by substitution and assimilation. The former is carried out by replacing pagan cultic elements with Christian one. By assimilation, the church adopted pagan rituals and gestures into which she infused with Christian meanings.[18] However, it was at the Second Vatican Council that the concept was fleshed out and given impetus. In its reform of the Roman Rite, the council set the criteria of adaptation when it says, "Even in liturgy, the Church has no wish to impose a rigid uniformity in matters which do not involve the faith or the good of the whole community. Rather she respects and fosters the spiritual adornments and gifts of the various races and peoples."[19] The council further teaches: "In some places and circumstances, however, even more radical adaptation of the liturgy is needed and entails greater difficulties."[20] The council's document on the liturgy, *Sacrosantum Concilium*, offers one instance in which a radical adaptation is necessary for mission territories: "In mission lands initiation rites are found in use among individual peoples. Elements from these, when capable of being adapted to Christian ritual, may be admitted along with those already found in Christian tradition."[21]

In its decree on the missionary activity of the church, *Ad Gentes,* Vatican II also calls for a form of missionary adaptation that covers, among other things, methods of evangelization, forms of worship, and so forth that are in consonance with the culture of each people. The council maintains that "the faith must be

---

[16] Ibid., 183.

[17] Ibid.

[18] Anscar Chupungco, *Cultural Adaptation of the Liturgy* (New York: Paulist Press, 1982), 23-24.

[19] *Sacrosantum Concilium,* # 38.

[20] Ibid., #40.

[21] Ibid.

taught by an adequate catechesis celebrated in a liturgy which harmonizes with the genius of the people, and introduced into upright institutions and local customs by appropriate canonical legislation."[22] Inasmuch as the council recognized cultural pluralism and did not wish to "impose rigid uniformity" and advocated for cultural adaptation,[23] it seems that its insistence on preserving the "substantial unity of the Roman rite" as *conditio sine qua non* for all liturgical adaptation falls short of a genuine inculturation. On the contrary, it promotes adaptation.

Because adaptation tends to substitute and/or replace western categories and concepts with local equivalents, it is perceived as theological substitution. Thus, it must be recognized that adaptation is not synonymous with inculturation.[24] It is not surprising, therefore, that Robert J. Schreiter observes that adaptation is replete with categories, names, and concerns of a local culture, which look like western theology and are easily understood by Westerners.[25] Adaptation's primary concern is to find similarities between western Christianity and other cultures it encounters.

Contextualization

Contextualization is closely related to adaptation. As the name implies, contextualization, used within a theological context, concentrates more directly on the cultural context in which Christianity takes root and receives expression.[26] As a theological method, contextualization is employed more in the field of biblical exegesis than in other theological branches. By the same token, the interest of biblical exegetes, among others, is to make the Gospel take deep root in the full life of their communities and, thereafter, to grow into its full stature in the people's cultural contexts.[27]

Contextualization suggests that individuals can respond and interpret the Scripture within the gamut of their cultural situation. Bruce J. Nicholls notes that theology, including biblical theology, is culturally conditioned and, therefore,

---

[22] *Ad Gentes,* # 19.

[23] *Sacrosantum Concilium,* # 37-38.

[24] Eugene Hillman, *Inculturation Applied Toward an African Christianity* (New Jersey: Paulist Press, 1993), 86.

[25] Robert Schreiter, *Constructing Local Theologies* (New York: Orbis Books, 1985), 10.

[26] Ibid., 12.

[27] Chris Manus Ukachukwu, "Methodological Approaches in Contemporary African Biblical Scholarship: The Case of West Africa," *African Theology Today,* ed. Emmanuel Katongole (Scranton: The University of Scranton Press, 2002), 7-8.

cannot but be contextualized.[28] Nicholls goes on to assert, with some exaggeration, that because missionaries to Africa and other continents did not contextualize the Gospel, the Gospel was presented in an inchoate way, devoid of the people's cultural expressions.[29]

Contextualization did not gain much popularity because of its narrow and limited audience. It is concerned more with cultural identity, contextual biblical interpretation, and so forth. Contextualization easily lends itself to crass relativism. Besides, contextual theology is ethnographically constricted.

Inculturation: Theological Underpinning

There is no one single overarching and acceptable definition of inculturation. We shall consider some salient theories of inculturation. Aylward Shorter defines it as "the on-going dialogue between faith and culture or cultures . . . the creative and dynamic relationship between the Christian message and a culture or cultures."[30] For Ary Crollius, SJ, inculturation is the integration of the Christian experience of the local church into the culture of its people in such a way that this experience not only expresses itself in elements of this culture but also becomes a force that animates, orients, and innovates this culture.[31] This force creates a new unity and communion not only within the culture in question but also in the universal church.

Pedro Arrupe (former superior general of the Society of Jesus) brought to the fore the concept of inculturation in theological circles. He defines inculturation as:

> The incarnation of Christian life and the Christian message in a particular cultural context, in such a way that this experience not only finds expression through elements proper to the culture in question (this alone would be no more than a superficial adaptation) but becomes a principle that animates, directs and unifies the culture, transforming it and remaking it so as to bring about a new creation.[32]

---

[28] Bruce J. Nicholls, *Contextualization: A Theology of Gospel and Culture* (Downers Grove, IL: Intervarsity Press, 1979), 25.

[29] Ibid., 28.

[30] Aylward Shorter, *Toward a Theology of Inculturation,* 11.

[31] Ary A. Crollius, *What is so New about Inculturation?* 4.

[32] Pedro Arrupe, "Father General's Letter on Inculturation to the Whole Society," *Jesuit Formation and Inculturation in India Today.* Cited in Aylward Shorter, *Towards a Theology of Inculturation,* 11.

A critical look at Arrupe's definition reveals some underlying fundamental paradigms for the evangelization of any culture. In the first instance, inculturation as a theological method for evangelization is analogous to the mystery of the incarnation of Jesus Christ as a human being. Second, the object referent of inculturation is the incarnation of the Gospel into a hitherto non-Christian culture.

One can argue that the mystery of Christ's incarnation is the model for inculturation par excellence. The incarnation analogy is adopted as a suitable principle of inculturation because its *leitmotif* is to make Christ incarnate and relevant to a people within the ambience of their culture. This ensures that Christianity is at home in the evangelized culture, becoming a way of life or part of a people's culture.[33]

The incarnation of Christ is at the heart of human culture. By becoming human, Jesus became incarnated in a particular culture. While carrying out his ministry, he made use of the cultural elements, wisdom, values, parables, and traditions of his time and people. Following in the model of the incarnation, inculturation incarnates the Gospel in any given culture that it encounters. Thus, in order to ensure a proper evangelization of a people, "The Church," as Vatican II notes, "must become part of all these groups for the same motive which led Christ to bind Himself, in virtue of his incarnation, to the definite social and cultural conditions of those human beings among whom He dwelt."[34] The council goes on to say:

> There are many links between the message of salvation and human culture. For God, revealing Himself to His people to the extent of a full manifestation of Himself in His Incarnate Son, has spoken according to the culture proper to different ages. Living in various circumstances during the course of time, the Church, too, has used in her preaching the discoveries of different cultures to spread and explain the message of Christ to all nations, to probe it and more deeply understand it, and to give it better expression in liturgical celebrations and in the life of the diversified community of the faithful.[35]

The analogy of the incarnation of Christ as the paradigm for inculturation brings to light the indispensability of culture for effective evangelization of the people. The parallel between incarnation and inculturation as a theological method means that Christ is the subject referent of inculturation at any point in time. Therefore, it necessarily follows that African cultures and, specifically, Igbo culture are indispensable for the evangelization of the people of Africa. The

---

[33] Aylward Shorter, *Toward a Theology of Inculturation*, 62.
[34] *Ad Gentes*, # 10.
[35] *Gaudium et Spes*, # 58.

mystery of the incarnation of Christ did not render cultures redundant, but rather it elevates human culture to a higher pedestal.

Shorter is right when he observes that there could have been no earthly ministry for Jesus if he had not adopted the cultural concepts, symbols and behavior of his hearers. "His cultural solidarity with the Palestinian communities of his day was a necessary condition for communication with them. The same is true of the church in every age and place. Inculturation is a necessity for the continuation of Christ's mission."[36]

The Christocentric underpinning of the theology of inculturation as a method for evangelization has many positive aspects as well as potential limitations. On one hand, the incarnation parallel ensures that Jesus remains the subject referent of inculturation. In Jesus Christ can be seen "the appearance of the universal within the particular, the entry of the absolute into the relative, the manifestation of the eternal within the temporal, the revelation of the Infinite with the finite."[37] On the other hand, inculturation ensures that the people are adequately evangelized.

The process of inculturation is also transformative. Just as Jesus challenged the culture and unjust social structures of his time, inculturation challenges the culture of the evangelized, bringing out what is best and enabling a culture to realize its potential of being transformed.[38] Consequently, the process of inculturation involves a two-way mutually critical dialogue, with faith and culture reciprocally interacting with and enriching each other. This equally constitutes the criteria for determining the relative adequacy of a culture in the process of inculturation.

Some theologians find the analogy of the incarnation to be inadequate. First, the analogy tends to suggest that its primary focus is the socialization and/or education of Jesus by his culture. If that is the case, inculturation will simply be the initial incarnation of the Gospel into a culture.[39] Hence, the ongoing process of conversion and dialogue between faith and culture is overlooked and muffled. Second, the concept of inculturation can easily fall into cultural relativism or culturalism and syncretism. However, it is important to underscore the fact that Christianity is not free from syncretic practices. Some of the rituals, feasts, and rites of the church are emendations of pagan and Judaic practices, which the church adopted into its liturgical worship.

---

[36] Aylward Shorter, *Toward a Theology of Inculturation*, 80

[37] D. Lane, *The Challenge of Inculturation*. Cited in Bartholomew Winters. *Priest as Leader*, 40.

[38] T. H. Groome, "Inculturation: How to Proceed in a Pastoral Context," *Christianity and Cultures,* eds. Greinacher, N. and Mette, N. (London: Maryknoll, 1994), 120.

[39] Aylward Shorter. *Toward a Theology of Inculturation*, 81.

A way out of the critical limitations of the incarnation analogy of inculturation is to understand the incarnation in its full sense, which is inextricably bound with the paschal mystery of Christ. The purpose of the incarnation of Christ became manifest in his ministry and paschal mystery. Inculturation can analogously be connected to the ministry, passion, death, and resurrection of Christ as well as his incarnation in human flesh. As Christ became accessible to people of every culture through his incarnation, ministry, and paschal mystery, inculturation must analogously follow a similar pattern. In other words, in any encounter between the Gospel and culture, the culture must undergo a *metanoia*. As Christ died and rose again, so must a culture die and rise again when the Gospel confronts it.

> The Gospel invites people to reappraise their cultures in the light of radically new values that turn human thinking upside-down. Cultures are to be evangelized and to undergo *metanoia* or conversion at their profoundest level. They must "die" to all that is not worthy of humanity in their tradition, all that is a consequence of accumulated guilt and social sin. If human structures can be vitiated by sin, then human cultures can be similarly vitiated.... Faced by the challenge of the One who died and rose again, cultures are called to die in order to rise to a greater splendour.[40]

In summation, inculturation entails the "death" of a culture with the purpose of being transformed by the risen Christ. The culture must continuously be engaged in a radical transformation of itself. Because of this "death," the faith adopts a multiplicity of cultural identities when members of any given culture accept it. The obvious theological implication for us is that inculturation makes the faith acceptable to people of diverse cultures. This means that the church, while speaking from within a culture, should be conscious of the fact that no fragment of culture or human experience is foreign to Christ.[41]

Inculturation: A Panacea to Authentic Evangelization

The word evangelization is derived from the Greek *euangelion* and the Latin *evangelizare* meaning "to convey the good news of wedding, party, athletic victory or such like."[42] The term evangelization was later transposed into Christianity to

---

[40] Ibid., 83-84.

[41] Francis E. George, *Inculturation and Ecclesial Communion: Culture and Church in the Teaching of Pope John Paul II* (Rome: Urbaniana University Press, 1990), 224.

[42] Robert J. H., "Distinctive Qualities of Catholic Evangelization," *The New Catholic Evangelization,* ed. Boyack K. (New York: Paulist Press, 1992), 14.

denote preaching, witnessing, and proclamation of the Gospel (Good News) of Jesus Christ. In the New Testament, St. Paul uses the term *euangelizo* primarily as a missionary term to mean "Announcing the Good News of Jesus" (Eph. 1:22; Col. 1:18).

Given the missionary character of the church, evangelization and mission basically came to denote the spreading of the Good News or, as Pope Pius VI puts it, "Bringing the Good News into all the strata of humanity, and through its influence transforming humanity from within and making it new."[43] Thus, evangelization primarily is directed toward proclaiming anew and spreading the Good News of Jesus Christ to both believers and nonbelievers.

Inculturation as a theological method for evangelization makes it possible for every culture to hear the message of the Gospel in their language and cultural context. As Pope Paul VI clearly notes, the Gospel and, therefore, evangelization are certainly not identical with culture. The Gospel is independent of all cultures. Nevertheless, the Kingdom, which the Gospel proclaims, is lived by people who are profoundly linked to a culture. Thus, the building up of the Kingdom cannot avoid borrowing the elements of human cultures.[44]

Though independent of cultures, the pope insists that the Gospel and evangelization are not incompatible with all culture; rather, they are capable of permeating all cultures without becoming subject to any one of them.[45] In essence, Pope Paul VI hinges his teaching on the fact that the Christian faith cannot exist without cultural forms. By the same token, the Gospel, as Cardinal George notes, while always expressed in cultural forms, transcends all cultures.[46] Also, to define inculturation as a dialogue between faith and culture is tantamount to speaking of a dialogue between a culture and the faith in a cultural form, that is, a dialogue between the Christianized culture of the missionary and the hitherto un-Christianized culture to which the missionary comes.[47] The necessity of inculturation as a theological method for evangelization cannot be overemphasized. Inculturation is an assuredly critical means through which Jesus Christ enters into a living relationship with a cultural tradition.

The Special Assembly for Africa of the Synod of Bishops took up the issue of inculturation as a theological method for evangelization. The synod fathers were confronted with two fundamental challenges and/or questions: (1) how must the church carry out its evangelizing mission at the dawn of the third millennium (twenty-first century) and (2) how can African Christians become ever more

---

[43] Pope Paul VI, *Apostolic Exhortation: Evangelii Nuntiandi* (London: Catholic Truth Society, 1975), # 18.

[44] Ibid., # 20.

[45] Ibid.

[46] Francis George, *Inculturation and Ecclesial Communion*, 12.

[47] Aylward Shorter, *Toward a Theology of Inculturation*, 12.

faithful witnesses to the Lord Jesus Christ? Addressing these challenges and questions, the synod fathers held that inculturation will help to actualize these goals. This assertion substantiates the fact that inculturation "seeks to dispose people to receive Jesus Christ in an integral manner. It touches them on the personal, cultural, economic, and political levels so that they can live a holy life in total union with God the Father, under the action of the Holy Spirit."[48]

Pope John Paul II, responding to the two questions and challenges, which the synod fathers grappled with, called for a more profound evangelization that is rooted in the theology of inculturation. John Paul II believed that inculturation is not only necessary but of urgent priority for the firm rooting of the Gospel in Africa and a requirement for the full evangelization of Africa.[49] The underlying rationale behind the pope's insistence on the urgent need for inculturation is that human beings are deeply tied to culture and cannot be evangelized unless they are addressed in terms of their culture, and as David Bosch suggests, "there is no such thing as a 'pure' gospel, isolated from culture."[50]

His Beatitude Stephanos II, Patriarch of Alexandria for the Egyptian Coptic church, aptly captures the essence of inculturation when he says, "If one wishes to guarantee the survival of Christianity and to safeguard the faith and the essence of the ecclesial tradition in our African countries, inculturation in evangelization is absolutely imperative."[51] Stephanos II goes on to insist that the task of inculturation in Africa is a matter of urgent priority. He contends that the churches of North Africa (the Maghreb), which were thriving in the early centuries of Christianity at the time of St. Cyprian and St. Augustine, unfortunately have not survived and have virtually no indigenous members because of the lack of inculturation. "At the same time," he says, "the Coptic churches of Egypt and Ethiopia remain very much alive, despite the most atrocious persecution and vicissitudes of all kinds through the centuries due to real inculturation."[52]

The process of inculturation, as a theological method of evangelization, is analogous to the modus operandi of anthropological concepts of enculturation and acculturation. As a person is inserted into his or her own culture, or undergoes the process of socialization (enculturation) or encounters another culture (acculturation), the faith is also inserted analogously into a culture. During the insertion or encounter between the faith and a culture, the culture undergoes a measure of reformation and reinterpretation. The concomitant result is a critical

---

[48] Maura Browne, *The African Synod: Documents, Reflection, Propositions*, # 32, 97.

[49] John Paul II, *Ecclesia in Africa*, # 46.

[50] David J. Bosch, *Transforming Mission: Paradigm Shifts in Theology of Mission* (New York: Orbis Books, 1991), 297.

[51] *L'Osservatore Romano*, # 19, weekly edition (May 11, 1994), 12.

[52] Ibid.

symbiosis of the faith and culture or, rather, a situation where, as John Paul II contends, the faith becomes culture, thereby synthesizing humankind's entire existence around Christ, the Wisdom of God.[53] The culture becomes enlivened by the faith. Similarly, just as enculturation is an ongoing process in the life of an individual, the same is applicable to the process of inculturation in the church.

The choice of inculturation over other methods or paradigms invariably portends that missionaries would no longer go into a culture as people who assume they have answers to every question. Rather, they would go as learners and participants in dialogue with the culture. They will not seek to "bring Christ" to the people, but they would enable the people they meet to recognize and discover the presence of Jesus Christ in their own cultural context. John Paul II made this clear in one of his pastoral visits to Africa in Nairobi, Kenya, in 1980 when he said, "In you, Christ has himself become African."[54] This is the core of inculturation—the incarnation of Christ in African or, more specifically, in Igbo culture.

Suffice it to note that inculturation does not mean a total endorsement of a culture in its encounter with the Gospel. On the contrary, inculturation adopts a mutually critical approach to a culture, resulting in a constant dialogue. It challenges and critiques a culture with the purpose of stripping it of all elements that impede the full theophany of God's truth and love. In the encounter between culture and the Gospel, inculturation aims at what I would call a *culturization* of Christianity and a Christianization of culture. The Gospel, while remaining what it is, becomes a true cultural reality.

Scriptural Foundation of Inculturation

As we pointed out earlier in another section, inculturation is not, per se, a new concept in theology nor is it relevant only to African churches. In fact, in the Bible, there are several applications of inculturation method. This section will discuss the scriptural foundation and bases of inculturation. It is important to note that the Scripture did not use the term inculturation, but its application is obvious from scriptural texts.

Biblical scholars (for instance Maher) argue that because of Israel's encounter with other cultures, the book of Genesis is a collection of literature from many centuries and cultures. Cardinal Francis George supports this view when he says that Old Testament writers borrowed from Semitic cultures and from peoples around them in order to talk of the cosmos and of the dealings of God with his people.[55] Oliver Onwubiko shares similar views when inter alia, he opines:

---

[53] John Paul II, *Familiaris Consortio*, # 10.
[54] *African Ecclesiastical Review* 22, # 4, (1980), 198.
[55] Francis E. George, *Inculturation and Ecclesial Communion*, 166.

> In the Old Testament, the influence of the Nations in the purification of Israel's monotheistic beliefs are good reference points of inculturation... for instance, Israel copied three basic Canaanite agricultural festivals, whose fertility aspects they ignored, but reinterpreted in the light of Israel's divine history and gave them salvific importance. "Pagan" symbols, like the Temple, were integrated, justified religiously and theologically. Rituals too were taken over from the Arabians and Mesopotamians; the Holocaust is a typical example.[56]

It is a well-known fact that the authors of Hebrew scriptures were deeply influenced by the cultures of the surrounding nations. One can then infer that God's self-revelation to the people of Israel and the tremendous influence of the "nations" were at the heart of the documentation of the Word of God. René Latourette strongly argues that the literary laws of the "nations" and sapiential literatures, which belong to an "international current of thoughts" from Greece, Egypt, Babylon, Phoenicia, were transformed into an instrument of divine revelation in Israel.[57] Actually, it was during the exilic period that the Word of Yahweh was written.

John Bright suggests that there is a massive influence of the "nations" on the Hebrew scriptures, which cannot be glossed over. Bright contends that Pentateuchal law exhibits numerous similarities to the law codes of second-millennium Mesopotamia (the Code of Hammurabi and others). Thus, some connection must be assumed.[58] For Bright, "The Decalogue, entirely apodictic in form and for the most part negatively stated, is the outstanding example of this."[59] Bright, however, argues that this borrowing was not directly from Mesopotamia but probably from people absorbed into Israel's structure who were of the same stock as her ancestors, whose legal tradition was ultimately of Mesopotamian origin.[60] Bright goes further to surmise that the book of Genesis in its creation and flood narratives (Gen. 1, 2, 6, 9) borrowed extensively from the ancient creation myths and epic legends of Mesopotamia.[61] It is equally true that the Torah is in many ways similar to the Assyrian, Sumerian, and Hittite law codes, all of which predate it. The examples cited above all point to some form of inculturation at work during the formation of Hebrew Scripture, theology, and culture. What is at issue here

---

[56] Oliver Onwubiko, *Theory and Practice of Inculturation*, 72.

[57] René Latourette, *Theology of Revelation* (New York: Alba House, 1967), 27.

[58] John Bright, *A History of Israel*, 2nd edition (Philadelphia: The Westminster Press, 1972), 165.

[59] Ibid.

[60] Ibid., 166.

[61] Ibid.

is that God's self-revelation (theophany) was made manifest within the cultural ambient of Jewish people and the surrounding nations.

In reading the New Testament, the question of the fundamental role of culture comes to the fore. The mystery of Jesus' incarnation on which the theology of inculturation is anchored cannot be understood without some knowledge of both Jewish and Hellenistic cultures.[62] While carrying out his mission, Jesus made use of the cultural elements of his people. He used the local food and wine to institute the Eucharist at his last Passover meal. He equally made use of the local idioms, parables, and stories of his Jewish culture to give emphasis and impetus to his teachings. Jesus gave new orientation to Jewish rites, imbuing them with his own mystery. For example, "the Last Supper is a case of reinterpretation of the paschal meal: no longer a memorial of the exodus, but of his passing over from this world to the father for the salvation of mankind."[63] Nevertheless, it must be noted that Jesus did not give blanket approval of all cultural practices of his people. He was very critical of certain customs and norms of his society. He challenged certain cultural practices that were inimical to and constituted obstacles to salvation and the liberation of his people. His opposition to these aspects of Jewish culture earned him the hatred and hostility of the religious authorities and led inevitably to his passion and death.[64]

The Acts of the Apostles, which recorded the history and practices of the first Christian communities, offers us deep insights into the challenges the first Christians faced as they took the Gospel to other cultures and outside Jewish territories. The celebrated first Council of Jerusalem, recorded in Acts 15, was convened principally to deal with a cultural issue—whether or not to require circumcision from non-Jewish (Greek and gentiles) converts to Christianity. In the end, the Council of Jerusalem established the church's criteria for determining the proper relationship that should exist between faith and other cultures in the course of evangelization.[65] Some of the criteria include:

- Circumcision is not required for membership of the church.
- Profession of faith in Jesus Christ.
- Baptism in the lord, and so forth.

The decision of the council not to encumber the new converts with Jewish cultural and religious practice is a classic example of inculturation. The apostles under the guidance of the Holy Spirit were able to distinguish and separate the faith from cultural practices. Conversion does not necessarily require the convert

---

[62] Aylward Shorter, *Toward a Theology of Inculturation*, 84.
[63] Anscar Chupungco, *Cultural Adaptation of the Liturgy*, 7.
[64] Aylward Shorter, *Toward a Theology of Inculturation*, 120.
[65] Oliver Onwubiko, *Theory and Practice of Inculturation*, 74.

to give up his or her culture for another. Onwubiko believes that in hindsight, the purpose of the Council of Jerusalem was to establish the church's principles for interacting with other cultures in carrying out its missionary mandate.[66]

Paul, the great apostle to the gentiles, was instrumental in shaping the decision of the Council of Jerusalem not to require gentile converts to submit to Mosaic Law but to keep the faith and refrain from what was unbecoming of Christians. Inasmuch as Paul was critical of the Greek and Roman philosophies, he nevertheless embraced every culture he encountered. Paul felt free to identify with any culture or social category. His goal was to become all things to all men and women (1 Cor. 19-23). Paul took the cultures of those he came to evangelize seriously, using them as staging grounds to engage each culture in dialogue with the Gospel. What mattered most to Paul was not culture but obedience to the Gospel. Revisiting the issue of circumcision, Paul's admonition to his Corinthian Christian community is very insightful:

> I give this order in all the churches. Was someone called after he had been circumcised? He should not try to undo his circumcision. Was an uncircumcised person called? He should not be circumcised. Circumcision means nothing and uncircumcision means nothing; what matters is keeping God's commandments [obedience to the Gospel]. Everyone should remain in the state in which he was called (1 Cor. 7:17-20).

In the light of Paul's missionary activities to the gentile world, exercised within the cultural framework of Greco-Roman matrix, it seems that Paul laid the groundwork for inculturation as an effective method of evangelization. Paul refused to accept the uncritical Judeo-Christian form of the Gospel that did not take into account the cultures of the gentile converts, which culminated in the Council of Jerusalem as noted above. The same arguments can be propounded when it comes to the evangelization of Africans.

This discourse on the scriptural foundation of inculturation leads to these conclusions: (1) The faith is a catalyst in human history and a product of inculturation. (2) God's self-revelation is made intelligible in human cultures. (3) This self-revelation does not preclude any particular culture from serving as a means through which God's self-revelation is made manifest. (4) Faith transcends every culture, but it cannot be transmuted by one culture. (5) Because of the importance of Jerusalem, both as the "mother church" and as the point of departure for the early Christians' missionary activities to the gentile and Hellenistic world, it remains a focal point and paradigm for inculturation process.[67]

---

[66] Ibid., 75.

[67] Francis E. George, *Inculturation and Ecclesial Communion*, 168.

It does not follow that we have to do away with the scripture because of its Mediterranean cultural heritage. On the contrary, the Bible remains indispensable to the Christian faith. However, the history of our forebears in faith is taken up through Christ into our history and transformed into a faith that is authentically African and Christian at the same time. Thus, it is important to underscore the fact that the prophets of the Old Testament, the apostles, the early Christians were very critical, not only of each other but also of their societies. At the same time, they remained people of their culture and their own time.[68] For the same reason, Africans must be critical of themselves, their society and cultures, and must remain who they are—Africans and Christians.

Inculturation in the Patristic Age

In light of our contemporary understanding of inculturation, it is difficult to classify the works of most of the fathers as promoting inculturation. This reluctance stems from the fact that the fathers borrowed, or rather substituted and "baptized," many pagan practices and incorporated them into Christianity. Evidence of such substitutions or borrowings abounds in liturgical, sacramental, and even in doctrinal formulations of the church.

When the church encountered the Greco-Roman cultures, it absorbed its symbols of authority, language, institutions, legal systems, and military terminologies.[69] An example of such transmutation is the celebration of the birth of Christ (Christmas), which replaced the celebration of the birth of the "sun-god" in Mithriac religion.[70] Another classic example is found in the *Didaché* (written between AD 90 and AD 120). The *Didaché* has instructions for the substitution of some Jewish prayers with prayers centered on Christ. While not rejecting Jewish prayers, the *Didaché* makes them Christocentric.

St. Justin Martyr (d. 165), a teacher of philosophy, who was one of the early fathers blazed the trail in the adoption of an inculturation-like methodology to evangelize and offer an *apologia* of the Christian faith. One of Justin's major contributions to Christian theology was his idea of *Spermatic Logos*. Justin, in explaining the Christian faith, used a "pagan" term, *spermatikos logos*, seed-bearing word, to refer to Jesus Christ. Justin argues that the *spermatikos logos* became human in the incarnation. He goes on to say that the *spermatikos logos* is implanted in the heart of every human culture, since all things were created through him and

---

[68] Ibid.

[69] Oliver Onwubiko, *Theory and Practice of Inculturation*, 75.

[70] Anscar Chupungco, *Cultural Adaptation of the Liturgy* (New York: Paulist Press, 1982), 24.

in him.[71] Justin's innovative contribution consists of what in hindsight we will call an inculturation of the "pagan" *spermatikos logos* into Christology and his use of this method to teach about the incarnation of Christ in every culture. Justin goes at length to postulate that those who lived before Christ in accordance to reason are Christians, though they did not see or hear about Christ:

> But lest some should, without reason, and for the perversion of what we teach, maintain that we say that Christ was born one hundred and fifty years ago under Cyrenius, and subsequently, in the time of Pontius Pilate, taught what we say He taught; and should cry out against us as though all men who were born before Him were irresponsible—let us anticipate and solve the difficulty. We have been taught that Christ is the first-born of God, and we have declared above that He is the Word of whom every race of men [humankind] were partakers; and those who lived reasonably are Christians, even though they have been thought atheists; as, among the Greeks, Socrates and Heraclitus, and men [people] like them; and among the barbarians, Abraham, and Ananias, and Azarias, and Misael, and Elias, and many others whose actions and names we now decline to recount, because we know it would be tedious.[72]

Justin used his philosophical knowledge to advance the Christian faith. He drew parallels between the Christian faith and the works of pagan philosophers. His major contribution to inculturation was his insistence that Logos is implanted in every human culture. Thus, the task of every missionary is not to bring Christ to the pagan culture, but to discover Logos in the culture, language, proverbs, and rituals of the people to be evangelized.

Anscar Chupungco, elucidating on the overt influence of the Greco-Roman cultures on the formation of Catholic liturgy, argues that the early church adapted rituals of pagan and Greco-Roman culture. Chunpungco goes further to say, "This practice became an enduring principle for succeeding centuries."[73] Interestingly, Chupungco maintains that liturgical and theological adaptations were not the fruit of previous theological reflections. "The preoccupation at that time," Chupungco says, "was how to preserve the Jewish heritage and at the same time maintain the newness of Christianity."[74] The model that was operative in this era was either

---

[71] Aylward Shorter, *Toward a Theology of Inculturation*, 76.
[72] St. Justin Martyr, *Apologia 1*, XLVI. Emphasis mine.
[73] Anscar Chupungco, *Cultural Adaptation of the Liturgy*, 13.
[74] Ibid.

substitution or assimilation. Oliver Onwubiko calls this model "the principle of *like* replacing *like*."[75]

The principle of adaptation, substitution, or assimilation continued into the seventh century until relative uniformity was established in liturgical celebration and in theology. When the church began to send missionaries to cultures outside the Greco-Roman world, the relationship of faith and culture assumed a different dimension. While some missionaries made efforts to engage in dialogue with the different cultures they came in contact with as a means of evangelization, their efforts were scuttled by papal authorities in Rome. The case of Mateo Ricci (which will be discussed in another section of this chapter) is a classic example. In summation, it seems that though the fathers of the church were not engaged in inculturation, as we know it today, their works and theology laid the foundation for theology of inculturation.

Inculturation in the Medieval and Reformation Era

During the period under review, the church's encounter with non-Christian cultures outside the Greco-Roman culture was long and tumultuous. Attempts by missionaries to engage non-Christian cultures in dialogue and to inculturate some aspects of these cultures into the church were stifled by Rome. Efforts were concentrated on the *Latinization* and uniformity of the church, including mission territories. Shorter observes that the Latin Church at the end of the middle ages was culturally different from what it had been in the fifth and sixth centuries. During this period, the missionary fervor went hand in hand with a zeal for the spreading of the Latin language and culture, as well as the direct intervention of the papacy in the affairs of particular churches.[76]

The Latin Church was enthralled with the classicist view of culture and, as such, sought not only to evangelize non-Christian cultures, but also to "civilize" them. The case was different in the churches of the East, which were more tolerant of other cultures.

The efforts of Saints Cyril and Methodius during the ninth century to engage non-Christian cultures in dialogue were particularly successful in this regard. We will examine the missionary method of Cyril and Methodius in the next section of this chapter.

The Roman Church's insistence on *Latinization* and its attempt to bring uniformity to the church contributed to the Reformation. One of the greatest achievements of the reformers was the breaking of the monopoly of Latin and the subsequent translation of the Bible, liturgy, and other relevant religious literatures

---

[75] Oliver Onwubiko, *Theory and Practice of Inculturation*, 76.

[76] Aylward Shorter, *Toward a theology of Inculturation*, 150.

into vernacular languages. This led to some measure of plurality and freedom from the Latin Church by the reformers in Europe. Shorter offers us some insights into what transpired during this period when he says:

> At the Reformation, the cultures or sub-cultures of Europe came into their own. The period of gestation had been long indeed, and it had been lengthened by the imposition of the dominant Latin culture. The yoke had been finally thrown off and Protestant nations were tempted to go to the other extreme of cultural incapsulation, as well as to compromise the unity of faith, the Christian term, as we have called it, of inculturation.[77]

The Catholic Church Counter-Reformation, which culminated in the Council of Trent (1545-1563), led to a sweeping standardization and uniformity of theology and liturgy. Trent did not make any distinction between theology and its historical and cultural forms.[78] In essence, Trent promoted and entrenched a monocultural church rather than the pluralistic church advocated by the reformers. The standardization of clergy formation in seminaries, which was to be the same throughout the world, is a classic example of uniformity in the church.

Saints Cyril and Methodius

Cyril and Methodius were brothers, born in Thessalonika in 825 and 826, respectively. Originally monks, they were sent by Emperor Michael to evangelize the Khazars in Russia in 861. Two years later, they were sent to evangelize Moravia, now part of the modern Czech Republic. Their missionary ingenuity arguably marked a watershed in missionary evangelization. It also earned them ecclesiastical wrath from Rome. The two brothers adopted inculturation as a method for evangelization of the Slavs, and they succeeded to a great extent. Their major contributions consisted of (1) the invention of Cyrillic alphabets adapted to the phonetics of the Slavonic language, (2) the translation of the Bible into Slavonic, (3) the embracing of the Slavic culture in the course of evangelizing it.[79]

Pope John Paul II in his Encyclical letter to commemorate the eleventh centenary of the evangelizing work of Sts. Cyril and Methodius called them the Apostles of the Slavs.[80] They earned this title from the pope because of their

---

[77] Ibid., 153.

[78] Ibid., 154.

[79] Ibid., 144.

[80] John Paul II, *Slavorum Apostoli* (Boston: Pauline Books, 1985), # 1.

diligent zeal and methodic inculturated evangelization of the Slavic people. John Paul II notes that the value of Cyril and Methodius' contribution to evangelization, which they carried out as pioneers in a territory inhabited by Slavs, contains both a model of what today is called inculturation—the incarnation of the Gospel in native cultures and also the introduction of these cultures into the life of the church.[81]

Cyril and Methodius' method of evangelization did not involve bringing Christ to the Slavs, but rather they sought to find Christ among the people in their own culture. They believed that all nations, cultures, and civilizations have their own part to play in God's mysterious plan and in the universal history of salvation.[82]

As the two brothers engaged the Slavonic cultures in dialogue with the Christian faith, they realized that the faith does not exist as a disembodied reality; people in a particular culture embody it. Their successful evangelization of the Slavs was because of their genuine efforts to inculturate the faith into the people's culture.

Matteo Ricci (1552-1610)

The missionary work of Matteo Ricci, an Italian Jesuit, is another classic example of authentic inculturation. As a missionary to China, Ricci sought to penetrate the Chinese culture from within; hence, he initially adopted the style of life of a Buddhist monk. He later adopted the identity of a Confucian scholar when he realized that Buddhism was not the dominant religious culture of China.[83] Ricci and his fellow Jesuit missionaries embarked on a profound dialogue with the religious culture of the Chinese. Their goal was "to achieve a Christian reinterpretation of Chinese culture which would in turn, provoke a Chinese interpretation of Christianity presented in this sympathetic Chinese form."[84] Describing the ancestral cult, Ricci writes:

> The most solemn thing among the *literati* and in use from the king down to the very least being is the offering they annually make to the dead at certain times of the year of meat, fruits, perfumes, and pieces of silk cloth—paper among the poorest and incense. And in this act they make the fulfillment of their duty to their relatives, namely, "to serve them in death as though they were alive." Nor do they think in this matter that the dead will come to eat the things mentioned or that they might

---

[81] Ibid., # 21.

[82] John Paul II, *Slavorum Apostoli*, # 19.

[83] George Minamiki, *The Chinese Rites Controversy: From Its Beginning to Modern Times* (Chicago: Loyola University Press, 1985), 20.

[84] Aylward Shorter, *Toward a Theology of Inculturation*, 158.

need them; but they say they do this because they know of no other way to show their love and grateful spirit toward the dead. And some of them told us that his ceremony was begun more for the living than for the dead, that is, to teach the children and the ignorant ones to honor and serve their living relatives, since they (children) see serious people doing even after death the offices for the relatives that they were wont to do when they (the relatives) were alive.[85]

Ricci and his fellow Jesuit missionaries developed a "Chinese rite" by inculturating the Chinese ancestral cult into the liturgy as a means of evangelizing the Chinese people. Ricci was aware of the superstitious nature of the ancestral cult, but he sought to evangelize and make it compatible with Christian faith.[86]

Ricci's missionary approach was as controversial as it was innovative. He was accused by church authorities in Rome of practicing syncretism by using secular Chinese rites to honor the dead in Catholic requiem masses. By the time of Ricci's death in 1610, thousands of people had been baptized. Sadly, after Ricci's death, church authorities rejected his methodology for evangelization. Missionaries in China were ordered under pain of excommunication to stop such innovative practices by the decree of Pope Innocent X in 1645.[87] It took more than two hundred years for the church to rescind the blatant condemnation of Ricci's missionary method. Pope Pius XI made the rescission in 1939.[88]

John Paul II hailed Ricci as the model for a truly successful dialogue between cultures and the modern missionary. The pope, speaking in glowing terms, maintained that Ricci brought "the Christian revelation of the mystery of God to China in a way that did not destroy Chinese culture." His achievement, the pope goes on to say,

> Lay above all in the realm of *inculturation*. Father Ricci forged a Chinese terminology for Catholic theology and liturgy, and thus created the conditions for making Christ known and for incarnating the Gospel message and the Church within Chinese culture . . . Matteo Ricci made himself so "Chinese with the Chinese" that he became an expert Sinologist, in the deepest cultural and spiritual sense of the term, for

---

[85] Pasquale M. D'Elia, ed., *Fonti Ricciane: Storia dell'Instroduzione de Christianesimo in Cina Scritta da Matteo Ricci S.I.* (Rome: La Libreria dello Stato, 1942-1949), vol. 1, 114-115. Cited in George Minamiki, *The Chinese Rites Controversy: From Its Beginning to Modern Times* (Chicago: Loyola University Press, 1985), 17-18.

[86] Pasquale M. D'Elia, ed., *Fonti Ricciane: Storia dell'Instroduzione de,* 17-18.

[87] George Minamiki, *The Chinese Rites Controversy: From Its Beginning to Modern Times*, 28.

[88] Ibid., 197.

he achieved in himself an extraordinary inner harmony between priest and scholar, between Catholic and Orientalist, between Italian and Chinese.[89]

While absolving Ricci of any blame, John Paul II asked for forgiveness for the errors that the Catholic Church had committed in the past against Ricci and others. The pope expresses deep sorrow and regrets for the lack of respect and esteem for the Chinese people.[90] It is curious that the missionaries who blazed the trail in evangelization were first condemned and later praised after so much harm had been done.

Inculturation in Magisterial Documents

There is a vast documentation of magisterial pronouncements on inculturation and more specifically, on the relationship of faith to non-Christian cultures. I will discuss a few of these magisterial documentations dated from the seventeenth century to the present period in this section.

Pope Urban VIII

The founding of the *Congregatio de Propaganda Fide* (now Sacred Congregation for the Evangelization of Peoples) in 1622 by Pope Urban VIII marked a formal establishment of an office responsible for coordinating missionary activities and evangelization around the world. The congregation abrogated the notion of ideal culture, which hitherto had become the bane of missionary evangelization. In a letter written to the vicar apostolic to China, dated 1659, the congregation reminded missionaries of the absurdity of transplanting European cultures:

> Do not in any way attempt, and do not on any pretext persuade these people to change their rites, habits and customs, unless they are openly opposed to religion and good morals. For what could be more absurd than to bring France, Spain, Italy or any other European country over to China? It is not your country but your faith you must bring, that faith which does not reject or belittle the rites or customs of any nation as

---

[89] John Paul II, *Message to the Fourth Centenary of the Arrival in Beijing of the Great Missionary and Scientist Matteo Ricci S.J.* # 2.
[90] Ibid.

long as these rites are not evil, but rather desires that they be preserved in their integrity and fostered.[91]

The letter is very instructive and remarkable in many ways. First, it reminded the vicar apostolic to China and other foreign missions of the ludicrousness and Sisyphean nature of imposing their culture on the evangelized. Second, the instruction laid out the principle of what will be called inculturation. Third, it clearly distinguished between the faith and its Euro-cultural expression declaring that faith does not repudiate nor destroy the rites and customs of any people in so far as they are not contrary to faith and morals.[92] Thus, missionaries were not to confuse the faith with their own expression of it. They were also not to demean or demonize local cultures. Unfortunately, the significance of this instruction went unheeded by many missionaries, especially in Africa. Even when attempts are made to inculturate the faith into local cultures, it has always been cautious and limited to substitution.

Pope Benedict XV

Pope Benedict XV in his encyclical *Maximum Illud* of November 30, 1919, took up the question of the place of faith in its encounter with local cultures again. The encyclical appeared one year after the end of the World War 1. In it, Benedict XV recalled the works of eminent missionaries who introduced the faith into various parts of the world, such as Cyril and Methodius among the Slavs, Francis Xavier in India and Japan, and Bartolomeo de las Casas in Latin America.[93] The pope goes on to insist that the implantation of the faith in mission countries must take into account the uniqueness and dynamics of each people.[94]

Benedict XV urged missionaries to master the language of the people, eschew any form of nationalism, and avoid relegating the mission of the church to secondary status.[95] These noble admonitions, if not commands, stem from the lackadaisical attitudes of missionaries toward their host cultures. Missionaries often feel that they came not only to evangelize but also to civilize. With this kind of mindset, most missionaries did not deem it vital to learn the language of the non-Christian people or even to study the cultures of their host. On the contrary, the evangelized

---

[91] *Collectanea Sacrae Congregationis de Propaganda Fide Seu Decreta, Rescripta pro apostolicis missionibus,* vol. 1, 42 (Rome, 1907), # 1109. Cited in Francis, George E. *Inculturation and Ecclesial Communion,* 168.

[92] Anscar J. Chupungco, *Cultural Adaptation of the Liturgy,* 39.

[93] Pope Benedict XV, *Maximum Illud,* # 3-4.

[94] Ibid.

[95] Ibid., # 4.

were expected to learn the language of the missionary and abandon their cultures in place of the missionaries. In fact, French colonists and missionaries in certain parts of Africa introduced a policy known as French assimilation. The colonized Africans were expected to adopt the French language, culture and tradition. For the colonists, it was only when cultural submission was achieved that the missionaries would consider their evangelization a success.

Correlated to the question of respect for evangelized cultures is the great concern Benedict XV highlighted regarding the training of indigenous clergy. The pope called upon apostolic vicars and missionaries to train indigenous clergy who would eventually succeed the missionaries.

> There is one . . . very important point for anyone who has charge of a mission. He must make it his special concern to secure and train local candidates for the sacred ministry. In this policy lies the greatest hope of the new churches. For the local priest, one with his people by birth, by nature, by his sympathies and his aspirations, is remarkably effective in appealing to their mentality and thus attracting them to the Faith. Far better than anyone else he knows the kind of argument they will listen to, and as a result, he often has easy access to places where a foreign priest would not be tolerated.[96]

The role of indigenous clergy cannot be overemphasized. They understand their people more than foreign missionaries do. They are best suited to carry out inculturation since they know their home cultures firsthand. Thus, they can be seen as the hope of the church in mission territories. Because of their vantage point, they should be the ones to initiate the dialogue between faith and culture and to perpetuate the mission of the church.

Benedict XV insisted that the local clergy should not be trained merely to perform the humbler duties of the ministry, acting as the assistants of foreign priests. On the contrary, the pope says, "They must take up God's work as equals, so that someday they would be able to enter upon the spiritual leadership of their people."[97] To be fair, the early missionaries who traveled to Africa were not adequately equipped to deal with the local cultures they encountered in the course of their evangelizing mission. These missionaries were not cultural anthropologists, and many of them did not know how to deal with cultures that were diametrically different to theirs. They acted in good faith. But what can be said about modern missionaries who still function in the mode of their predecessors? As noted in a previous chapter, Africans have become missionaries unto themselves; nevertheless, the mistakes of the early missionaries are still replicated.

---

[96] Ibid.
[97] Ibid., # 15.

THE THEOLOGY OF INCULTURATION

Vatican II Council

The Second Vatican Council marked a watershed moment in the church's self-understanding of its nature and mission to the world. It was truly an *aggiornamento*, a great renewal for the church. One remarkable achievement of the council among others was the new understanding of the church as a mystery that is both universal and locally situated. The church is in the world, not separate from the world. At the same time, the church is on a mission to the world.[98] Because the church is missionary in character, it must engage all the cultures of the world in dialogue. This new disposition led to the affirmation of cultural plurality, liturgical reforms, and, by necessity, the theology of inculturation.

Although the council adopted the terminology of cultural adaptation with regard to non-Western culture, it nevertheless laid a solid foundation for a new method of evangelization and for the theology of inculturation. Inculturation is possible today because of Vatican II's recognition of the church as a communion of people of diverse cultures and races and, importantly, their idea that local churches contain in themselves all the elements necessary for salvation and a full manifestation of the universal church.

Beginning with the document *Sacrosanctum Concilium*, the council discussed the practical questions of reformation of the liturgy and cultural adaptation. The key passages in this regard are articles 37 and 38 of the *Sacrosanctum Concilium*. In providing for a single, reformed Roman Rite, the document made provision for the legitimate adaptation of local customs:

> Even in the liturgy, the Church has no wish to impose a rigid uniformity in matters which do not involve the faith or the good of the whole community. Rather she respects and fosters the spiritual adornments and gifts of the various races and peoples. Anything in their way of life that is not indissolubly bound up with superstition and error, she studies with sympathy and, if possible preserves intact. Sometimes in fact she admits such things into the liturgy itself, as long as they harmonize with its true and authentic spirit.[99]

Article 37 cited above has remained very contentious. Given the fact that the church's rituals, rites, and doctrine developed from superstitious and pagan practices in the Mediterranean world, it is curious that the council was against the acceptance and purification of certain superstitious practices in mission territories.

---

[98] *Lumen Gentium*, # 1, *Ad Gentes*, # 1.
[99] *Sacrosanctum Concilium*, # 37.

All the same, the provisions of the *Sacrosanctum Concilium* are remarkable and certainly a step away from the monoculturalism that enveloped the church prior to the council. However, these provisions are not sufficient. It seems to me that cultural adaptation of the liturgy as elucidated by the council with its attendant translation of liturgical texts into the vernacular is a superficial form of inculturation. The revision of the rites and its subsequent translation into local languages is at best only a beginning. A legitimate liturgical reform demands a radical inculturation, that is, the creation of new rites with an African hue that is in tandem with local cultures.

Vatican II dealt with the question of the relationship between faith and culture extensively in other conciliar documents such as *Lumen Gentium, Gaudium et Spes,* and *Ad Gentes.* In its pastoral constitution on the church in the modern world, *Gaudium et Spes,* the council teaches that there is a link between the message of salvation and human culture. According to the council, the church is sent by her Lord to every people and culture to proclaim the Good News of Jesus Christ. Consequently, the church is not tied exclusively to any race or nation, nor to any particular way of life or any customary pattern of living, ancient or recent. Thus, in fidelity to its mission and at the same time conscious of her universal mission, she can enter into communion with various cultural modes, to her own enrichment and those cultures too.[100] The council further teaches that the church takes nothing away from the temporal welfare of any people by establishing that kingdom. Rather, she fosters and takes to herself, insofar as they are not contrary to the Gospel the ability, resources, and customs of each people. Taking them to herself, she purifies, strengthens, and ennobles them.[101]

In its decree on the church's missionary activity, *Ad Gentes,* Vatican II made a more definitive pronouncement on the importance of inculturation of local cultures as a *sine qua non* for the authentic evangelization of the people. For the council:

> The work of planting the Church in a given human community reaches a kind of milestone when the congregation of the faithful, already rooted in social life and considerably adapted to the local culture, enjoys a certain stability and firmness. This means that the congregation is now equipped with its own supply, insufficient though it is, of local priests, religious, and laymen. It means that it is endowed with those ministries and institutions, which are necessary if the People of God are to live and develop its life under the guidance of its own bishop.[102]

---

[100] *Gaudium et Spes,* # 58.
[101] *Lumen Gentium,* # 13.
[102] *Ad Gentes,* # 19.

The means for the implantation of the faith, the council goes on to say, is by teaching the faith through adequate catechesis that is celebrated in a liturgy, which harmonizes with local customs by appropriate canonical legislation.[103] By doing so, the church becomes part of local churches.

John Paul II

John Paul II, in the course of his papacy, wrote extensively on the theology of inculturation, though always cautiously. As noted earlier, John Paul II was the first pope to use the terms acculturation and/or inculturation in a papal document. The pope called inculturation a neologism, which expresses very well one factor of the great mystery of the Incarnation.[104] For the pope, the Gospel must engage each culture in dialogue with the purpose of evangelizing and transforming that culture. This ensures that Christianity is deeply rooted in any culture.

John Paul II notes that catechesis, as well as evangelization in general, is called to bring the power of the Gospel into the very heart of people and their cultures. For this purpose, catechesis will seek to know these cultures and their essential components; it will learn their most significant expressions; it will respect their particular values and riches. In this manner, it will be able to offer these cultures the knowledge of the hidden mystery and help them to bring forth from their own living tradition original expressions of Christian life, celebration, and thought.[105] John Paul II, however, cautions that two things must be borne in mind.

> On the one hand the Gospel message cannot be purely and simply isolated from the culture in which it was first inserted (the biblical world or, more concretely, the cultural milieu in which Jesus of Nazareth lived), nor, without serious loss, from the cultures in which it has already been expressed down the centuries; it does not spring spontaneously from any cultural soil; it has always been transmitted by means of an apostolic dialogue which inevitably becomes part of a certain dialogue of cultures. On the other hand, the power of the Gospel everywhere transforms and regenerates. When that power enters into a culture, it is no surprise that it rectifies many of its elements. There would be no catechesis [evangelization] if it were the Gospel that had to change when it came into contact with the cultures.[106]

---

[103] Ibid.
[104] John Paul II, *Catechesi Tradendae*, #95.
[105] Ibid.
[106] Ibid., # 53. Emphasis mine.

In essence, John Paul II affirms that for evangelization to be successful, it must be guided by respect for any cultures it encounters. Missionaries must always endeavor to distinguish between what constitutes faith and its cultural expressions.

In the course of his extensive travels around the world, especially to Africa to confirm the faith of his brethren, John Paul II unceasingly urged the people to take seriously the question of inculturation to ensure that the Gospel is proclaimed and deeply rooted in African cultures. In his first pastoral visit to the continent of Africa in 1980, the pope spoke on the necessity and expediency of inculturation as tool for a new evangelization:

> One of the aspects of this evangelization is the inculturation of the Gospel, the Africanization of the Church. Several people have told me that you set great store by it, and rightly so. This is part of the indispensable efforts to incarnate the message of Christ. The Gospel, certainly, is not identified with cultures, it transcends them all. But the kingdom that the Gospel proclaims is lived by men deeply tied to a culture; the construction of the kingdom cannot dispense with borrowing elements of human cultures. Indeed evangelization must help the latter to bring forth out of their own living tradition original expressions of Christian life . . . you wish to be at once fully Christians and fully Africans.[107]

John Paul II, in this address, confirms what Pope Paul VI said in his *Evangelii Nuntiandi* (#20). Almost a week later, the pope reiterated the importance of inculturation as an evangelization method when he spoke to Kenyan bishops thus: "Inculturation . . . will truly be a reflection of the Incarnation of the Word, when a culture, transformed and regenerated by the gospel, brings forth from its own living tradition original expressions of Christian life."[108] In the same address, the pope succinctly says, "There is no question of adulterating the Word of God, or of emptying the cross of Christ of its power, but rather of bringing Christ into the very nature of African life and of lifting up all African life to Christ. Thus, not only is Christianity relevant to Africa, but Christ, in the members of his Body, is himself Africa."[109]

John Paul II, in his *Redemptoris Missio*, articulates further his understanding of inculturation vis-à-vis its relation to creation, incarnation and evangelization. The pope maintains that the church, while carrying out its missionary activity,

---

[107] John Paul II, *Address to the Bishops of Zaire*, May 3, 1980, AAS 72, (1980): 430-439, 4. Cited in Francis E. George. *Inculturation and Ecclesial Communion*, 112-113.

[108] AFER, vol. 22, 4, (August, 1980): 198.

[109] Ibid.

encounters different cultures and becomes involved in the process of inculturation. Thus,

> Through inculturation the Church makes the Gospel incarnate in different cultures and at the same time introduces peoples, together with their cultures, into her own community . . . through inculturation the Church, for her part, becomes a more intelligible sign of what she is, and a more effective instrument of mission. Thanks to this action within the local Churches, the universal Church herself is enriched with forms of expression and values in the various sectors of Christian life, such as evangelization, worship, theology and charitable works. She comes to know and to express better the mystery of Christ, all the while being motivated to continual renewal.[110]

Pope John Paul II enjoins missionaries who come from other cultures not only to move beyond their own cultural limitation but also to immerse themselves in the cultural milieu of those to whom they are sent. Thus, missionaries must be well acquainted with the language, customs, and traditions of the people they have come to evangelize.[111]

The 1985 Extraordinary Synod of Bishops convened by John Paul II dealt with the question of inculturation. In its report, the synod says:

> Because the Church is communion, which joins diversity and unity in being present throughout the world, it takes from every culture all that it encounters of positive value. Yet inculturation is different from a simple external adaptation, because it means the intimate transformation of authentic cultural values through their integration in Christianity in the various human cultures.[112]

The synod unmistakably drew a distinction between adaptation (which is external and superficial) and inculturation (which aims at a fuller understanding of culture and of the interplay between the Gospel and every culture).

Finally, John Paul II in his Apostolic Exhortation, *Ecclesia in Africa*, which was issued after the first ever Synod of Bishops for Africa, stresses the urgency of inculturation for the church in Africa. Drawing copiously from the propositions of the synod, the pope teaches:

---

[110] John Paul II, *Redemptoris Missio* (Boston: Pauline books, 1990), # 52.

[111] Ibid., # 53.

[112] The Final Report of the 1985 Extraordinary Synod of Bishops, Section D, # 4.

> On several occasions the Synod Fathers stressed the particular importance for evangelization of inculturation, the process by which 'catechesis takes flesh in the various cultures. Inculturation includes two dimensions: on the one hand, "the intimate transformation of authentic cultural values through their integration in Christianity" and, on the other, "the insertion of Christianity in the various human cultures." The Synod considers inculturation an urgent priority in the life of the particular churches, for a firm rooting of the Gospel in Africa. It is a requirement for evangelization, a part toward full evangelization, and one of the greatest challenges for the Church on the Continent on the eve of the Third Millennium.[113]

John Paul II did not hesitate to urge African bishops during his numerous visits to Africa and ad limina visits of bishops from Africa, to take seriously the issue of inculturation and evangelization if the Gospel must become incarnate and deeply rooted in Africa. At the same time, the pope equally cautions that inculturation must be in harmony with the deposits of faith and not contradict the Gospel.[114] The pope urged African bishops to take note that inculturation includes the whole life of the church—theology, liturgy, and structures.[115] This is very instructive because it appears inculturation had principally been limited to the liturgy and translations of scriptural and liturgical texts. Several years after *Ecclesia in Africa*, the church in Africa has yet to articulate a systematized ecclesiology and theology of the church that is anchored in inculturation.

In proposing the theology of inculturation to Africa, the pope, however, cautioned that inculturation must remain faithful to the Gospel and the apostolic tradition. The pope particularly insisted that inculturation must be compatible with the Christian message and communion with the universal church, avoiding all forms of syncretism.[116]

African theologians are in disagreement particularly as to what constitutes syncretism. It seems that much of what is called apostolic tradition was originally syncretic and imbued with pagan practices before they were inculturated by the church. Thus inculturation in Africa cannot but undergo similar process that apostolic tradition went through during its early formation. It seems to me that the same Holy Spirit, which inspired the early church as they dialogued and inculturated pagan rites, rituals, ideology, ceremonies into the church, is equally leading the church in Africa, particularly among the Igbos, to fashion an adequate ecclesio-missiology.

---

[113] John Paul II, *Ecclesia in Africa*, # 59.
[114] Francis E. George, *Inculturation and Ecclesial Communion*, 115.
[115] John Paul II, *Ecclesia in Africa*, # 62.
[116] Ibid.

Thus far, the magisterial documents I have considered present a solid theological base for the theology of inculturation as a method for evangelization. Various popes in the course of their pastoral visits to Africa have called for a deep rooting of the Gospel and for a harmonious relationship of the faith and culture. Yet good will is often lacking when it comes to the actual implementation of inculturation. Notwithstanding the papal pronouncements on inculturation and its indispensability to evangelization of cultures, it is disheartening that church authorities continue to resist efforts to promote a genuine theology of inculturation. Serious attention has not always been paid to inculturation; at best, it has received superficial attention. Such efforts have been limited mainly to translations of scriptural and liturgical texts or the allowance of liturgical dances, local drums used in liturgical music, and so forth.

Chapter 5

TOWARD AN ECCLESIO MISSIOCENTRIC THEOLOGY OF THE CHURCH

The model of the church as a family of God is not, per se, a new theological model. The concept is an ancient model, but its deep theological significance remains unexplored and untapped. The model does not influence the ecclesial-missiocentric nature of the church. The predominant images or models of the church in the documents of Vatican II, which were explored in the previous chapter, continue to shape and determine the church's nature and mission to the world.

In this chapter, we shall continue to explore how the Igbo concept of *ezi-na-ulo,* extended family, provides the theological and theoretical frameworks for constructing an ecclesio-missiology for the evangelization of Igbos in their cultural matrix. It is my hope that this model will accentuate the Igbo consciousness of the nature and mission of the church, as well as provide a method for evangelization. In view of the sacrosanct nature of the family as a sacred institution among Igbos, the concept of the church as family of God has theological relevance and validity. It also provides a natural appeal to Africans, and indeed to Igbos, in their quest to deepen their understanding of the church, which promotes evangelization.[1]

The Theology of the Church as the Family of God

The theology of the church as the family of God takes its cue from a nexus of interrelatedness and participation that undergirds the inner workings of the Trinity. The church understands the Trinity in terms of a community of the persons of the Father, Son, and the Holy Spirit. The three persons have at the same time the

---

[1] Joseph Healy et al., "Our Five year journey of SCCs from Dec. 1991 to Oct.1996: The Evolving Sociology & Ecclesiology of Church as Family in East Africa," *AFER* 39, no 5 & 6, (1997): 300.

same divine nature, essence, and substance, yet they remain distinct from one another.[2] For John Zizioulas, a Greek Orthodox bishop and theologian, it is only in terms of relationship can the identity of each of the three persons have ontological significance.[3]

In the inner working of the Trinity, there is a distinction of functions and persons: God the Father creates, God the Son redeems, and God the Holy Spirit sanctifies. However, there is no distinction or emphasis in precedence, status, or essence. Each of the persons of the Trinity exists because the others exist. Thus, the three persons form a unity in the Godhead. Similarly, Africa's ontological principle—"I am because we are," analogously mirrors the relationality and communion of the three divine persons of the Trinity. This principle, while respecting the individuality of each person in the community, emphasizes the relationality and the unity of individuals in the community.

African people enjoy close interpersonal ties and relationships based on a kinship bond and belief in the common origin of members of the same community. Because the extended family is the bedrock of society and consists of a communion of persons, it is, therefore, not surprising that the *Message of the Synod* of Bishops for Africa expresses the view that, "the Church-Family has its origin in the Blessed Trinity at the depths of which the Holy Spirit is the bond of communion. It knows that the intrinsic value of a community is the quality of relations which makes it possible."[4] The synod fathers strongly maintain that this model definitely serves a useful and effective means to promote and enhance sincere relationships and responsibility at various levels of church life in Africa.[5]

The egalitarian nature of the three persons of the Trinity challenges the church as the extended family of God to go beyond kinship and consanguine ties. Therefore, the theology of church as family of God is not based on biological ties but is inspired by the Trinity. Within this trinitarian union, the church must also see herself as professing the unity and solidarity of the three divine persons. This unity challenges us to promote *koinonia* among all God's people. It is no wonder that the Synod of Bishops for Africa jubilantly asserts:

---

[2] Karl Rahner, "Trinity, Divine," *Sacramentum Mundi: An Encyclopedia of Theology*, vol. 6, ed. Karl Rahner (New York: Herder & Herder, 1970), 297.

[3] John Zizioulas, *Being as Communion* (New York: St. Vladimir Seminary Press, 1997), 88.

[4] Maura Browne, ed., "Message of the Synod, # 20," *The African Synod: Documents, Reflections, Perspectives* (New York: Orbis books, 1996), 76.

[5] Msafiri G. Aidan, "The Church as a Family Model: Its Strengths and Weaknesses," *African Theology Today*, vol.1, ed. Emmanuel Katongole (Scranton: The University of Scranton Press, 2002), 88.

> Christ has come to restore the world to unity, a single human Family in the image of the Trinitarian Family. We are the Family of God: this is the Good News! The same blood flows in our veins, and it is the blood of Jesus Christ. The same Spirit gives life, and it is the Holy Spirit, the infinite fruitfulness of divine love.[6]

It appears the synod fathers adopted the image of the church as the family because of its inclusivity, and most importantly, it resonates with African cultures, emphasizing the solidarity, unity, relationality, and communion that characterize the African notion of the family. The new family of God embraces the whole human race without any iota of discrimination on the basis of race, sex, gender, culture, language, or class.

Lisa Sowle Cahill observes that although the family as a bonded kinship group is ever an occasion of temptation to sublimate self-interest into dedication to one's mate, offspring, or kinship groups, the specifically Christian meaning of family does not stop with biology, but transcends it.[7] What the church as family of God demands, is, therefore, the sublimation of kinship loyalty to identify all human beings as "God's children" or our "brothers and sister in Christ."[8] The church as family of God lays emphasis on the fact that Christians and indeed every human being belong to the one large family of God. For Father Michael Amaladoss, the church as the family of God:

> Is not bound by national economic or caste barriers. It is not only comfortable with multi-culturalism, but sees it as the creative variety and richness of the human race. Its model of community-in-difference is neither architectonic like a building or temple nor even organic—like a tree or a body—but human-divine like a family or the Trinity itself. We would not dare to propose the Trinity as a model, if Jesus himself had not done so.[9]

Our oneness is actualized through the baptismal covenant in Jesus Christ. The sacrament of Baptism links each member of the church as family of God vertically with God and horizontally with the entire human family.[10]

---

[6] Maura Browne ed., *Message of the Synod*, # 25.

[7] Lisa Sowle Cahill, *Sex, Gender & Christian Ethics* (United Kingdom: Cambridge University Press, 1996), 201.

[8] Ibid.

[9] Michael Amaladoss S.J., "Mission in a Post-Modern World: A Call to be Counter-Cultural," *SEDOS Bulletin*, 28: 8/9 (Aug. 15-Sept. 15, 1996): 238-9.

[10] Patrick C. Chibuko, *Paschal Mystery of Christ* (New York: Peter Lang, 1999), 63.

Correlated to the trinitarian underpinning of the extended family model is the Christological grounding of the image. As the firstborn of all creation (Col. 1:15), Christ recognized and appreciated the human family, but he was not tied down to a particular family. Though he never repudiated his immediate family, as some have argued elsewhere (Ruether, Hauerwas), Jesus Christ nevertheless transcended it to create a new dynamic family where everyone has equal rights.[11] For example, when told that his family was looking for him, Jesus replied, "Here are my mother and my brothers. For whoever does the will of my heavenly father is my brother, and sister, and my mother" (Matt.12:49-50).

The church as the family of God can be promoted through a rich Christology of Christ as not only its *Pater familias* but also, as in the words of Benezet Bujo, "Africa's proto-ancestor" and the founder of a new community of God.[12] For Bujo, Jesus symbolically replaces the twelve tribes of Israel by choosing the twelve apostles. However, by restoring the symbolic "people of the twelve tribes," Jesus made it clear that he is the "tribal father" of the eschatological Israel, a term that ultimately encompasses all people without distinction.[13] As a result, African ecclesiology of the church as the family of God sees Jesus in the context of "Proto-ancestor." As the Proto-ancestor, he establishes the new, eschatological family (church) in its bipolar dimension of the living and the dead.[14] Jesus is the real life-giving source.

The Relationship between Faith and Culture

The relationship between faith and culture is critical to understanding the significance of the role of inculturation in the evangelization of the Igbos. A good understanding of this relationship will serve as a *preparation* for the theology of inculturation.

Opinions remain divided as to what should constitute the proper relationship between faith and culture. During the apostolic age, it took a council (Jerusalem) to convince some of the apostles that those who were not circumcised (as required by Jewish custom) could be accepted into the Jerusalem Church (see Acts 15).[15]

---

[11] Ibid., 60.

[12] Benezet Bujo, "On the Road Toward an African Ecclesiology: Reflections on the Synod," *African Synod: Documents, Reflections, Perspectives*, ed. Maura Browne (New York: Orbis Books, 1996), 140-141.

[13] Ibid.

[14] Ibid.

[15] Jerusalem is assumed to be the terminus a quo for the Christian mission to the Hellenistic and gentile worlds. Whatever happened in the Jerusalem Church became a point of reference for other churches.

With the expansion of the church into Greco-Roman societies, the relationship between faith and culture was at first frosty, but it seems that in order to be relevant to the new cultures, the early Christians inculturated many elements of the cultural practices of their societies in the church. Their faith easily blended with the cultural practices of their people. The early Christians expropriated cultural values, rituals, feasts, and so forth of their host cultures. For example, the feast of Christmas, the use of statues, holy water, Mass vestments, cult of saints, rites and rituals, and so forth emanated from the Mediterranean and western cultures. It can be said that these cultures provided the *seminal verbum* for the implantation of the faith.

As the Christian faith moved into non-Western world, the relationship between faith and culture developed differently. For example, when missionaries came to Africa, instead of the faith inculturating African languages and cultures, missionaries made concerted efforts to make the African cultures and people accept and adopt the faith couched in the missionaries' own cultures. In return, the recipient culture was rejected as primitive, barbaric, and satanic. This approach resulted in Christianity being in seeming perpetual conflicts with non-Western cultures.

Another reason that accounts for the conflict between faith and culture, especially in mission territories, is the expression of cultural and religious superiority by missionaries. The feeling of superiority dates back to ancient Greeks who called other nations *barbaroi*.[16] Romans and members of other "civilization" likewise looked down upon others. When the church and empire united to become the politico-religious system known to history as Christendom, Roman monoculturalism received a powerful reinforcement. This led to the identification of the superior world culture with diligent study of the ancient Latin and Greek authors, scholastic philosophy and theology, music, art, etc.[17] Missionaries were admonished to proclaim the Gospel in mission territories in a single cultural form. Any variation, Shorter argues, "was deemed to be either a deviation or a stage of development toward the, as yet, unrealized ideal."[18] David Bosch shares a similar opinion when he opines that, more often than not, such feelings of superiority flowed from the powerful and dominant culture toward the weak and dominated culture.[19]

Bernard Lonergan offers an insightful view on the philosophy that promoted the identification of Christianity with one culture by church officials, theologians, and missionaries in the past. According to Lonergan, "Culture was conceived

---

[16] David J. Bosch, *Transforming Mission: Paradigm Shifts in Theology of Mission* (New York: Orbis Books, 1991), 291.

[17] Bernard Lonergan, *Method in Theology* (Toronto: University of Toronto Press, 1971), 326.

[18] Aylward Shorter, *Toward a Theology of Inculturation*, 18.

[19] David J. Bosch, *Transforming Mission*, 291.

not empirically but normatively. It was a matter of acquiring and assimilating the tastes and skills, the ideals, virtues and ideas that were pressed upon one in a good home and through a curriculum in the liberal arts."[20] For the classicists, church dogmas are permanent not so much because they represent revealed truths, but because they are rooted in a universal, permanent culture and in the existence of immutable substances and meanings.[21] It must be acknowledged that there are obvious constituents of human nature and activity that are common to the human race, such as the demands of human reason, sickness and health, procreation, dying experiences, etc. Yet differences abound in worldviews, rituals, religious claims of truths, and so forth.

The church at the time failed to recognize differences in culture. Rather, it clung to the notion of monoculturalism for over sixteen centuries. This world culture was in practice identifiable with the culture of Europe. The faith and Europe were almost synonymous. In light of this, the classicist normative views of culture undergird missionary activities to the "heathens." It prevented the church from recognizing the value of cultural pluralism and distorted the church's self-understanding of her image. It further fueled the unnecessary conflict between faith and culture.

Unfortunately, missionaries to Africa carried such feelings of superiority with them and made no concerted effort to distinguish between religious and cultural superiority. What applied to one, applied axiomatically to the other.[22] The result was the blistering condemnation of African cultures as savage and irredeemable. For missionaries, a sure sign of being a good African Christian is the untrammeled renunciation of one's culture while accepting the evangelizer's faith and culture. Consequently, churches in "mission fields" were structured on exactly the same line as those on the missionaries' home front, where a completely different socioeconomic and cultural system existed.[23] In the process, the western form of Christianity and theology were transmitted uncritically and unchallenged to mission territories. No efforts were made to give some autonomy or to find any vestiges of Christianity in the receiving cultures. Even church architectures were patterned after those found in the missionaries' homeland.

It is worth noting that the attitude of the church toward cultural pluralism and the importance of culture in the evangelization of a particular people have changed significantly. The role of culture in evangelization and deepening the faith is now taken seriously. The church recognizes that there is no such thing as a heavenly, perfect, or model culture through which the Gospel must be proclaimed. As Pope Paul VI observes, "The Kingdom which the Gospel

---

[20] Bernard Lonergan, *Method in Theology*, 301.

[21] Aylward Shorter, *Toward a Theology of Inculturation*, 19.

[22] David J. Bosch, *Transforming Mission*, 291.

[23] Ibid.

proclaims is lived by men who are profoundly linked to a culture, and the building up of the Kingdom cannot avoid borrowing the elements of human culture or cultures."[24] Nevertheless, it must be observed that faith transcends every culture; hence, it cannot be reduced to mere forms of culture. At the same time, faith needs cultural formulations.

The realization of the symbiosis between faith and culture makes it imperative for an ecclesiology with an Africa hue. Our position is predicated on the fact that the Gospel does not come as a disembodied message but as a message that must be communicated in the language and culture of those to whom it is addressed. It has to be clothed in cultural symbols that are meaningful to the evangelized. Hence, a genuine ecclesiology and evangelization among Africans must take cognizance of its culture.

Inculturation, Theological Pluralism, and One United Church

The ever-increasing awareness of pluralism in Christian theology draws our attention to the realization that there is no single way or, "a made-to-fit-all" understanding of the nature and mission of the church to the world. Theological pluralism urges us to look beyond the status quo and what, for ages, has been normative. As membership of the church cuts across different ethnicities, races, languages, and cultures, there will be plural ways and methods of understanding the nature and mission of the church. However, this awareness of plurality does not call for a discontinuity with the past. On the contrary, it invites all to harness the contributions of early and past theologies, which were plural.

Plurality enriches the church and promotes unity in diversity in the one, holy, catholic, and apostolic church of Christ, where people of every race, language and culture use their cultural matrix to enrich and enliven the life of the church. St. Gregory the Great (540-604) could not have said it better when he asserts, *in una fide, nil officit consuetude diversa* (in the one faith there is no harm in diverse custom).[25] To argue that there is plurality in theology is to assert that there are different ways of speaking and understanding God's self-revelation through His Son, Jesus Christ.

While the basic purpose of theological reflection has remained the same, theology is best expressed in concrete life situations and circumstances. As such, the response to the Gospel will vary from culture to culture. The realization of this leads us to insist that there are plural ways of speaking about God or Christ's transforming and redemptive events.

---

[24] Pope Paul VI, *Evangelii Nuntiandi*, # 20.

[25] James C. Okoye, *The Eucharist in African Perspective* http://www.sedos.org/english/okoye_2.htm (accessed February 19, 2007).

Theological plurality is further accentuated by a growing sense that the theologies inherited from the older churches of the North Atlantic community did not fit well into different cultural circumstances.[26] Theological pluralism exists "as forms of theological reflections with the same corpus of orthodox theology. The endemic tension between Augustinians, Franciscans, Dominicans, Thomists, and Jesuits, as a way of preserving their peculiar theological systems, is evident in academic theology."[27] Thus, Robert Schreiter, an American theologian, convincingly observes that it is becoming increasingly evident that the theologies once thought to have a universal and even enduring or perennial character were but regional expressions of certain cultures.[28]

David Tracy, while celebrating the reality of pluralism within theologies contends that the New Testament itself is internally pluralistic. Tracy, asserts that diversity in the New Testament is self-evident and should be clear to any reader. For Tracy, that such diversity is enriching to all should be clear to any contemporary Christian who has experienced the event known as ecumenism.[29] Tracy further notes that the beauty of theological pluralism lies in the fact that "it allows each theologian to learn incomparably more about reality by disclosing the really different ways of viewing both our common humanity and Christianity."[30]

Because there is no one way of speaking of God, theological pluralism has to be recognized as a characteristic of our contemporary Christianity as manifested in different theologies and methods. It does not mean that the essential doctrinal teachings of the church are jeopardized, but rather the diverse and plural nature of Christianity are affirmed and recognized. To put it in another way, theological plurality affirms unity and not uniformity.

In various documents of Second Vatican Council, there are allusions and subtle references to possible theological pluralism within the church. For instance, in its decree on the missionary activities of the Church, *Ad Gentes*, the council teaches that:

> Theological investigation must necessarily be stirred up in each major socio-cultural area, as it is called. In this way, under the light of the tradition of the universal Church, a fresh scrutiny will be brought to

---

[26] Robert J. Schreiter, *Constructing Local Theologies* (New York: Orbis Books, 1985), 1.

[27] Oliver Onwubiko, *Theory and Practice of Inculturation*, 109.

[28] Robert J. Schreiter, *Constructing Local Theologies*, 3.

[29] David Tracy, *The Analogical Imagination: Christian Theology and the Culture of Pluralism* (New York: Crossroad, 1981), 249-250.

[30] David Tracy, *Blessed Rage for Order: The New Pluralism in Theology*, revised edition (*Chicago*, University of Chicago Press, 1996), 3.

bear on the deeds and words which God made known. Thus, it will be more clearly seen in what ways faith can seek for understanding in the philosophy and wisdom of these peoples. This will foster a better insight on how a people's customs, worldview, and social order can be reconciled with the manner of living taught by divine revelation.[31]

Vatican II, noting the difficulties involved in harmonizing different cultures with Christian teaching, was nevertheless optimistic that these difficulties do not necessarily harm the life of faith.

Indeed they can stimulate the mind to a more accurate and penetrating grasp of the faith . . . while adhering to the methods and requirements proper to theology, theologians are invited to seek continually for more suitable ways of communicating doctrine to the men (and women) of their times. For the deposit of faith or revealed truths are one thing; the manner in which they are formulated without violence to their meaning and significance is another.[32]

No wonder Pope Paul VI acknowledged theological plurality when he gladly notes, "Indeed we admit that a certain theological pluralism finds its roots in the very mystery of Christ, the inscrutable riches whereof (cf. Eph 3:8) transcend the capacities of the expression of all ages and all cultures. Thus the doctrine of the faith, which necessarily derives from mystery of Christ, calls for constant fresh research."[33]

From these conciliar documentations, we can draw two conclusions: (a) the council rejects the concept of a single theology made-to-fit-all cultures and era; (b) within the bounds of the unity of the church, theological pluralism, is not only necessary, but also expedient and legitimate. What is of utmost importance is to distinguish between, on one hand, revealed truths and, on the other hand, the manner in which they are expressed.

Pluralism and Ecclesio-Missiocentric Theology of Inculturation

The theology of inculturation, as we now understand it, is an offshoot of theological pluralism. An ecclesio-missiocentric theology of inculturation recognizes that one-method-fits-all is unacceptable and inadequate for evangelization.

---

[31] *Ad Gentes*, # 22.
[32] *Gaudium et Spes*, # 62.
[33] Pope Paul VI, *On Reconciliation within the Church: An Apostolic Exhortation*, # 4.

Inculturation is further inspired by the belief that the Spirit of God is redemptively present in African religions and cultures as it was in the Greco-Roman cultures and religions.

John Paul II, while affirming the reality of pluralism in general and its benefits to humankind's quest for answers to the questions of ultimate reality, nevertheless was critical of its tendency to relegate all truth claims to the same level. In his words:

> Recent times have seen the rise to prominence of various doctrines, which tend to devalue even the truths, which had been judged certain. A legitimate plurality of positions has yielded to undifferentiated pluralism, based upon the assumption that all positions are equally valid, which is one of today's most widespread symptoms of the lack of confidence in truth.[34]

The pope, while not totally against pluralism, expresses concern that it could lead to relativism, which suggests that no single religious tradition possesses the absolute truth.

The theology of inculturation, as an offshoot of theological plurality in the church, does not portend a relativization of church doctrines but holds that if the faith is to be genuine and fully lived in any culture, it must become inculturated. Faith must become part of the culture of the people. Hence, the goal of inculturation is not to question the doctrines of the church but to ensure that the Gospel takes deep roots in every culture and takes on the idiosyncrasies of that culture. The implication of this is that Rome's version of how things ought to be done would give way to the development of local theologies that are faithful to tradition and the scripture.

Since Vatican II spoke of the church as existing fully in both the particular and the universal, the theology of inculturation advocates an autochthonous church that reflects a faith that is expressed in cultural forms. This would encourage the recovery of and respect for the people's historical memory, idioms, language, culture, symbols, values, rituals, and so forth.[35] The nature of the autochthonous church envisioned is not a church that is independent of Rome, but a church that is homegrown and not directed by univocal formulae dictated by Rome.

The theology of inculturation draws our attention to the fact that the Gospel was not born in the West, but in the East and then passed to the West, where it adopted the cultural expressions of the West.[36] Kathryn Tanner, citing Ernst Troeltsch's contention that Christianity is the religion of the West, because of its

---

[34] John Paul II, *Fides et Ratio,* # 5.
[35] Robert B. Kaiser, *A Church in Search of Itself,* 107.
[36] Ibid., 106.

westernization, reiterates the fact that western culture has been decisively shaped by Christianity even as Christianity has been decisively shaped by it.[37] In light of this, the question "Why can't African cultures shape Africa Christianity as Christianity shapes African cultures" becomes more poignant.

The task of the theology of inculturation, as postulated from an African perspective, seeks to make Catholicism less "Roman" and more African. As Robert Kaiser succinctly notes, "African Catholics had no wish to write a new creed, or make the Trinity—the Father, Son and Holy Spirit—into a Happy Couple, or deny the resurrection. They did want to revisit a good many pieces of Church discipline that were man-made. If men could make the rules, then men could unmake them."[38] African Christians want African answers to questions of meaning and life, celibacy, the celebration of the Eucharist with African food and drink, the status of polygamous couples who convert to Catholicism, the ordination of women as priests and deacons, among others. It is also, in essence, a call to respect and adhere to the principle of subsidiarity.

Theology is a human activity; as such, it is socially and historically circumscribed. Theology cannot be engaged in or understood in isolation from the historical and cultural situations of a people; otherwise, it becomes a hollow enterprise. Hence, theology exhibits the particularities that distinguish specific cultures.[39] Another important factor that undergirds the theology of inculturation as an offshoot of theological pluralism is God's self-revelation in a historical human situation through the mystery of the incarnation in Christ. God continues to speak to people within their cultural ambient and historical situations. By the same token, every theologian and or Christian lives in a situation that shapes how he or she relates with God. In this regard, David Tracy is right when he argues that the "situation" serves as a point of departure for theologizing.

> Every theology lives in its own situation . . . in this move, theologians are no different from other cultural critics who bring their own orientation, questions and possible probable or certain modes of analysis and response to the situation encompassing all thinkers, not least the theologian . . . like all creatures . . . we are all in our culture and history: affected by it at every moment for good or ill, groping at every moment to understand, to discern how to live a worthwhile life in this place, at this moment.[40]

---

[37] Kathryn Tanner, *Theories of Culture: A New Agenda for Theology* (Minneapolis: Fortress Press, 1997), 62.

[38] Ibid., 138.

[39] Ibid., 64-65.

[40] David Tracy, *Analogical Imagination*, 339.

For Tracy, the situation in question is the ensemble of the cultural world in which the theologian lives and operates.

Tracy's notion of the "situation" differs from Paul Tillich's "situation." Tillich's situation refers to the scientific, artistic, economic, political, and ethical forms. Tillich's situation is the creative interpretation of existence, an interpretation that is carried on in every period of history under all kinds of psychological and sociological conditions. It is also that of meaninglessness.[41] The difference lies in the fact that Tracy's situation is marked by plurality and ambiguity and the emergence of the uncanny (mystery) in a religious experience.

Underlying both the situation and tradition, Tracy insists, "is the personal recognition of the presence of the uncanny as the presence of a power not of one's own. The disclosure of that power has the classic force of some recognition of the whole."[42] Thus, the presence of the uncanny in the situation discloses a religious dimension to the situation itself. It is against this backdrop that Tracy argues that since theology is not a direct statement from God, the Christian response to the uncanny and to the religious dimension is that of critical correlation, which results in a second order language.[43] A second-order language evidently leads us to contend that theology interprets the "situation" within the context of the theologian's cultural matrix. Since the "situation" is not always the same in all cultures, theological pluralism must be embraced.

The reality of theological pluralism makes it difficult, if not impossible, to accept one central theological interpretation of God's self-revelation and the Christ-event. Obviously, each culture will have a different response and approach. Again, Tracy strongly insists, "There is no one response, no single journey of recognition and expression of the Christ event's transformation of the situation and its transformation by the situation."[44]

Bernard Lonergan argues along the same line when he observes that the idea of a single interpretation or a single theology in the church is an illusion. For Lonergan, preaching the Gospel to all men and women requires many preachers. This in turn requires each of the preachers to get to know the people to whom he or she is sent, their ways of thought, their manners, and their style of speech.[45] Pluralism, Lonergan contends, "is pluralism of communications rather than of doctrines. But within the limits of undifferentiated consciousness, there is no

---

[41] Paul Tillich, *Systematic Theology* (Chicago: The University of Chicago Press, 1951), 4.

[42] David Tracy, *Analogical Imagination*, 374.

[43] Ibid.

[44] Ibid., 372.

[45] Bernard Lonergan, *Method in Theology*, 276.

communication of doctrine except through the rituals, narrative forms, titles, parables, metaphors that are effective in the given milieu."[46]

Pluralism offers an inexorable richness to Christian theology. Thus, the theology of inculturation understood through the prism of plurality has much to offer to enrich Christian theology. It brings to the fore the African situation and the dynamics of African ecclesiology. It is an African perspective and interpretation of the Christ-event and its overarching implications for missio-ecclesiology in Africa. Consequently, western theology, particularly Catholic theology, has nothing to fear from engaging African cultures and inculturating African culture in its theology. On the contrary, we ought to be fearful if both theology and African cultures are not engaged in any interactive dialogue

---

[46] Ibid.

Chapter 6

LEADERSHIP IN THE CHURCH AS THE EXTENDED FAMILY OF GOD

The present church leadership structure does not have any semblance to nor reflect the model of the church as the family of God. African ecclesiology continues to reflect a systemic structure that is decidedly hierarchical, clerical, and patriarchal. Hardly any layperson is placed in a leadership position in most dioceses in Africa. For example, priests hold all the leadership positions and heads of departments in the Catholic Secretariat of Nigeria.[1] The case is the same in most dioceses in Nigeria. In fact, the Catholic Church in Igboland is called *uka fada*, or, the priest's church. It is so called because of the excessive dominance of the clergy. The laity is hardly involved in decisions that affect them. Many bishops rule their diocese like benevolent medieval monarchs. No one dares disagree or challenge their authority without incurring the "ire of the monarch." There is little, if any, collaboration between many bishops and their priests in the administration of the diocese. In fact, there seems to be mutual mistrust and recrimination between many priests and their bishops. Father Richard McBrien, lamenting on the general deficient collaboration between priests and their bishops says: "Many priests do not perceive themselves to be close collaborators with their bishops, as Second Vatican Council envisioned them to be. Too few bishops reach out to their priests to ask for their honest opinions about anything that seriously affects the life of the church and the priesthood."[2] The situation is more poignant in many an African diocese.

Many African bishops are not accountable to anyone in their dioceses except to Rome. They hardly, if ever, publish the financial accounts of their dioceses. Lay people and, in many cases, the priests of the diocese do not know, for example, how the diocesan temporal patrimony is administered. There are hardly any functional

---

[1] CBCN, www.cbcn.org (accessed May 25, 2006).

[2] Richard McBrien, "Alternate views in the 'Year for Priests,'" *National Catholic Reporter*, Vol. 46, (2010), # 1, 27.

diocesan financial committees. In dioceses where such committees exist, they exist on paper as rubber stamps to give the impression of compliance to canonical directives that all dioceses must have a finance committee.

The apparent lack of accountability and openness hearkens back to the practices of the medieval feudal system, in which monarchs were not obligated to anyone. Sadly, this is the structure of the church in many Africa dioceses in the twenty-first century.

The First Nigerian National Pastoral Congress of the Catholic Church acknowledged that the structure inherited from the missionary church was clerical and hierarchical. The congress boldly asserted that church structure was organized to serve this model.[3] The *Lineamenta* of the Pastoral Congress acknowledged the overbearing centralization of authority and power in Rome with its attendant muzzling of the principle of subsidiarity.[4] Surprisingly, the *Lineamenta* contradicted itself when it identified church structure as being hierarchical.[5]

The Pastoral Congress bemoaned the dismal state of the laity in the church, particularly in the Nigerian context, but failed to address the non-involvement of the laity in the affairs of the church. According to the Pastoral Congress:

> The lay population is yet to be fully integrated and legitimately involved in the pastoral life of the Church. It cannot be said that our lay people have found their identity and mission in the Church and in the world. Lay people are sometimes mobilised solely to serve the specific interest of the hierarchy. They are hardly empowered to act in their areas of specialisation.... The laity generally complain of the Church's elitist and clericalist views that downgrade their intelligence and competence.[6]

The Pastoral Congress failed to address how this anomaly could be corrected. It also failed to craft a new leadership structure of the church that is consistent with the model of the church as the extended family of God, which the Synod of Bishops for Africa and John Paul II adopted as particularly fitting for the African church.

The failure of the Pastoral Congress to articulate a church structure that is in consonant with the image of the church as the family of God can be understood against the backdrop of the canonical roles of bishops. Canonically, bishops enjoy a high degree of autonomy and authority in the church. By their episcopal consecration, bishops exercise three functions: sanctifying, teaching and

---

[3] Lineamenta, *Church in Nigeria: Family of God on Mission* (Lagos: Catholic Secretariat of Nigeria, 1999), # 176.
[4] Ibid., # 177.
[5] Ibid., # 179
[6] Ibid., # 182.

governing.[7] These roles seem to have been rooted in St. Ignatius of Antioch's *ubi episcopus, ibi ecclesia* (where the bishop is, there is the church). Suffice it to add, though, that while the bishop might be the head of the church, the head cannot exist or function in isolation from the body of the church.

I believe, inculturating the extended family leadership structure into the church will not only erase the erroneous perception of the church as simply *uka fada,* it will lead to the recognition of the church as truly the family of God. It will also redress the overbearing influence of bishops and priests in the church.

Toward an Ohacratic Structure of the Church

The church is a living and dynamic organism, always renewing and reforming itself. The model of the church as the extended family of God provides a veritable ground for the church in Africa to renew itself. Time is ripe for the church to give up the vestiges of its medieval feudal heritage and inculturate the extended family model and structures of authority and leadership. Of particular concern is the place of bishops and priests in church governance. While not advocating the abrogation of the office of the bishop, it is important that such office ought to be fulfilled within the ambit of the extended family model. The bishop remains the center of unity of the local church.

The present ecclesiastical structure leaves less to be admired. Under the present dispensation, the bishop is more of a chief executive officer and less of a servant and shepherd of his flock. Moreover, the enormous bureaucracy in the church, orchestrated by centralization of authority in the pope and Vatican Curia, gives the impression that bishops are vicars of the pope, who have been appointed to carry out the pope's instructions. Such an impression runs contrary to the teaching of Vatican II—that bishops are vicars of Christ.[8]

A church structure and leadership that do not listen to the voices of its members contradicts the image of the church as the family of God. The church as family of God strongly evokes the Igbo's deep and acute sense of solidarity and relationality, which are the hallmarks of the family. The deep sense of solidarity and relationality is concretized in the role of *oha* and *umunna*. Because the *oha* component of the family is deeply rooted in Igbo ontology and in the concept of being as belongingness, it is at the heart of a just *ohacratic* society.[9] It seems that a recovery of the indispensable role of *oha* and *umunna* in the society and their

---

[7] Lumen Gentium, # 21.

[8] Ibid., # 21.

[9] Pantaleon Iroegbu, *African Vicious Triangles: The Option for Ohacracy.* www. estes.ucl.ac.be/publications/DOCH/DOCH/DOCH/%2039%20(Iroegbu).pdf (accessed May 1, 2006).

inculturation into church structure will not only lead to decentralization of authority and leadership but will also lead to entrenching the principle of subsidiarity in the church. This will give the laity a leadership role and voice in the church.

Previously, I underscored the fact that elders exercise legislative and executive functions. The extended family model recognizes the role and place of bishops as elders in the extended family of God. Nevertheless, they should not be the only elders. A problem arises when a young bishop or a priest takes the place of elders. Could such a young bishop or priest be called an elder? The issue is resolved on two Igbo ontological principles. First, one becomes an elder based on wisdom accumulated over the years; therefore, the bishop or the priest could qualify as an elder because of his training and wisdom acquired during his priestly formation. Second, the Igbo have the adage *nwata kwo aka ofuma, osoro eze rie nri* (when a child washes his hand properly, he dines with kings). A young fellow could join the council of elders, not necessarily because of his or her age, but because of what he or she has been able to accomplish in the society. Bishops and priests on this basis qualify as elders. However, there is the danger of neglecting the fundamental role of the extended family in the community if the bishops and priests are merely perceived as substitute elders and allowed to exercise their eldership as "monarchs over their fiefdoms."

Father John Mary Waliggo, a Ugandan theologian, cautions against the uncritical adoption of bishops and priests as substitute elders and leaders of the extended family of God. For Waliggo, this could easily slip into patriarchalism. Waliggo warns that the theology of the church-as-family is a two-edged sword: "It can be profitably used but may also lead to benign paternalism. We should not once again end up with a pyramid structure of the church but rather a circular one of communion."[10] Waliggo goes on to argue forcefully that before the model is applied, it must be fully liberated.[11] The church as the family of God should not be a patriarchal structure in which bishops, priests, and other religious figures are the parents/elders, and the laity are their children.

Eugene Uzukwu similarly observes that shortly after the Synod of Bishops for Africa, bishops connected the notion of family with the "spiritual paternity" of priests and bishops. Uzukwu cautions that this metaphor must be stripped of all the characteristics of patriarchal dominance, and that the novelty of the Gospel must predominate.[12] For Uzukwu, "the novelty of the gospel introduces a mode of being into the African family experience similar to the way Jesus lived family in order to reassemble the new family of God or new People of God based on a

---

[10] John Mary Waliggo, "The Church as Family of God and Small Christian Communities," *AMECEA* 40 (1994), 1.

[11] Ibid.

[12] Eugene E. Uzukwu, *A Listening Church: Autonomy and Communion in African Churches*, 66.

new kind of relationship. This may not exclude division (Lk 12:52f); and it will certainly include an openness that knows no limits (Mk 3:31-35)."[13]

The derivative implication of the church as the extended family of God is that it must follow the structural ethos of the extended family model. Authority and leadership cannot be restricted to the bishops and priests. Priests and bishops will exercise leadership and authority in the extended family of God's church, not with tokens of magnanimous paternalism but in consultation with lay elders as spokespersons of the church. In other words, the structure of the church will not be the over-hierarchicalized and patriarchal model but an *ohacratic* one.

The lay faithful are members of the church; as such, they comprise the church as much as do bishops and priests. By virtue of their baptism, the laity shares in the priesthood of Christ. Therefore, they must play significant roles in the church.

Because of their singular and indispensable role in the church, they must have a voice in the "council of elders" in parish and diocesan administration.[14] The ancient maxim "Whatever concerns all must be discussed by all" is applicable in this situation.

Peter Osuchukwu is right when he argues that the structuring of the extended family allows all members to participate actively in the life of the church. "Ministries," he says, "should not be seen as the prerogative of the priest . . . the people should be led to realize that the whole community (as in the traditional *umunna*) is called to participate."[15] Consequently, there should be a wider distribution of ministries.

A major critical issue that the extended family model will tackle concerns the appointment of bishops. Oftentimes, Rome appoints bishops without consulting the laity. Their suggestions are hardly sought or even considered. In most cases, priests and the laity are rarely consulted before a bishop is appointed in their diocese. In cases where they are consulted, it is done secretly and leaves little to be admired. The seeming lack of consultations and the secretive nature in selecting a bishop have in some cases led to revolt and the rejection of a few bishops in some dioceses in Nigeria.

If anyone questions the rationale behind such structures, the answer is often given that the laity is not yet mature enough to be entrusted with such responsibilities. Yet the church in Igboland is over one hundred years old. One continues to wonder when the laity will be mature enough to be involved in the selection of bishops and administration of their church.

Eugene Uzukwu expresses his exasperation at the flagrant abuse of "sacred power" and denial of the rights of the laity in the running of the church when he

---

[13] Ibid. 67.

[14] John Mary Waligo, *The Church as Family of God and Small Christian Communities*, 144.

[15] Peter Osuchukwu, *The Spirit of Umunna*, 228.

avers that such abuses are based on "the naked denial of rights to lay people in the church because they neither belong to the clergy nor are they religious. In the words of the saintly Pius X, their 'one duty . . . is to allow themselves to be led, and, like a docile flock, to follow the pastors.' All decisions are taken by the hierarchy at their various levels of operation—parish, diocese, and Episcopal conference."[16] The church cannot truly be the family of God if most of its members are not consulted in matters that concern them and given leadership roles.

Correlated to the issue of church structure is the seemingly innocuous title of bishops as "lord" or "lordship." It is disheartening that African bishops have refused to relinquish this title. The title dates back to the medieval period when bishops were feudal lords and controlled both church and state affairs like masters and lords. Sadly, in our contemporary era, African bishops still cling to this title. In a society as Igboland, where there is a mad craze to acquire titles and to be addressed as such just to boost one's bloated ego, bishops could set example by jettisoning the title "my lord," "his lordship," and so forth. Addressing bishops as "lords" negates and undermines the servanthood/eldership of bishops in the church as the family of God model. The title connotes a master-slave relationship. Since bishops are servants and at the same time shepherds of the family of God, it seems appropriate for them to adopt family titles (for example *nna*) and to dispose of the medieval title "lordship." This title has no place in the church as the extended family of God. Priests and the laity are not servants of bishops. They are bishops' brothers and sisters, collaborators, fellow members of the extended family of God.

The Extended Family Structure and Collegiality

Collegiality, an ancient and pristine practice in the early church, is at the heart of the model of the church as the extended family of God. In the early period, the church was less hierarchical and institutionalized. Cardinal Joseph Ratzinger (now Pope Benedict XVI) underscores this point when he observes that the episcopal office in the early church had a horizontal structure. According to Ratzinger, "The relationship of the various churches to one another was described with Trinitarian language of unity amid equality." Ratzinger further says, "The early Church did indeed know nothing of the papal primacy in practice, in the sense of Roman Catholic theology of the second millennium."[17] In essence, Cardinal Ratzinger acknowledges that from the very beginning, spiritual leadership existed in the

---

[16] Eugene E. Uzukwu, *A Listening Church: Autonomy and Communion in African Churches*, 122.

[17] Joseph Cardinal Ratzinger, "Anglican-Catholic Dialogue: Its Problems and Hopes," *Insight* 1, no 3 (March 1983): 5.

church in various forms; it was fluid and open. Leadership was not restricted to bishops and priests. The laity played prominent leadership roles in the church.[18]

Since the church was constituted from the beginning as a family of God, as can be deduced from tradition and scriptures, the leadership structure was collegial. The apostles made decisions collectively, as evidenced in Acts of the Apostle 15 and in other instances. Although Peter was the head of the apostles (Matt. 16:18-19), he did not exercise primacy independent of his fellow apostles. He relied on and consulted with other apostles. The same can be said of the Apostle Paul and, of course, the early Christians.

Archbishop John Quinn argues that the practice of consultation among bishops was exercised by early Christians and beyond. In his words: "Bishops of the Church had a consciousness of an obligation to speak forth-rightly when they believed the way of Roman authority [pope] being exercised was excessive."[19] Quinn goes further to contend that there were diversity and collegiality in the ancient church, which raise the possibility that there could be room for variety in the structures and practices of the church.[20] The extended family model will help in the recovery of the early church's understanding of leadership and authority—collegiality.

It is preposterous to argue that the church has not been and is not a democratic institution. There is plentiful evidence to the contrary. The early Christians followed democratic principles in exercising authority and leadership in the church. However, the form of democracy that was operative differed from our contemporary constitutional democratic process of ballot box and one person one vote to elect political leaders.

The early Christians operated a "democratic system" through consensus, in the form of assent and sometimes, by popular acclamation in choosing their leaders. Decisions were not arbitrarily made by one person but by the consensus of the Christian community. For instance, when the Greek-speaking Christians complained that the Hebrew Christians neglected their widows, the apostles asked the Greeks to choose their own leaders. The Greeks chose the first seven deacons (Acts 6:1-7). In addition, the election of the apostle Matthias to replace Judas Iscariot was done by casting of lots and not by executive fiat of the first pope—Peter (Acts 1:15-26). In addition, when the question of admitting uncircumcised gentiles who converted to Christianity into the fold arose, the problem was not resolved by the fiat of the head of the church—Peter. The apostles and presbyters, in agreement with the whole church, decided that circumcision should not be a precondition for becoming a believer (Acts 15). The significance of the examples cited above, in my

---

[18] Ronald Modras, *In His Own Footsteps: Benedict XVI*, 14.

[19] John Quinn, *The Reform of the Papacy: The Costly Call to Christian Unity* (New York: The Crossroad Publishing Company, 1999), 27.

[20] Ibid.

understanding, hinges on the fact that important decisions were arrived at through "democratic processes." The whole church was involved in the decision process. The leaders listened to the community and responded to their needs accordingly.

One person did not write the church doctrines and articles of faith. Councils and synods formulated doctrinal articles of faith. These councils and synods were not the exclusive preserve of popes and bishops but included lay people as well.

St. Clement of Rome (c. 96), one of the successors to St. Peter, held that the apostles foresaw that there would be strife when the office of the episcopate became vacant. To obviate such strife, the apostles approved that those who are to succeed them as bishops must be appointed with the consent of the whole church.[21]

The election of St. Ambrose of Milan in 374 as a bishop was done by overwhelming popular acclamation, even though he had not yet been baptized.[22] These few instances point to the fact that the early Christians adopted democratic principles in the selection or election of church leadership. The laity was actively involved in the process of choosing whoever exercised leadership over them.

The church abandoned the democratic process of selection of presbyters and bishops from the fourth century when the Council of Nicaea (325) enacted canons eliminating the vote of the laity in the election or selection of bishops.

The church evolved from a persecuted group of small members to become the official religion of the Roman Empire under Emperor Theodosius in 380. From this period up to the medieval era, the church became increasingly involved in secular affairs and began to adopt feudal monarchical and institutionalized categories. The clergy grew increasingly powerful and stifled the participation of the laity in church governance.

The model of the church as the extended family of God challenges us to chart a new course for a leadership structure that is truly African. That structure is both relational and nonclerical. A distinction has to be drawn between the ministerial role of the clergy and their leadership role. Ordination to the priesthood is a call to service. Although service could also take the form of leadership, the two, however, are not the same. Non-ordained faithful can exercise leadership roles in the church without interfering in priestly services. In most traditional African communities, priestly roles are distinct from exercise of leadership and authority, which are exercised by the elders and *oha*, and in some instances in consultation with traditional priests.

Eugene Uzukwu demonstrates that Africa's culture offers a structural mechanism for leadership and authority in the church as the family of God model. Uzukwu notes that consultation and listening must be the guiding principles

---

[21] Clement of Rome, *First Letter to the Corinthians*, 44.

[22] Henry Chadwick, *The Early Church* Revised edition (London: Penguin Books, 1993), 167.

for the existence of a church, consistent with the family of God model. For Uzukwu, church leaders must develop "large ears." By listening to the voice of its lay members, solidarity, unity and communion will be realized.[23] Essentially, listening is a recognition of the indispensability of *participation* and *solidarity* that characterize Africa's extended family structure, which should be operative in the church.

Given the deep sense of communality and belongingness that pervade the entire spectrum of African worldview, the church family model would promote a fresh impetus to communion ecclesiology. Communion ecclesiology is understood here to mean that the church as family of God is a communion of not only the union of different bishops with the pope but also a union of different churches or communities.[24] Moreover, for the church to see itself as an extended family, its boundary has to go beyond clan or ethnic groups. Hence, the waters of baptism, through which all Christians are regenerated and initiated into the family of God, must be stronger than the blood of narrow clannishness, ethnicity, and tribalism.[25]

The extended family as a model for the church not only resonates with Africans' cultural values and sensibility, it also forms the basis for balancing the images of the people of God, the bride of Christ, the church as a communion, etc., which are all family-related images.[26] The model is also inclusive rather than exclusive. No one is excluded from the extended family of God.

The Igbo concept of the extended family is in many ways similar to the Hebraic and New Testament understanding of family. In the first instance, they show that the concept of family is not strictly defined in kinship or affinial terms. The overarching principle is not necessarily a consanguine relationship, but people who are bound together by other ties such as profession of common faith, belief, culture, etc. Consequently, one can argue that the Igbo concept of *ezi-na-ulo* with its cognate *umunna*, and *ikwu n'ibe* is comparable to the biblical understanding of family and household. The new family of God envisioned here goes beyond ethnic or consanguine lines.

Again, since the Igbo worldview and culture are communitarian and republican, if magisterial pronouncements on inculturation are to be taken seriously and not become mere *flatus vocis* statements, adopting the extended family structure, as the appropriate church structure will accentuate the Igbo understanding of

---

[23] Eugene E. Uzukwu, *A Listening Church: Autonomy and Communion in the African Churches,* 127.

[24] Maura Browne, *Message of the Synod,* #57.

[25] Joseph Healy and Donald Sybertz, *Towards an African Narrative Theology,* 149.

[26] Oliver Onwubiko, *The Church as the Family of God: Ujamaa* (Enugu, Nigeria: Fulladu Publishing Company, 1999), 2.

the nature and mission of the church. The extended family image of the church offers a veritable foundation and a new vista for the recovery of collegiality and decentralization of authority in the church. Thus, the church must move beyond the rhetoric of simply asserting that the church in Africa is the family of God by inculturating family structures of leadership and authority.

Chapter 7

WOMEN AND THE CHURCH AS THE EXTENDED FAMILY OF GOD

Before we go into the discussion of the status and role of women in the church as the family of God, we would first take a critical look at the situation, role, and status of women in African societies. History and experience present us with conflicting and ambiguous views on the status of women in African cultures. On one hand, women in Africa are generally regarded as the epitome of life in the community. They are the main transmitters of cultural values and traditions.[1] In addition, they play diverse roles, such as mothers, wives, religious leaders (diviners, seers, and priestesses), medicine women, and breadwinners in the family, etc. In fact, the most revered deity in Igbo traditional religion and in many African societies is the female earth goddess *ali*.

In Igbo traditional societies, women collectively exercise leadership roles as *umuada*. No one dares challenge their authority without incurring the ire of the community. Women in conjunction with men serve as traditional priests to the community deity. They offer sacrifices on behalf of the community.

On the other hand, the paradox of the status of African women reveals itself in the marginalization of women on an individual basis. As individuals, women remain disadvantaged in the society. Regarded as the weaker sex, women are often exploited, abused, and relegated to the background in the public square or forum. In certain societies, women are hardly educated by their parents. Preference is always given to the male child. Men are regarded as the heads of women. Women are essentially perceived more as mothers and wives and are expected to be submissive to their husbands and men. There are taboos that forbid women from performing certain functions in African societies. Women are regarded as

---

[1] Anne Nasimiyu-Wasike, "Acceptance of the total human situation as a precondition for authentic inculturation." *Inculturation: Abide by the Otherness of Africa and the Africans*, eds. Peter Turkson and Frans Wijsen (Netherlands: Kok Publishers, 1994), 50.

second-class citizens, as properties to be acquired by men for the purpose of childbearing and companionship.

Peter Stanford appositely encapsulates the ambivalence of the status of women in sub-Saharan African societies when he writes:

> African women's lives are understood in five stages of which three are highly desirable. While the birth of a girl is not a reason for celebration, the girl who has reached puberty, the virgin, has high value. A young mother of a male child is at the peak of her importance, whilst subsequent births just prove that she can give birth until finally, after menopause, she has lost this power.[2]

Paradoxically, after losing the biological power to give birth through menopause and well-advanced age, a woman gains another power—that of grandmother, mother-in-law—and in fact becomes highly important as a sort of honorary male.[3] Younger women are expected to acquiesce to men as if to a master because men are considered superior to women. It is only when a woman has attained the status of "honorary male" that she is to a certain degree free from patriarchalism.[4]

Patriarchalism exposes women to violence, rape, obnoxious widowhood rituals, and female genital mutilation. In many cases, women are denied rights of inheritance. Even in households that are headed by women as breadwinners, their often irresponsible husbands still assert their unfounded claims to superiority by resorting to violence.[5] As if these abuses are not enough, African women are still expected to cook, clean the house, feed the children, and engage in other domestic chores. They are expected to make coffee and tea and not participate in policy making even in matters that concern them.

The status of women in African societies is despicable and must be condemned. Unfortunately, the situation is not helped in any way by the Catholic Church's conflicting teachings and posture toward women. On one hand, the church teaches the equality of women and men. On the other hand, the attitude of the church toward women seems to suggest that women are not equal to men. For example, women are excluded from the hierarchy of the church. The church denies women ordination to either the diaconate or the priesthood simply because of their

---

[2] Peter Stanford, *The Legend of Pope Joan* (New York: Henry Holt and Company, 1999), 74.

[3] Ibid.

[4] The term patriarchism is derived from the Latin *patriarchia,* means the rule of the father. We use the term here to refer to "the rule and dominance of men over women."

[5] Reuben Abati, *Lagos: The Domestic Violence Bill,* http://www.nigeriavillagesquare.com/content/view/2857/96/ (accessed July 29, 2006).

anatomical constitution. Hence, they are excluded from the governance of the church.

Interestingly, women played important leadership roles among the early Christians. The Acts of the Apostles and the epistles are replete with numerous accounts of women who exercised leadership roles and ministry in the early church (Acts 12:11-17; 18:2, 18, 26; 1 Cor. 16:19). We shall revisit this issue later.

It was from the time of St. Augustine that women began to be relegated to the background. Augustine argued, "The woman together with the man is the image of God, so that the whole substance is one image. But when she is assigned as a helpmate, which pertains to her alone, she is not the image of God: however, in what pertains to man alone, is the image of God just as fully and completely as he is joined with the woman into one."[6] Augustine went further to say in his *City of God* that women are naturally the weaker sex and therefore should be submissive to the masculine sex.[7] Augustine's teaching on women fed into ideas that women are not able to withstand temptation and, therefore, cannot image Christ.

There were insidious ideas that contributed to the denigration of women. For example, women's menstrual blood was believed to turn wine sour, make crops barren, rust iron, and infect dog bites with poison. With such destructive power, the idea of women handling the body and blood of Christ as the priest and chief celebrant of the Eucharist was out of the question.[8]

From the high middle ages, antiwomen movement in the church reached its feverish hysteria with St. Thomas Aquinas arguing that the female sex is misbegotten male and, therefore, women were inferior by nature to men.[9] Aquinas and others relied heavily in hindsight on flawed anthropological understanding of women that was prevalent at their time to disparage women.

Carol Coston could not have been more right when she suggests that the residue of the thinking of church fathers and theologians like Thomas Aquinas still influences the position of the present church regarding the status of women. This,

---

[6] Augustine, *De Trinitate*, 12, 7, 10.

[7] Augustine, *City of God*, Book VI, Ch. 9; Book XIV, Ch. 11-12.

[8] Peter Stanford, *The Legend of Pope Joan*, 56.

[9] Thomas Aquinas, *Summa Theologiae 1*, q 92, 1, 1. In his reply to objection 1, Aquinas argues, "As regards the individual nature, woman is defective and misbegotten, for the active force in the male seed tends to the production of a perfect likeness in the masculine sex; while the production of woman comes from defect in the active force or from some material indisposition, or even from some external influence; such as that of a south wind, which is moist, as the Philosopher observes." Aquinas equally argues that the female sex cannot represent Christ because women are incomplete human beings and thus cannot be ordained to the priesthood. *S.Th. III Supp. 39, 1.*

Coston observes, accounts for why women are not allowed to actively participate in serious decision making or the fullness of ministry.[10]

Some feminists argue that the sexist language in the liturgy and church documents marginalize women by the excision of the feminine pronoun in prayers and articles of faith in the church. For example, "man" or "mankind" is always used in the generic sense without the mention of women in numerous church documents. The male pronoun is used in referring to God, giving the false impression that God is male.

Maureen Dowd, a New York Time columnist, citing Lisa Miller's blistering attack of the Catholic Church all-male hierarchy, says, "In the Roman Catholic corporation (church), the senior executives (hierarchy) live and work, as they have for a thousand years, eschewing not just marriage, but intimacy with women . . . not to mention any chance to familiarize themselves with the earthy, primal messiness of families and children."[11] For Dowd, the exclusion of women from the hierarchy is a contributive factor in the church's clergy hideous sexual abuse of boys and girls, cover up of these abuses and indifference to the welfare of victims. Dowd does not say how the exclusion of women from the priesthood is directly related to the sexual abuse of minors by priests or reconcile the fact that most sexual abuse of minors are perpetrated by parents.

Bernadette Kunambi raises yet another grave point about the status of African women in the church when she remarks that women are often puzzled by the faith as it is presented to them. "What puzzles African women," Kunambi contends, "is the set-up of the Church as brought to Africa. Women, find themselves at a loss as to know what their place is in the Church. The Church teaches equality of all men (which includes women) before God, and yet the woman often finds herself a second class, if not a third class citizen in the Church."[12] Concisely, the problem, according to Kunambi, is structural injustice (lack of representation of women in the hierarchy) and the ambiguous teaching of equality of men and women by the church.

The Synod of Bishops for Africa recognized the alienation and marginalization of women as one major form of the structure of sin engulfing African societies.[13] However, while calling for the rights of women to be respected and promoted in modern societies, the synod fathers failed to ask for equal rights for women and men in the church. Rather, the synod continued the stereotype of seeing women as mothers, wives, and sisters.[14]

---

[10] Carol Coston O.P., "Feminism, Value and Vision," *Network* 8, # 6 (Nov-Dec. 1980). Cited in Anne Nasimiyu-Wasike, *Acceptance of the Total Human*, 53.

[11] Maureen Dowd, "Worlds without Women," *The New York Times Sunday Opinion* (April 11, 2010), 20.

[12] Bernadette Kunambi, "The Place of Women in the Christian Community," *African Christian Spirituality*, ed. Aylward Shorter (New York: Orbis Books, 1980), 153.

[13] *Message of the Synod*, 65.

[14] Ibid.

The Inter-Regional Meetings of Bishops of Southern Africa acknowledged that "the church has not yet come to terms with the position of women in traditional and contemporary African society, and has not sufficiently recognized the various ministries they have. In this sense, the full potential of women in service to the church and society is not being attained."[15] Similarly, Archbishop Charles Palmer-Buckle of Accra, Ghana, concedes that the church and society in Africa have failed women. In his words:

> Women constitute about 55 to 60 percent of African society. They constitute about 70 to 75 percent of the church . . . yet when it comes to the leadership, they are a negligible minority . . . . The need to hear women, is a fact that we cannot run away. The only thing is how to make it effective, not just as decorative . . . but the tendency is to bring in just as choreography. That is not it. Bring them because they're qualified, because they have something to contribute.[16]

Cognizant of the fact that women have suffered and continue to suffer untold hardships in their families under the highly patriarchal African societies, the extended family model is susceptible to abuse. Critics argue that the model can exacerbate the spiral of violence against women and promote male dominance in the church rather than engender women's equality with men. This criticism is serious and cannot be glossed over. The challenges must be addressed, but before we do that, let us first elaborate on the challenges that face our model vis-à-vis the status of women in the church.

One scathing criticism against the model of the church as the family of God centers on the issue of patriarchalism. Feminist scholars contend that the image of the church as family of God is structurally patriarchal. Critics argue that the image fits into the already existing patriarchal and hierarchical structure of the church. For Elaine Leeder, patriarchy perpetuates the oppression of women, gender inequality, and discriminatory practices against women. "Patriarchy," she says, "is constructed in such a way that it maintains control over women with the tool of violence."[17] For feminist scholars like Leeder, the family is the place where this dynamic is most clearly played out. Therefore, a church that adopts the family as

---

[15] IMBISA, "The Challenge to the Position of Women," *Inculturation: The Faith That Takes Roots in the African Cultures,* 32, # 225. Cited by Agapit J. Mroso, *The Church in Africa,* 153.

[16] Charles Palmer-Buckle, *Ghanaian Archbishop says church has failed Africa,* National Catholic Reporter, http://ncronline.org/news/vatican/ghanaian-archbishop-says-church-has-failed-africa (accessed October 14, 2009).

[17] Elaine Leeder, *The Family in Global Perspective: A Gendered Journey* (Thousand Oaks, California: Sage Publications, 2004), 60.

its model is inextricably bound to perpetuate violence against women and relegate them to a second-class position.

Jane Anderson equally argues that the church perpetuates patriarchalism in the ecclesiastical discipline of celibacy. For Anderson, by accepting celibacy, priests sacrifice family-of-origin attachments and replace these with "Catholic kinship." In such a social system, priests are recognized as having sole control of the domestic church. This paternal dominance is upheld in part by the use of images that promote "spiritual fatherhood."[18] Anderson goes on to argue that:

> The pattern begins with God, who is said to resemble an omnipotent male parent who is celibate—for there is no Mother God. This God is addressed as "Father," a title and form of address that is echoed in many prayers of the church . . . . Next, comes the pope, from the Greek *pappas*, meaning "father." As "the Holy Father," he represents the definitive and morally perfect male celibate leader who oversees all other "Fathers." Further down in the hierarchy are the bishops who are regarded as *paterfamilias,* from the Latin, transliterated as "father head of the family." Lower still is the priest, referred to in everyday discourse as "Father."[19]

Anderson and others raise a legitimate concern in this regard. The image could serve as a tool for the continual subjugation of women.

Despite the negative connotations associated with the image of the church as the family of God such as patriarchalism, loss of values, dysfunctional families, the extended family of God remains the best model for the church in Africa. The church as family of God offers us the best structure to nurture spiritual ideals and to transmit a sense of the "unconditional love" that Christ promises the church.[20] If the family is truly a community of disciples, then it reflects the transforming power of the Kingdom of God, educating in solidarity and compassion for those excluded from the social, material, psychological, and spiritual conditions of human flourishing.[21] The model of the church as the family of God offers a veritable ground to confront patriarchalism in an *ohacratic* way.

Notwithstanding the seeming discriminatory stance and attitude toward women in the church, African women have made remarkable impacts in the church, especially in the areas of evangelization, sustenance and care of the church, liturgy,

---

[18] Jane Anderson, *Priests in Love: Roman Catholic Clergy and Their Intimate Relationships* (New York: Continuum, 2006), 140.

[19] Ibid., 140-141.

[20] Lisa Sowle Cahill, *Sex, Gender, and Christian Ethics* (United Kingdom: Cambridge University Press, 1996), 210.

[21] Ibid.

and so forth. Women continue to empower themselves through groups like the Catholic Women Organization (CWO), a powerful organization in the church in Nigeria. In fact, the church in Africa and among the Igbos can hardly survive or maintain its social structures without the contributions of the CWO. Women are also involved in catechetical instructions and lay parish administration. However, these involvements of women seem to be only tokens of goodwill gestures given to them not because they are worthy of it but presumably, because there are not sufficient men (priests) to perform these functions.

But the question remains, how do we reconcile our image of the church as family of God with the status of women in the church and in African societies with the coequality of men and women who embody the *imago Dei*? In this regard, the church must inculturate the *ohacratic* principle of the extended family.

It is not sufficient to call for the recognition of the equality of women and men in the church as family of God. Concrete steps must be taken toward actualizing it. At the universal level, one issue that seems to militate against the full equality of men and women in the church and remains contentious is the question of women ordination. Critics suggest that women can never be equal with men, unless they too can be ordained to the priesthood.

Pope John Paul II insists that the church has no right to ordain women to the priesthood because priestly ordination right from the apostolic time has been reserved to men alone. The pope maintains that it has always been the constant practice of the church, which has imitated Christ, to ordain only men to the priesthood; and the church's teaching authority has consistently held that the exclusion of women from the priesthood is in accordance with God's plan for his church.[22]

In 2010, the Congregation for the Doctrine of the Faith issued *Norms* codifying any attempted ordination of women as *delecta gaviora* (grave sins) against the sacrament of Holy Orders. According to the *Norms*, "With due regard for canon1378 of the Code of Canon Law, both the one who attempts to confer sacred ordination on a woman, and she who attempts to receive sacred ordination, incurs a *latae sententiae* excommunication reserved to the Apostolic See."[23]

Proponents of women ordination to the priesthood argue that for Catholic women around the world, the *Norms* classifying women ordination as a *delecta gaviora* "is a statement of profound spiritual violence against half of the human race already routinely victimized on the basis of their God-given anatomy."[24] For

---

[22] John Paul II, *Apostolic Letter, Ordinatio Sacerdotalis*, (May 22, 1994), # 4.

[23] William Cardinal Levada, *Normae de gravioribus delictis,* (May 21, 2010), Art. 5, #1.

[24] Jamie Manson, "*New Norms are much more than a PR Disaster,*" National Catholic Reporter, Vol. 46, #21 (August 6, 2010), 1.

Jamie Manson, this *Norms* demonstrate unequivocally a painful truth that, the church can be, and often is, a very toxic place for women.[25]

Critics of the church's stand against women ordination argue that given the patriarchal nature of the society in Jesus' time, his choice of men as apostles should not have come as a surprise to anyone. Jesus was influenced by the cultural milieu and circumstances of his time when he chose the twelve apostles.

Some feminist scholars point out that the New Testament presents two seemingly contrasting but positive positions regarding the role of women in the church. On one hand, there is the position that seems to suggest that a woman's place is in the home and public ministering belongs to men (Luke 10:38-42; 1 Cor. 14:34-35; 1 Tim. 2:11-12). Barbara Reid O.P. of Catholic Theological Union, Chicago, suggests that the author of Luke's Gospel gives this position validity by placing approval of the silent Mary on Jesus' lips (Luke 10:38-42).[26] Reid, however, argues that this passage needs to be understood against the backdrop of the fact that this Gospel incident may be more of a reflection of the situation of the Lucan communities and the questions they were trying to resolve. For Reid, what concerns Martha is *diakonia* and her distress over her sister leaving her to carry it out alone.[27] In other words, Jesus did not reproach Martha for serving but for, perhaps, concentrating all her energy on serving while neglecting the Word of God, which is equally important. Reid then suggests that the incident in Luke is not about preparing a meal, but rather, "Martha voices how burdened her heart is over the conflicts surrounding women's exercise of their ministries in the early church."[28] The question then is what did Mary do with the Word of God she learned while sitting at Jesus' feet?

On the other hand, in the New Testament, we find myriads of women playing active roles as evangelizers and teachers like Mary Magdalene, the first to witness to the resurrection of Christ (Mark 16:9-11); Prisca (Acts 18:26); Euodia and Syntyche (Phil. 4:3); women prophets like Philip's four daughters (Acts 21:9); women heads of house churches like Nympha (Col 4:15), Mary (Acts 12:12), Lydia (Acts 16:40), Prisca (Rom. 16:5; 1 Cor. 16:19), and Phoebe, who is named *diakonos*, deacon of the church at Cenchreae (Rom. 16:1).

Proponents of women ordination argue that if Mary Magdalene, a woman, was the first to witness to the Risen Lord (Matt. 28:9-10; Mark 16:9-11; Luke 24:9-10), a defining moment in the life of the church, and is called by the church, "the Apostle to the Apostles," the argument of the church for not ordaining women is tendentious. Proponents also surmise that if contemporary women can play active

---

[25] Ibid., 16.

[26] Barbara E. Reid, "A Woman's Place," *America: The National Catholic Weekly* (July 5-12, 2010), 38.

[27] Ibid.

[28] Ibid.

roles in the political and social arenas, which demonstrate their equality with men, the church cannot claim that the sexes are equal when the priesthood and diaconate are reserved to men alone. What this tantamount to is to imply that only men can act in *persona Christi*, and, therefore, only men can image Christ, whereas women are ontologically incapable of imaging or acting in *persona Christi*.

In light of the foregoing, it seems further study and discussions on the question of women ordination is necessary to discern what the Holy Spirit is saying to the church as the family of God in the twenty-first century.

Finally, as women all over the world work and fight for gender equality in the church and society, African women must join in the struggle for equality. They must realize that the church as the family of God belongs to them as well as to men. Thus, it is not sufficient for them to "pray and bemoan" their marginalization in the church and society. African women must, as Bernadette Mbuy-Beya, the Mother Superior of the Ursuline Sisters, Congo Democratic Republic, points out, "Cease waiting to be liberated from and by men or acting like defeated victims, but rather take full charge of themselves. The liberation of women is in their hands."[29] The church as the family of God must work toward the full realization of the equality of women and men in the church. It must be recognized that in the church as family of God, no gender is superior to the other. We all stand as equal brothers and sisters.

The church as the family of God model challenges us to question and examine critically the role of women in the church, especially in the light of certain African traditions that allow women to become priestess and to hold important positions in the community. The model also challenges us to discard old attitudes, stereotypes, and customs that are inimical to women as human beings and daughters of God.[30]

---

[29] Bernadette Mbuy-Beya, "Women in the Churches in Africa," *The African Synod*, 185.

[30] IMBISA, *The Challenges to the Position of Women*, # 117.

Chapter 8

TOWARD AN AUTHENTIC EVANGELIZATION OF THE IGBOS

The image of the church as family of God confronts us with the question of how the Church can carry out its evangelizing mission and deepen the faith of its members. The question challenges us to reevaluate and redefine the church's method of evangelization. The reevaluation is necessary in order to make Christianity properly situated in Africa. This quest is crucial for the church in Africa, especially since Africans have now become missionaries themselves. Moreover, the reality of theological plurality and diversity of cultures in the church challenges us to propose new methods of spreading the Good News and deepening the faith among believers.

In hindsight, one could argue that the inability of earlier evangelizers to deepen the faith among Africans emanated from the fact that missionaries were unable to draw a distinction between the Gospel and its cultural formulations. Their classicist understanding of culture constituted a hindrance to deeper evangelization of Africa. For most missionaries, their culture was best suited for evangelization, while African cultures were not. Africans were to be rescued and redeemed from their pernicious cultures. Bernard Lonergan observes that for missionaries with the classicist mentality of culture, "it was perfectly legitimate to impose their normative culture on others. Accordingly, to preach both the Gospel and their culture is for them to confer the double benefit of both the true religion and the true culture."[1] As I mentioned in an earlier chapter, one of the ways out of this quagmire, which will lead to authentic evangelization, is inculturation.

It is precisely because the early missionaries did not adopt inculturation that the Christian faith in Africa, after many centuries of existence and practice, continues to flounder. The flagrant condemnation of everything about Africa as barbaric,

---

[1] Bernard Lonergan, *Method in Theology* (Toronto: University of Toronto Press, 1979), 363.

primitive, and savage by pioneer Christian missionaries constituted an obstacle toward a genuine evangelization. For example, Father Joseph Lutz, a pioneer Catholic missionary in Igboland, admonished missionaries coming to Africa in these words: "All those who go to Africa as missionaries must be thoroughly penetrated with the thought that the Dark Continent is a cursed land, almost entirely in the powers of the devil."[2] Similar misperceptions of other African communities abound. With this bias, missionaries to Africa were determined to pass on an unadulterated faith insulated in European culture and its form of Christianity. With this methodology, the missionary zeal to evangelize and civilize African people became intertwined with the colonization of Africa.

Dialogue: The Methodology for an Inculturated Evangelization

In order for faith to take deep roots, it must engage every culture it encounters in a constructive dialogue. Dialogue between the Gospel and culture through the instrumentality of inculturation goes beyond an external adaptation of the faith to a given culture. Dialogue seeks for an inculturation, which will achieve "the intimate transformation of authentic cultural values through their integration in Christianity in the various human cultures."[3]

If we consider the historical development of Christianity spanning over two millennia, it has to be noted that this development was accentuated by the willingness of the faith to engage in dialogue with different philosophies and cultures, including the Jewish religion and the Greco-Roman cultures. Consequently, for the evangelization of Africans to be successful, the faith has to engage African cultures in dialogue. Such dialogue must recognize the religious and cultural experiences of Africans. Hence, dialogue becomes more poignant and an urgent priority in inculturating the extended family as an image of the church in Africa.

Dialogue as a method for evangelization does not entail compromising one's faith or uncritically accepting other religious or cultural experiences. Among other things, evangelization seeks to engage any culture in dialogue and accept whatever is true of the culture in question. Evangelization also seeks new forms of cultural expression of the unchanging faith. Pope John Paul II underscores the efficacy of dialogue as a missionary methodology when he says, "Dialogue is a part of the Church's evangelizing mission. Understood as a method and means of mutual

---

[2] Holy Ghost Congregation Archives, cited in Christopher Ejizu, *Ofo Ritual Symbols* (Enugu, Nigeria: Snaap Press, 1986), 148.

[3] The Final Report of the 1985 Extraordinary Synod, D, 4.

knowledge and enrichment, dialogue is not in opposition to the mission *ad gentes*; indeed, it has special links with that mission and is one way of its expressions."[4]

As Cardinal George rightly observes, inculturation dialogue requires clarity in distinguishing revelation from doctrine and both from theology.[5] Understanding this dynamic will help the church understand, in part, how the faith is trans-cultural and, yet, searches for new forms of particular expression.[6]

The essence of dialogue as a method for inculturated evangelization, therefore, is to learn incomparably about our common human experiences, differences, and similarities in culture, about God's self-revelation in Christ, and, lastly, about how each culture experiences and expresses faith in Christ.

To engage constructively in inculturation dialogue, the dialogue partners must not engage in a "monologic dialogue" in which conversation partners talk at each other. In a "monologic dialogue," each interlocutor is unresponsive to what the dialogue partner says but is preoccupied with preconceived notions and bent only on presenting his or her views. On the contrary, dialogue becomes meaningful when its participants converse with open minds and exhibit a willingness to acknowledge whatever is noble and salvific in each religious tradition and culture. Thus, dialogue demands a close contact with and a great sensitivity to the spiritual and human values that are enshrined in any religious tradition and culture.[7] The bottom line here is that while engaging a culture in dialogue, the faith seeks to understand the culture in question. I believe such openness can help to dispel the cloud of suspicion, mistrust, prejudice, mutual recrimination, etc., that distort the work of evangelization in Africa. This element was totally lacking during the first evangelization of Africa. Now that Africans have become missionaries to themselves, they are best suited to dialogue with their own cultures than the early missionaries.

In view of the fact that Christianity is witnessing a seismic shift in its religious history in Africa, and while it is true that there is an unprecedented explosion in the number of Africans who are converting to Christianity (with more than 50 percent of Africans converted to Christianity),[8] we should be cautious about believing in numbers. Numbers do not tell the whole story about African Christianity, or rather what Lamin Sanneh calls the "religion of the colonizers," which is growing so fast in Africa.

---

[4] John Paul II, *Redemptoris Missio*, # 55.

[5] Francis E. George, *Inculturation and Ecclesial Communion*, 343.

[6] Ibid., 349.

[7] Vatican Pontifical Council for Inter-Religious Dialogue & Congregation for the Evangelization of Peoples, *Dialogue and Proclamation*, # 14.

[8] Lamin Sanneh, "Why is Christianity, the Religion of the Colonizer, Growing so Fast in Africa," *The Santa Clara Lectures* 11 (May 11, 2005), 13.

As I pointed out in preceding chapters, a critical assessment of the state of Christianity in Africa reveals that much still need to be done. Despite the remarkable success recorded by the missionaries, the Christian faith, at best, remains superficial. African traditional religion (ATR), which so-called Christians are abandoning for Christianity, continues to wield enormous influence on the life of most African Christians and the followers of other religious traditions. The situation makes dialogue with ATR not only necessary but imperative. Dialogue and inculturation are necessary to ensure that the errors of past missionary evangelization are not repeated.

It is sad to note that although Africans have become missionaries to themselves there is scarcely any ongoing dialogue with ATR. The past missionary method of blatant condemnation of local customs and traditions continue to be the tool of choice for evangelization. There is neither a dialogue *ad intra* nor *ad extra*. What we witness most often is the "dialogue of the deaf" with ATR. The African church, still heavily clothed in European theology, continues to engage in the "dialogue of the deaf" with itself and remains unwilling to engage in constructive and mutually informative dialogue with African cultures. Denis Isizoh, a Nigerian theologian, suggests that this lack of dialogue stems from the belief that adherents of ATR will all convert to Christianity.[9] More often than not, such conversions do not take place; even when they do, as evidenced by the phenomenal growth of Christianity in Igboland, such conversions remain shallow. Many converts continue to adhere to the tenets of ATR. Bolaji Idowu, the Methodist Archbishop of Nigeria, encapsulates this point when he laments:

> It is now becoming clear to the most optimistic of Christian evangelists that the main problem of the Church in Africa today is the divided loyalties of her members between Christianity with its western categories and practices on the one hand, and the traditional religions on the other. It is well known that in strictly personal matters relating to the passage of life and crises of life, African Traditional Religion is regarded as the final succour by Africans.[10]

Idowu's view is quite instructive. It reminds us of the reality of African Christianity, and that the faith is far from being deep-rooted.

The problem of African Christianity makes dialogic inculturated evangelization an urgent necessity. The obvious implication of dialogue as a tool for inculturation

---

[9] Denis Chidi Isizoh, *Dialogue with Followers of African Traditional Religion: Progress and Challenges*, http://www.afrikaworld.net/afrel/dialogue-with-atr.htm (accessed Sept. 5, 2006).

[10] Bolaji Idowu, *African Traditional Religion: A Definition* (New York: Orbis Books, 1973), 205.

is that evangelization would be understood, essentially, as not going to convert a people, but to engage them and their culture in dialogue. Thus, evangelization would not be about the proclamation of the Good News in abstract terms couched in foreign cultures, but it becomes realistically concrete when evangelizers work toward understanding a culture. Dialogue would achieve its purpose when participants get to know and respect one another's religious beliefs, forge friendships, and help to overcome hostilities.

It is important to outline the fundamental criteria for dialogue as a method for an inculturated evangelization. The overarching criteria for dialogue, as David Tracy points out, are "to recognize the other as the other, the different as different and also to acknowledge other words of meaning as in some manner, a possible option for myself."[11] Tracy offers more insights into the rules of engagement in dialogue or conversation when he contends that conversation is akin to a game with some hard rules:

> Say only what you mean; say it as accurately as you can; listen to and respect what the other says, however different or other; be willing to correct or defend your opinions if challenged by the conversation partner; be willing to argue if necessary, to confront if demanded, to endure necessary conflict, to change your mind if the evidence suggests it.[12]

Awareness of this facticity beckons on the church to have what Paul Knitter calls a "personal existential awareness of the other." By this, he means, "We have to experience and feel the beauty, authenticity, power, inspiration and truth of another religious tradition and culture, not in books or films, but in friendship and community."[13] In other words, dialogue as a method for evangelization must be primarily existential. Hence, it is necessary not to begin dialogue with doctrinal issues. This would be pointless.

Experience has shown that interreligious or cultural dialogues have been most fruitful when issues that cut across the spectrum of the religious divide like justice, peace, hunger, violence, wars, and values constitute the points of departure in dialogue. Conversely, dialogues that begin with the most sensitive and disputed issues often crumble as soon as they begin.

---

[11] David Tracy, *Dialogue with the Other: The Inter-Religious Dialogue* (Louvain: Peeters Press, 1990), 41.

[12] David Tracy, *Plurality and Ambiguity: Hermeneutics, Religion, Hope* (Chicago: The University of Chicago Press, 1987), 19.

[13] Paul Knitter, *Jesus and the Other Names: Christian Mission and Global Responsibility* (New York: Orbis Books, 1996), 28.

For Avery Dulles, dialogue partners will generally do better to begin with topics on which there are promise of achieving a significant measure of consensus. Dulles lists the possible common grounds for dialogue with cultures and different religions: religious freedom, human interdependency, social welfare and civil order, religious themes such as the value of prayer and the nature of mystical experience, which seem to occur in similar ways in different religious traditions. Other possible dialogue themes include suffering and happiness, life and death, speech and silence, mystical experience, and so forth.[14] The essence of dialogue then is to affirm similarity in difference and difference in similarity. When dialogue partners are able to establish trust among themselves, any discussion on the doctrinal aspects of religion would be meaningful and possibly lead to conversion.

Dialogue requires openness to the other and respect for what is good in the other. Consequently, for evangelization to be fruitful among Africans, the church as family of God must engage not only in dialogue with itself but also in dialogue with African traditional religion and cultures. The essence of dialogue *ad intra* is to lead to the re-evangelization of the members of the church by giving fresh impetus to the faith. On the other hand, dialogue *ad extra* provides the platform for meeting the Igbo culture and traditional religion.

At this juncture, it is important to point out that dialogue as a tool for inculturated evangelization does not replace proclamation; rather, both are integral. Shorter aptly argues that dialogue is in some sense a prerequisite for proclamation. Without proclamation, faith cannot be deepened or expressed, nor can inculturation take place.[15] Because the church is missionary in character, it has the right to proclaim and invite people to fellowship without any form of coercion.

In fact, as Pope Paul VI points out, "There is no evangelization if the name, the teaching, the life and kingdom and the mystery of Jesus of Nazareth, the Son of God are not proclaimed. The history of the church, from the discourse of Peter on the morning of Pentecost onwards, has been intermingled and identified with the history of this proclamation."[16] Elucidating further on the content of proclamation, the pope teaches that evangelization has as its focal point a clear proclamation that in Jesus Christ, who died and rose from the dead, salvation is offered to all men and women as a gift of God's grace and mercy.[17]

The African Synod squarely addressed the necessity of dialogue and proclamation of the Gospel in Africa with ATR. The synod fathers note that ATR

---

[14] Avery Dulles, "Christ Among the Religions," *America* 186, # 3, (February 4, 2002): 19.

[15] Aylward Shorter, *Evangelization and Culture*, 42.

[16] Pope Paul VI, *Evangeli Nuntiandi*, # 22.

[17] Ibid., # 27. John Paul II takes up this theme in his *Redemptoris Missio* # 44-45. There he argues that just as the whole economy of salvation has its clear center in Christ, so too all missionary activities are directed to the proclamation of this mystery.

still has an influence on Africans and often directs the way of life of even the best of African Catholics.[18] Thus, in order to sustain the momentous growth of Christianity in Africa, the old missionary methodology for evangelization must be jettisoned for a dialogic incarnated inculturation. Unless Christianity becomes incarnated in African cultures, it will continue to remain the "religion of the colonizers." Insofar as it remains an alien religion, the phenomenal growth in the number of converts to Christianity will not perdure. Dialoguing with ATR will help Christianity to discover why ATR continues to hold a strong appeal among the best of Christians and which aspects of it can be inculturated into the Catholic faith.

---

[18] African Synod, *Propositions*, # 42.

Chapter 9

LITURGICAL INCULTURATION

Liturgical inculturation is critical for an effective inculturated evangelization of Africans. Africans' deep sense of the sacred and their religiosity impel them to celebrate different stages of life in the sacred cosmic order. Birth, puberty, coming of age, marriage, planting, harvesting, death, worship, veneration of ancestors, and other sacred events are marked by special ceremonies.[1] Various rites and rituals distinctively characterize these celebrations.

In African culture and religion, the Supreme Being, deities, spirits, and human beings communicate and interact through the media of rites and rituals. Rites and rituals are fundamental parts of African cultures and, therefore, characterize them. Rite or ritual is a set form of carrying out a religious action or ceremony: a means of communicating something of religious significance through words, symbol, or action.[2] Rites and rituals reflect the totality of life in a community. At the same time, they are symbolic and generate group identity, providing a sense of continuity. They also serve as codes through which a particular culture expresses its insertion into the world.

A worshipping community uses religious rituals to reaffirm its foundation; making the community experience its existence and participation in a transcendental realm.[3] Through rites and rituals, the power of tradition is expressed from generation to generation, and the lore of the society is transmitted to ensure cohesion and continuity.[4] Thus, it is not an overstatement to assume that there is

---

[1] Benignus C. Ogbunanwata, *New Religious Movements or Sects: A Theological and Pastoral Challenge to the Catholic Church* (Frankfurt: Peter Lang, 2005), 53.

[2] John S. Mbiti, *Introduction to African Religion*, 131.

[3] Eugene E. Uzukwu, *Worship as Body Language: Introduction to Christian Worship, an African Orientation* (Collegeville, Minnesota: The Liturgical Press, 1997), 41.

[4] Bronislaw Malinowski, *Magic, Science and Religion and Other Essays* (New York: Anchor Books, 1992), 40.

an existential dynamic relationship between rites/rituals and African communities. It inexorably follows that for evangelization to be effective, it must inculturate the people's rites and rituals as the fundamental means of communication between the divine and human beings.

Because the liturgy is the favored place where human beings and divine unite, it is, as Vatican II teaches, "the outstanding means by which the faithful can express in their lives, and manifest to others, the mystery of Christ and the real nature of the true Church."[5] As a human action, the liturgy uses rituals and symbols to express and manifest the redemptive and sanctifying mystery of Christ. Hence, "the sanctification of human beings is manifested by signs perceptible to the senses and is effected in a way which is proper to each of these signs."[6] Certainly, there are no "heavenly made" rites and rituals and symbols through which the sanctification of human beings is actualized in the liturgy. The liturgy embodies the rites, rituals and symbols of a people.

The Roman liturgy, which unmistakably developed from the Jewish tradition and Greco-Roman cultures in their cultic worship, serves as the means through which western Christianity gives accent to and responds to God. Christianity was able to flourish in the west because it inculturated the religious and cultural rites, rituals, and symbolisms in which it found itself—the Mediterranean world. Thus, for liturgy to achieve its purpose—the sanctification of believers, it must reflect some measure of Africanness; that is, the liturgy must be perceptible by the African cultural sensibility. Otherwise, it becomes an impotent and empty ritual.

Liturgical inculturation is undoubtedly mired in controversy. The controversy stems from the perception that it would lead to syncretism. Vatican II cautioned against uncritical liturgical adaptation when it warned against the adaptation of a way of life that is indissolubly bound up with superstition and errors.[7] Precisely what is meant by "bound up with superstition and errors" has remained a point of contention. It equally constitutes a clog in the wheels of liturgical inculturation. Bearing in mind that Christian liturgy from the earliest times evolved from pagan cults in the Greco-Roman world, which were invariably bound up with superstition; one wonders if this caveat is necessary. According to Eugene Uzukwu, the Roman Eucharistic prayer is "heavily dependent on pagan Greco-Roman prayer patterns. The cults of saints, anointing with oil, Christian feasts like Christmas, and so forth have pagan roots."[8] These ritual and festivals were part of the Greco-Roman cultures before they were inculturated into Christian liturgical celebrations.

Since the main objective of inculturation is to sanctify every culture that the Gospel encounters, liturgical inculturation should equally sanctify and redeem

---

[5] *Sacrosanctum Concilium*, # 2.
[6] Ibid., # 7.
[7] Ibid., # 37-40.
[8] Eugene E. Uzukwu, *Worship as Body Language*, 18.

the rituals, festivals, and symbols of Africans. The present rites and rituals in the church do not fully serve this purpose because they do not resonate with Africa's religiosity. Of what use are rituals and symbols that convey mixed meanings or have no significance to a culture?

An effective African liturgical inculturation would entail that the texts, rituals, and symbols used in liturgical celebrations by the local church would be drawn from African culture and absorb its language, rituals patterns, and symbols.[9] An inculturated liturgy disposes people to participate actively in liturgical celebration through the instrumentality of their own cultural symbols and rituals.

The goal of liturgical inculturation in the extended family model concept of the church is to ensure that the liturgy is not construed as an alien imposition but that it becomes part of the people. This objective ensures that the church become part of every culture.

Inculturating African Food and Wine into the Eucharist

The Vatican II Council Constitution on the Sacred Liturgy *Sacrosanctum Concilium* initiated liturgical reforms in the church. The council opened a new vista on the liturgical life of the church by encouraging active participation in the liturgy. The council recognized that active participation in the liturgy is bolstered if there is less uniformity and when local customs and languages are inculturated into the liturgy. Taking steps to ensure active participation in the liturgy, the council teaches: "Even in the liturgy, the Church has no wish to impose a rigid uniformity in matters which do not involve the faith or the good of the whole community. Rather she respects and fosters the spiritual adornment and gifts of the various races and people."[10] Vatican II's teaching gave relief to millions of Catholics all over the world who had longed to worship God in their own language and culture and to incorporate their arts, music, rituals, and symbols into the liturgical life of the church.

As the church in Africa was grappling with how to make the liturgy truly African by inculturating local customs, the 1983 Code of Canon Law was promulgated. Regarding Eucharistic celebration, the code expressly forbade the use of anything other than wheat bread and grape wine for the celebration of the Eucharist. "The most sacred Eucharistic Sacrifice must be celebrated with bread and wine, with which a small quantity of water is to be mixed. The bread must be

---

[9] Anscar Chupungco, *Liturgies of the Future: The Process and Methods of Inculturation* (New York: Paulist Press, 1989), 29.

[10] *Sacrosanctum Concilium*, # 37.

only wheat and recently made so that there is no danger of spoiling. The wine must be natural from the fruit of the vine and not spoiled."[11]

The underlying reasons behind the promulgation of this canon are, first, to maintain unity and uniformity in the celebration of the Eucharist and, second, to remain faithful to the Gospel and Apostolic tradition. It is the belief of the magisterium that Jesus used wheat bread and grape wine in the institution of the Eucharist; hence, the church must remain faithful to this tradition. The problem with this law lies in the belief that the efficacy of the Eucharist depends on the materiality of the bread and wine used in the celebration of the liturgy. The canon rendered moot the possibility of using African food and wine to celebrate the Eucharist.

Tradition is often invoked in justifying the doctrinal teachings and liturgical practices of the church. Sometimes the argument goes thus: "The church has always taught or believed . . . hence it must be right." It is a fact that the early Christians lived in a period that is completely different from ours. The early Christians were people of their time. They did not live outside the world nor did they adopt a culture that was different from theirs. They used what was operative in their time to worship God. They transformed pagan practices into Christian rituals. It is true that the church has not followed consistently all that the early Christians believed and practiced. Differences have always existed in the choice of bread and wine used in liturgical celebrations from the first century of the church until the ninth century and beyond.

Eucharistic celebrations, rites, and rituals have undergone several dramatic changes over the course of the history of the church. The early Christians did not celebrate the Eucharist with wafers but with real bread baked by families, which they equally consumed at home. The emphasis for them was not on the specific bread and wine they used but on the memory of Jesus giving himself through bread and wine. It was not a memory about the specific bread and wine that shaped their understanding of liturgical celebration. For Edward Foley, "The early Christians emphasized the symbolic meal of the Eucharist rather than the use of unleavened or leavened bread and grape wine."[12]

At any rate, the actual bread and wine Jesus used for the Passover meal is not the same kind of bread and wine that is in use today. The Eucharistic elements have undergone changes, adapting to the needs and circumstances of a particular culture. Father François Kabasele, an African theologian, could not have been more correct when he argues that the host and wine used in Mass today are certainly not the same bread and wine that Jesus used in the first Holy Thursday liturgy. For Kabasele, "What is important . . . as far as the Eucharistic elements were concerned, was

---

[11] *Code of Canon Law*, 924, §1-3.

[12] Edward Foley, *From Age to Age: How Christians Celebrate the Eucharist* (Chicago: Liturgical Training Publication, 1991), 83.

the 'bread' and not the unleavened nature of the bread."[13] Father James Okoye shares a similar view when he suggests that Jesus may have used another form of bread. Okoye argues that, "Jesus used the elements of food and drink available in his culture; the sacramental sign is not seen to inhere in the particular form of food and drink. In fact, it is questioned whether he actually used wheaten bread. Passover was the time of barley harvest; the harvest of wheat did not usually come till about Pentecost."[14] To become fixated on the specific bread and wine to be used in the Eucharistic celebration negates the reality of Jesus' intention. Jesus gave himself to his loved ones as the food that sustains life, urging them to do likewise for others and to keep the memorial of this salvific event alive.

Insisting on using wheat bread and grape wine creates an undue sociocultural and economic burden on Africans. Since wheat and grapes do not grow in most parts of Africa, it is costly and inconvenient to use these items in the celebration of the Eucharist. How should this dilemma be solved? Should the local church be importing foreign wheat bread and grape wine in order to celebrate a valid and licit Eucharist? The issue of using wheat bread was laid to rest in 1983 when the military government in Nigeria banned the importation of certain foods including wheat flour. The church began using local grains to produce the bread for the Eucharist. However, grape wine continues to be imported. It is against this backdrop that I argue for the use of palm wine for the liturgical celebration.

Palm wine is produced from palm trees that grow almost everywhere in sub-Saharan Africa. It can be considered the Igbo equivalent of grape wine. All natural, it has an alcoholic content of about 12 percent but is usually diluted with water before it is drunk. Palm wine can also be bottled and preserved for a long period. The palm tree from which palm wine is produced is quite useful and rich in symbolism. For example, the tree produces oil for cooking; the kernel is used in the production of soap, body cream, etc. Furthermore, to hold a palm frond in time of war or violence is equivalent to holding an olive tree branch, signifying peace. Palm wine is the choice of wine in any traditional celebration such as a marriage, funeral, communal festival, or a libation to the ancestors or gods. Even though it is easily available and freely drunk among the Igbos, it is nevertheless held sacrosanct. A ceremony could not be said to have taken place in a typical Igbo feast if another type of wine is used in the place of palm wine. This symbolism makes palm wine the best alternative to grape wine. Other African nations have their own local wines and food that can fulfill this role.

Critics of an inculturated African Eucharist argue that the color of palm wine is not red and as such cannot symbolize the blood of Jesus. It seems to me

---

[13] François K. Lumbala, *Celebrating Jesus Christ in Africa: Liturgy and Inculturation*, trans. Jean Smith (New York: Orbis Books, 1998), 51.

[14] James C. Okoye, *The Eucharist in African Perspective,* http://www.sedos.org/english/okoye_2.htm Date accessed February 19, 2007.

that, although most often red wine is used in the liturgy, we are not certain of the color of wine Jesus used in instituting the Eucharist. Besides, white grape wines are frequently used in most churches in America and Europe. Moreover, as I mentioned earlier, the liturgy evolved over a long period, adapting to the changing needs of people. Moreover, there have never been uniform rituals for the liturgy in the church. Some of the early Christians did not even use wine for the liturgy. For instance, the Aquarians[15] of the third century refused to celebrate the Eucharist with wine because they saw it as something that corrupts the senses.[16] This makes me wonder whether the emphasis should be on minute details, like of the color of wine, its material elements, or on the symbolic meaning of the Eucharist. Put in another way, is the saving efficacy of the Eucharist, which recalls the passion, death, and resurrection of Christ, intrinsically bound with the material elements that constituted a Jewish culture?

Insistence on the use of grape wine and wheat bread over the local food and wine of Africans raises a larger question: Since Jesus was a Jew, must one be a Jew in order to become a Christian? Why do we not use grape wine and wheat bread specifically made in the Mediterranean region? If Jesus were an African, would he not have used African food and wine to institute the Eucharist? Do we have to wait for African political leaders to ban the importation of grape wine, as most did with regard to the importation of wheat bread, before we inculturate palm wine? Are African symbols and rituals incapable of being transformed by Christ?

It is my view that the Eucharist is not the sacrament of wheat bread and grape wine. It is an *Anamnesis* of the passion, death, and resurrection of Jesus, a saving act perpetuated by the church through rites, rituals, and symbols in a sacrificial meal. It is not a memorial or a celebration of Western culture, or as Lumbala rightly notes, "Mediterranean agriculture or [a] paschal meal located within the ambient of Jewish liturgical customs."[17] The materiality of wheat bread and grape wine does not constitute a theological necessity for salvation. Thus, the insistence on the materiality of bread and red grape wine is untenable. It seems that insisting on maintaining a uniform liturgical celebration without due deference to African cultures is to suggest that African food and drink are irreconcilable with

---

[15] Aquarians were several sects in the early Church like the Ebionites. They venerated water (*aqua*), which they regarded as the source of life. The Aquarians are so called because they used water instead of wine in the celebration of the Eucharist. The name, however, seems to have been given chiefly to the followers of Tatian. At the time of St. Cyprian, the practice existed in some parts of Africa of using water instead of wine in the celebration of the Eucharist. St. Cyprian strongly condemned it in one of his letters, ascribing it, however, to ignorance and simplicity rather than to a heretical spirit. http://www.newadvent.org/cathen/01660d.htm (accessed July 2, 2006).

[16] François K. Lumbala, *Celebrating Jesus Christ in Africa*, 52.

[17] Ibid., 54.

the Gospel. This to me smacks of hanging on to an antiquated classicist view of monoculturalism with its tendency to impose a "superior" culture on others.[18]

The catechism of the Catholic Church teaches that in the Eucharist, earth and heaven unite.[19] The "hypostatic union" of heaven and earth is brought about through the instrumentality of bread and wine and the action of the priest. The union of heaven and earth should not be restricted to the materiality of wheat bread and wine from vine but through each people's food and drink in so far as they bring nourishment to the human person. Using imported wine for Eucharistic celebration alienates the Igbos not only from attaining the "hypostatic union" of heaven and earth but also from the salvific mystery of Christ in the Eucharist. Again, the Eucharist has a cosmic dimension, and if Africans cannot celebrate it with their local food and drink, certainly, African cosmos is excluded from this cosmic reality. Insisting on maintaining the status quo (only unleavened wheat bread and wine from vine) for the celebration of the Eucharist sends a mixed message to a people whose land does not grow grapes. First, although the wine, as the church prays in the offertory, "is gift of the earth and work of human hands," this does not ring through for Africans because it is not truly the work of African participants nor is it produced from their soil.[20] Second, insisting on using wheat bread and grape wine, which do not grow in many parts of Africa, seems to suggest that African food and wine are not capable of undergoing transubstantiation and, therefore, incapable of being sacramentalized. Of course, it is not correct because as Eugene Uzukwu rightly notes:

> The unique transformation of the Jewish ritual by Jesus does not lie in the domain of elements. He ate and drank like any other Jew the products of the land . . . . Jesus used the food items of his culture because he was establishing the Eucharist in the context of a meal. This means that the question of the use of wheat or barley bread and grape-wine, is not a dogmatic but a disciplinary issue. We have to celebrate the Eucharist memorial with food and drink but this food and drink do not necessarily have to be wheat bread and grape wine.[21]

Charles Cummings shares similar perspective when he argues that in designating which food would contain his presence, "Jesus did not insist on something exotic or imported. Instead, Jesus was content to use the bread and wine of the Passover meal—ordinary, everyday items. The bread was made at home;

---

[18] Bernard Lonergan, *Methods in Theology*, 363.
[19] Catechism of the Catholic Church, # 1326.
[20] Emmanuel Chukwu, *Ezi-na-Ulo. 394.*
[21] Eugene E. Uzukwu, "Food and Drink in Africa and the Christian Eucharist," *Bulletin of African Theology* 2, # 4, (1980): 183-184.

the wine was readily obtainable if not homemade. These were the staple foods of the populace at that time: their common daily nourishment."[22] The point I would like to underscore in Cummings's view is that Jesus used the staple food of his people. To insist on the use of wine made from grape vines when there are viable alternatives denies Africans the sacramental realization of their bio-region and makes them feel that their land is incapable of being transformed by the mystery of Christ's salvation.[23] As the favored place where a community of believers gives witness and expression to God through the instrumentality of rituals and symbols, the Eucharist must be celebrated in every culture in such a manner that will lead to the realization of the Lord's intentions. African rites, rituals, and symbols must be inculturated into the liturgy as the church has done with Western symbols and rituals.

A negation of an inculturated liturgy will make Africans continue to view the liturgy as an alien imposition. The liturgy will become for Africans, in the words of François Lumbala, "a museum where one goes to mediate on ancient artifacts or to study history; where one learns to admire its heraldry. In this way the anthropological dimension of the Eucharist is eliminated and ultimately, the fundamental meaning of the memorial simply disappears."[24]

To argue that an inculturated African liturgy would exacerbate division in the church is to fall into historical error. In fact, there are several rites in the Catholic Church: Syrian, Byzantine, Coptic, Ethiopian, Chaldean, Alexandrian, Melkite, Malankara, Ambrosian, Syro-Malankara, Syro-Malabar, Roman, etc. These rites are peculiar and unique to the people who use them. The question then is what is wrong with having an African rite that would advance the genuine evangelization of the people?

The so-called Zairean (Congo) liturgy that was approved in the 1960s is heavily Roman—the language of the liturgy is Latin—the rite does not permit the use of African food and wine in the celebration of the Eucharist. Thus, it is not truly an African liturgy. Vatican II's insistence on not imposing rigid uniformity and adapting local cultures in the liturgy is a step in the right direction. Unfortunately, Rome has yet to fully implement this reform.

Opposition against an African rite, which, of course, includes the use of palm wine for liturgical celebrations, leads into the larger issue of domination and cultural imperialism. The Evangelization of African cultures by Euro-American missionaries was couched in Western culture, which is tendentiously presented as superior to African cultures. Africans were and are called upon to give up

---

[22] Charles Cummings, "Fruit of the Earth, Fruit of the Vine," *Embracing Earth: Catholic Approaches to Ecology,* eds. Albert J. Lachance, and John E. Carroll (New York: Orbis, 1994), 157.

[23] Emmanuel Chukwu, *Ezi-na-ulo,* 394.

[24] François K. Lumbala, *Celebrating Jesus Christ in Africa,* 55.

their cultural heritage for the Western form of Christianity. African cultures were perceived as not worthy of being Christianized. The "superior" Western cultures remain the preferred channel for any encounter between Africans and Christ. Again, Lumbala is right when he insists that the search to impose uniformity reveals a temptation to pride, which makes a group in power pretend to possess God fully and to be able to impose limits on how God is revealed in other cultures.[25] It is obvious that this approach has not achieved the much desired result—genuine evangelization. This accounts for why the faith is not deeply rooted in Africa.

African scholars (Lumbala, Uzukwu, Okoye, etc.) reject the imperialistic hue of uniformity in liturgical celebration as flawed and lopsided. Such imposition undermines the theological foundation of the incarnation of Christ on which the theology of the inculturation is rooted. Christ, by taking flesh and becoming human, is at the heart of all cultures. He is inexorably present in all cultures even before the Gospel is explicitly proclaimed. Christ adopts a multiplicity of cultural identities when members of each culture become his followers through faith and baptism.

An African-inculturated Eucharist is not just about using local food and drink. For the Eucharist to be truly African, it must incorporate fundamental elements of Africa's religious and cultural sacrificial meal. In a typical African communal sacrificial meal, every member of the community is expected to share in the meal for reconciliation or the celebration of a festival. In such instances, the object of sacrifice is distributed to various groups in the community. Ancestors are also called upon to participate in the meal. The sacrificial meal embodies the entire community and brings it into the sphere and sanction of the invisible world.[26] To participate in the community's sacrificial meal, one must be in communion with the community. Where there is conflict between community members or offence to the ancestors, reconciliation must precede the meal. In this sense, the Igbo sacrificial meal mediates harmony, healing, and reconciliation between people and between them and invisible powers.[27]

Although Christianity in Africa has made much progress, it is not yet African in content and outlook. Many African Christians remain unwilling to relinquish their traditional culture and religion. In my judgment, only an inculturated Christianity can free African Christians from this quandary. In order to make the Eucharist truly African, it must incorporate African symbols and ways of

---

[25] Ibid., 6.

[26] James Okoye, *The Eucharist in African Perspective* http://www.sedos.org/english/okoye_2.htm (accessed February 19, 2007).

[27] Ibid.

worship to draw Africans more fully into the self-giving of Christ to God and to His community.[28]

What Is Lost and What Is Gained in Liturgical Inculturation?

Africans are warm and unabashedly communitarian, celebrating life and death through active participation of the community. The church in Africa needs a liturgy that is vibrant in character. Liturgical inculturation guarantees this. The expediency of liturgical inculturation cannot be overemphasized. It will help steep the Igbos in a deeper appreciation of the sacraments. Liturgical inculturation will bring new impetus and meaning into the paschal mystery of Christ and thereby engenders authentic evangelization. Evidence abounds to buttress the fact that the church has survived and flourished where it has respected and followed the path of inculturation. Conversely, evangelization has been stifled where inculturation was not taken seriously. A typical example is the Jesuit missionary activity led by Matteo Ricci in China. Ricci and his fellow missionaries embarked on a profound dialogue with Chinese culture. Their goal was to achieve a Christian reinterpretation of Chinese culture, which in turn, would provoke a Chinese interpretation of Christianity presented in Chinese form. Ricci constructed a Chinese rite, which led to massive conversion of Chinese into Christianity. Sadly, his success was short-lived because the Vatican rejected Ricci's methodology and regarded the Chinese rite as being incongruent with Christian faith and morals. The rejection of the Chinese rites was a tragedy. "It spelled the loss of China and Indochina to the Church."[29]

Christ promised to send the Holy Spirit, to guide and animate us always and never to leave us orphans (John 14:18). The Holy Spirit, which guided the early apostles and the early Christians during the formative periods of the church and beyond, was not more present to them than it is to us in the contemporary church. Thus, inasmuch as we cannot do away with tradition and the deposits of faith of the church, it has to be borne in mind that tradition is a living organism, always in a state of development. The church cannot remain ossified in the past in the name of tradition but must constantly renew itself.

As a living organism, the church must always adapt to the changing world; otherwise, it will become irrelevant to the people it is called to serve. Even if African rituals and symbols are superstitious, it is the task of inculturation to make them *graceable* and salutary. Finally, liturgical inculturation must not be limited only to the Eucharist. It must involve every facet of the church's sacraments and life.

---

[28] Ibid.

[29] Anscar Chupungco, *Cultural Adaptation of the Liturgy*, 38.

Chapter 10

SMALL CHRISTIAN COMMUNITIES AS THE BASIC STRUCTURE OF THE CHURCH AS THE EXTENDED FAMILY

The extended family model implies that the church must truly be family in structure and operation. The model proposes the creation of Small Christian Communities (SCCs) that would adequately cater to the needs of its members and, at the same time, promote evangelization and deepen the faith. The organization of the church as SCCs means developing an ecclesiology with a local content, recognizing the needs, hopes, and aspirations of the community.

The concept of SCCs, or as some would prefer Basic Ecclesial Communities, originated in Latin America in the 1950s. It began as a movement for educating the poor masses by forming them into small groups by the creative pastoral effort of the laity.[1] Philip Knights distinguishes between the key terms in the concepts of the Christian Communities. He argues that in Latin America the key adjective is *Basic*, while in Africa, it is *Small*.[2]

SCCs were born out of the experience of people without priests but conscious of their priestly roles by virtue of their baptism. For Pope Paul VI, Small Christian Communities spring from the need to live the church's life more intensely or from the desire and quest for a more human dimension that larger ecclesial communities can only offer with difficulty, especially in big cities.[3] Thus thee rationale behind the creation of SCCs is anchored on the need to break the anonymity that pervades parish structures especially in urban areas. People gathered to share the Word of God, relating it to their story and struggle for liberation. There is no question about the validity of SCCs, since they remain firmly attached to the local church and to the universal church.

---

[1] Pernia A. M., "The Ecclesiology of the Base Ecclesial Communities," *Studies in Philosophy and Theology,* vol. xv, # 2 (1990), 56.

[2] Philip Knights, *The African Synod in Rome, 1994: Consequences for Catholicism.* http://www.martynmission.com.cam.ac.uk/CAfrica.htm (accessed February 10, 2007).

[3] Pope Paul VI, *Evangelii Nuntiandi,* # 58.

The SCC is a practical and rational way of organizing the church from grassroots. Since African families are large and inclusive, organizing a SCC as a communion of members of large families in the same geographical areas who share the bond of fellowship in Christ to enhance their understanding of the church will advance the model of the church as the extended family of God. Moreover, as Pope Paul VI says:

> Such communities can quite simply be in their own way an extension on the spiritual and religious level—worship, deepening of faith, fraternal charity, prayer, contact with pastors—of the small sociological community such as the village, etc. Or again their aim may be to bring together, for the purpose of listening to and meditating on the Word, for the Sacraments and the bond of agape, groups of people who are linked by age, culture, civil state or social situation . . . in still other cases they bring Christians together in places where the shortage of priests does not favour the normal life of a parish community.[4]

The 1994 Synod of Bishops for Africa, in proposing the family as the model of the church suitable for Africa, adopted the SCC structure, because it provides the framework for structuring the church as the family of God. In its *Final Message*, the Synod contends, "The Church, the Family of God, implies the creation of small communities, which are cells of the Church-as-Family, in which one is formed to live concretely and authentically the experience of fraternity."[5] The *Final Message* further says such communities will provide the best means to fight ethnocentrism within the church itself and, more widely, within our nations. These individual churches-as-family have the task of working to transform society.[6] Also, such communities would foster the spirit of disinterested service, solidarity, and a common goal.

The synod fathers insisted that the church-as-family cannot reach its full potential unless it is broken up into SCCs, which are small enough to permit close human relations. The Assembly described the characteristics of such communities as follows:

> Primarily they should be places engaged in evangelizing themselves, so that subsequently they can bring the Good News to others; they should moreover be communities which pray and listen to God's Word, encourage the members themselves to take on responsibility, learn to live an ecclesial life, and reflect on different human problems in the

---

[4] Ibid.
[5] *African Synod: Message of the Synod*, # 28
[6] Ibid., 28.

light of the Gospel. Above all, these communities are to be committed to living Christ's love for everybody, a love that transcends the limits of the natural solidarity of clans, tribes or other interest groups.[7]

At any rate, SCCs engender the traditional values of solidarity and communality and somehow mirror the structure of the early churches, which were constituted by small number of Christians. Heads of households led these church communities. The early church had family characteristics and structures that served as the bedrock for evangelization. Because the Gospel is lived in a concrete cultural context, SCCs are well situated, and predisposed for the successful inculturation of the Gospel and deepening of the faith.

SCCs make inculturation possible because authentic inculturation begins from the grassroots—from "bottom up" and not a "top-down" enterprise. SCCs provide a veritable ground for the Gospel to permeate the roots of cultures and to incarnate in the people's present historical moments. The SCCs will equally renew the impulse of evangelization, deepen the faith, and inspire an honest response from the culture.

The Association of Member Episcopal Conferences in Eastern Africa (AMECEA) underscores the invaluable contribution of SCCs in inculturation and deepening the faith when it says:

> Small communities also seem the most effective means of making the Gospel message truly relevant to African cultures and tradition. By participating in the life of the Church at this most local level, Christians will foster the gradual and steady maturing of the young Church. As their sense of responsibility for the Church grows, ordained and non-ordained Christians will discover the meaning of a truly African expression of the Christian faith and thus be able to respond to Pope Paul VI's challenge in Kampala, Uganda in 1969: 'You may and you must, have an African Christianity.'[8]

SCCs promote shared authority and responsibility, in contrast to the overbearing hierarchical model of the church. The AMECEA stresses that SCCs are the most local expression of the church and the groundwork for the structure of the whole church.[9] They shape and aid its members in their understanding of the meaning and nature of the church in the African context.

---

[7] John Paul II, *Ecclesia in Africa*, # 89.

[8] 1979 AMECEA Plenary Study Conference, 270. Cited in Joseph Healey & Donald Sybertz, *Towards an African Narrative Theology*, 150.

[9] Joseph Healey & Donald Sybertz, *Towards an African Narrative Theology*, 39.

SCCs at every level are legitimately the church because the risen Christ is present to them. Thus, they remain firmly attached to the local church out of which they develop and to the universal church.[10] SCCs situated within the parameters of the extended family provide a fundamental base for our inculturated ecclesio-missiocentric church. They are communities where love, care, and solidarity abound and are a fertile ground for an inculturated evangelization.

Aylward Shorter posits that because SCCs are essentially cells of committed Christians at the service of the church and the world, evangelization becomes most effective when it operates through interpersonal relationship and through the charity and concern of Christian neighborliness.[11] These values are at the heart of African concepts of communality and relational ontology.

The establishment of SCCs does not mean that parish and diocesan structures should be dismantled. An SCC is a communion of individuals, a parish will become a communion of SCCs, and the diocese will become a communion of parishes. The universal church is a communion of dioceses throughout the world. At every stage of communion, the exercise of leadership and authority will no longer be the prerogative of clergy but will become inclusive and involve the clergy as well as the laity.

Every SCC is built on the Word of God, making it a praying, meditating, and sharing community.[12] These activities bind Christians together, deepen solidarity, and raise their consciousness of being members of the family of God. Concomitantly SCCs are a veritable ground for evangelization as centers of formation and deepening of the faith.

It is my hope, along with the synod fathers, that creating SCCs will lead to a genuine evangelization of such African communities.

---

[10] Pope Paul VI, *Evangelii Nuntiandi*, 58.

[11] Aylward Shorter, *Evangelization and Culture*, 159.

[12] Agapit J. Mroso, *The Church in Africa and the New Evangelization: A Theologico-Pastoral study of the Orientation of John Paul II* (Vatican City: Editrice Pontificia Universita Gregoriana, 1995), 125.

Chapter 11

ANCESTRAL ECCLESIOLOGY

One aspect of an African traditional worldview and cosmology that the church as family of God must inculturate into its ecclesiology is the role of ancestors in the life of Africans. Ancestors are integral to African religiosity and social structures. They are the pillar on which a community or clan rests. Ancestors constitute the unity of the community and represent the pivotal point from which all actions of the members of clan take their legitimacy.[1] They also occupy an exalted position in the Igbo and Africans' consciousness.

Ancestors are the disembodied spirits of departed relatives who lived virtuous lives, passed away peacefully because of old age, and were accorded all the necessary rites of passage to ensure their successful entry into the noble status of ancestorhood. Of course, not all dead persons automatically become ancestors. Those who lived wicked and immoral lives or died in unnatural circumstances do not qualify for such honors. The Congolese theologian, Father François Kabasele Lumbala, offers some insightful general criteria, which qualifies a person for ancestorhood:

> To have followed the laws, not to have been found guilty of theft or debauchery; not to have been angry or quarrelsome; not to have been tempted by sorcery; to have been an agent of communion among people. To have had a descendant, since the life received must be communicated; the ancestor may not be a barrier to life, which would be the case without descendant ... to have died well, which means first of all to have died a "natural" death; that is to say, to have lived many

---

[1] Bénézet Bujo, "On the Road toward an African Ecclesiology: Reflections on the Synod," *African Synod: Documents, Reflections, Perspectives*, 140.

years, to have transmitted one's message to one's family, and to have been buried.[2]

It is worth noting that ancestorhood is not restricted to old people. Young people can also qualify as ancestors. The Igbo proverb, *Nwata kwo aka ofuma, osoro eze ri nri* (if a child washes his hands well, he or she will dine with the king), encapsulates this exception. A young man or woman who died while undertaking heroic acts on behalf of the community could join the rank of ancestors. Ancestors are perceived as hero or heroines and role models for their families and societies; everyone is enjoined to emulate their sterling and exemplary qualities. Although physically dead, ancestors are believed to be present in the lives of the surviving members of the lineage. Hence, they are called the living-dead.[3]

Belief in ancestors is inextricably linked to the Africans' understanding of death as a gateway into another realm of life. Ancestors are believed to have survived death. While living in the spiritual world, they take an interest in the affairs of their families.[4] A continuity of interaction exists between ancestors and the living in the Igbo worldview. There are countless vivid anecdotes of ancestors' interventions in the life of their progeny. Most often, the interventions are for good.

Not all ancestors are identifiable and honored individually; there are ancestors who are "unsung." Such ancestors did not leave any distinctive footprints behind in the community; neither did they cause any perceptible harm. They form the great mass of ancestors, and when libations are poured to the ancestors generally without calling names, they are also included.

Because ancestors constitute an invisible genealogical continuum with the living, they are honored and revered. It must be emphasized that ancestors are not "worshipped" in the strictest sense of the word but "honored."[5] It is erroneous to believe that Africans worship their ancestors as one would worship the gods. Inasmuch as Africans build shrines for their ancestors and offer food and prayers to them, they are conscious that these departed relatives are not gods. African worldview draws a clear distinction between the concept of God as the Supreme Being, lesser divinities, and ancestors. Each has its distinct role and place in cosmology. John Mbiti clearly articulates this point when he argues that "acts of respect for the departed do not amount to worshipping them; they show

---

[2] François Kabasele Lumbala, *Celebrating Jesus Christ in Africa: Liturgy and Inculturation* (New York: Orbis Books, 1998), 43.

[3] Christopher I. Ejizu, "Traditional Igbo Religious Beliefs and Ritual," *Groundwork of Igbo History,* ed. Adiele E. Afigbo (Lagos: Visita Books, 1991), 812-813.

[4] Geoffrey E. Parrinder, *African Traditional Religion,* 3rd ed. (Westport, Connecticut: Greenwood Press, 1970), 58.

[5] Victor C. Uchendu, *The Igbo of Southeast Nigeria,* 102.

people's belief that the departed of up to four or five generations should not be forgotten."[6]

Among the Igbos, there are different types of deities in contradistinction to the ancestors. Some of the deities include *Anyanwu*—sun god, *Amadioha*—god of thunder and lighting, *Ala*—the earth goddess and fertility, *Ahianjoku*—the god of farm work, *Agwu nsi*—god of divination, *Ikenga*—god of adventure in hunting and business enterprise, and so forth. Sacrifices are offered to these gods either in thanksgiving for favors received or to appease their wrath when things go wrong in the family or community.

Africans hold their ancestors in high esteem, invoking their protection and help in times of peril and in times of joy and thanksgiving. They are honored and invoked by family members and the community through sacrifices and libations. Shrines are erected in their honor. These shrines also serve as places where sacrifices could be offered to them. In this way, ancestors constitute an integral part of African traditional religions.

Ancestors play important roles in human beings' relationship with God. In African cosmology, it is considered rude to approach God directly unless it is absolutely necessary. God, as I noted earlier, is understood as *amama amacha amacha*, the unknowable mystery who cannot be approached directly. Nevertheless, God can be approached through the ancestors and lesser divinities that are closer to God. Thus, prayers and libations are offered to the ancestors in the belief that they will relay human beings' concerned and prayers to God.[7] Ancestors act as intermediaries or rather mediators between God and human beings. People invoke them for guidance and protection.[8]

As I have argued previously in this book, Christianity did not begin in the abstract. Christianity exists in human culture, adopting various traditions as it develops and spreads out. Thus, inculturating Africa's veneration of ancestors who inexorably remain part of the extended family into Christianity is vital to evangelization.

Some African theologians have wrestled with the question of the place of Christology in relationship to Africa's ancestral cult. Bénézet Bujo expresses the view that Jesus, by choosing twelve apostles to symbolically represent the twelve tribes of Israel, made himself the eschatological tribal father of the new Israel and the people of God, thereby replacing Abraham the primal ancestor of Israel.[9] Bujo then argues that the primordial ancestor, to whom the founding of a community is

---

[6] John S. Mbiti, *Introduction to African Religion*, 2nd ed. (Oxford: Heinemann Educational Publishers, 1991), 18.

[7] Ibid., 130.

[8] Sindima J. Harvey, *Drums of Redemption: An Introduction to African Christianity* (Westport, Connecticut: Greenwood Press, 1994), 136.

[9] Bénézet Bujo, *On the Road Toward an African Ecclesiology*, 140.

attributed, plays an indispensable role in that community. By way of correlation, Bujo contends that Africans can connect to Jesus as the primordial tribal father and ancestor of Christians.[10]

The overarching reason that supports the categorization of Jesus as the "proto-ancestor" is that through his death, resurrection, and ascension, he returns to the realm of the spirits and, therefore of power. From the standpoint of Akan (Ghana) traditional beliefs, "Jesus has gone to the realm of the ancestor spirits and the 'gods' . . . but if Jesus has gone to the realm of the 'spirits and the gods,' so to speak, he has gone there as Lord over them in the same way that he is Lord over us. He is Lord over the living and the dead, and over the 'living-dead,' as ancestors are also called."[11] Since it is by baptism that one is regenerated into the church as the extended family of God and since Jesus is the first born of all creation, he is by the same token, the "Proto-Ancestor" who vivifies the eschatological family (church) of the living and the dead.[12] Therefore, the church as family of God is grounded on the "Proto-Ancestor"—Jesus Christ.

The perception of Jesus as our common ancestor strengthens the image of the church as the extended family of God and reinforces the bond of brotherhood and sisterhood of all believers in Christ. As a "proto ancestor," Jesus transcends Africa's concept of ancestor, giving it new impetus and understanding. By his incarnation, Jesus achieved a far more profound solidarity with us in our humanity than our natural ancestors. At the same time, he transcends our ethnic and lineage ancestors by his divinity.[13] Through his incarnation, passion, and resurrection, Jesus brings into being a new family of God. He becomes the ultimate embodiment of all the virtues of the ancestors.[14] Kwame Bediako demonstrates very clearly how Jesus Christ is actually the only real and true ancestor and source of life for all humankind. Let me quote him at length:

> By his unique achievement and perfect atonement through his own self-sacrifice, and by effective eternal mediation and intercession as God-man in the divine presence, he has secured eternal redemption (Hebrews 9:12) for all who acknowledge who he is for them and what he has done for them, who abandon the blind alleys of merely human traditions and rituals, and instead, entrust themselves to him. As mediator of a new and better covenant between God and humanity

---

[10] Ibid., 141.

[11] Kwame Bediako, *Jesus and the Gospel in Africa: History and Experience.* (New York: Orbis Books, 2004), 26-27.

[12] Ibid.

[13] Ibid.

[14] Bénézet Bujo, "African Theology in its Social Context," *Christian Leadership in Africa Series*, trans. O'Donohue J. (Nairobi: St Paul Publications, 1992), 80.

(Hebrews 8:6; 12:24), Jesus brings the redeemed into the experience of a new identity in which he links their human destinies directly and consciously with the eternal, gracious will and purpose of a loving and God (Hebrews 12:22-24). No longer are human horizons bounded by lineage, clan, tribe or nation. For the redeemed now belong within the community of the living God.[15]

In the Catholic theology of the communion of saints, one can see a parallel between ancestor veneration and the Christian veneration of saints. Africans' reverence of ancestors is akin to the Christian cult of saints. The cult of Christian saints evolved from Greco-Roman pagan religions, which had altars and shrines dedicated to different pantheons. The inculturation of pagan cults and rites by the early Christians was a way of gaining converts and purifying their cultures of pagan practices. It seems that by Christianizing pagan cults, rites, and rituals, the early Christians were able to evangelize the people of their time and culture. It invariably follows that for Christianity to permeate African cultures and for evangelization to be effective, Africans' reverence of their ancestors must meld and be inculturated into the church as the family of God.

Because the saints are closer to God than humans are, they serve as intermediaries between God and human beings. By the same token, a parallel could be drawn between the cult of saints and ancestor veneration among Africans. First, certain practices associated with the cult of saints, like Christians visiting the tombs of martyrs and other saints to offer prayers, are no different from Africans' veneration of their ancestors. Second, Christian saints lived heroic and exemplary lives; so have our ancestors. Third, in African cosmology, African ancestors are believed to be closer to the transcendent God so are the Christian saints. Thus, ancestors play mediatory roles between God and human beings as the saints do.

> Ancestors continue to support members of the family alive on earth, just as saints support the family of Christians through their prayers and merits. Ancestors are at a key juncture in communion of life and their descendants; in somewhat the same way as the life of Christ is the link between the Christians on earth and the saints. Ancestors receive their power from the Supreme Being, just as the saints were moved by the power of Christ. Ancestors provide an example to follow, just as the saints do for Christians.[16]

Since ancestors are intrinsically part of the Igbo family and worldview, it is erroneous to suggest that ancestral veneration is superstitious, which the early

---

[15] Kwame Bediako, *Jesus and the Gospel in Africa*, 30.

[16] François K. Lumbala, *Celebrating Jesus Christ in Africa*, 46.

missionaries branded a religious experience they did not understand. Bolaji Idowu encapsulates the gross prejudice western people have against other cultures in this scintillating anecdote:

> We may call to mind here the popular story about the Englishman who went to place a wreath on the tomb of a deceased relative at the same time that a Chinese was putting rice on the tomb of his own deceased relative: The Englishman characteristically asked the Chinese, "My friend, when is your relative going to eat the rice that you are offering?" To which the Chinese promptly replied, "When yours smells your flowers." [17]

This story illustrates the stereotypical rush to judge or disparage other people's cultures by people with a monocultural mentality without giving much thought to apparent discrepancies and ambivalence in their own culture.

African ancestors spring from the family structure.[18] They represent a more enduring reality in African worldview than do divinities, nonhuman spirits, amulets, and charms.[19] A genuine evangelization of Africans within the context of the extended family image of the church must take cognizance of the ancestor veneration. Our ancestors are our saints and role models. It would be a disservice to the African church to present unknown saints in place of known ancestors as patrons and models for Christian virtues.

---

[17] Bolaji E. Idowu, *African Traditional Religion* (London: SCM, 1973), 179.

[18] Oliver A. Onwubiko, *African Thought, Religion and Culture* (Enugu, Nigeria: Snaap Press, 1991), 61.

[19] Kwame Bediako, *Christianity in Africa: The Renewal of a Non-Western Religion* (New York: Orbis Books, 1995), 216.

Chapter 12

IMPLICATION OF THE MODEL OF THE CHURCH AS THE EXTENDED FAMILY OF GOD

In evaluating the image of the church as the extended family of God, a plethora of consequential implications and challenges emerges. Among these are ecclesial, economic, and sociopolitical implications. These implications and challenges affect not only the African church but also the universal church.

Ecclesial Implications

From the ecclesial point of view, the image of the church as family of God challenges us to revisit western ecclesiology and theology of the church and to chart a new course in church structure. What is at stake is church leadership and authority. The church cannot be a family unless it also inculturates Africa's family structure of leadership and authority. The laity has to be included among the elders of the church.

The model of the church as the extended family of God recovers the pristine Christian life of the early disciples who lived communally, sharing all they had in common, with no one suffering want (Acts 4:32-34). Again, if the nature and mission of the church is understood in terms of the common brotherhood and sisterhood of all believers, this will help build bridges across races and nations, not only in Africa but all over the world. The church can do this through evangelization of Africa and re-evangelization of the Western world to curb excessive capitalism with its attendant individualism and unbridled depersonalization of the human person. It will equally motivate the West to relate to Africans as equal brothers and sisters, since as Mbiti pointed out, "A human person is because we are;" a person is primarily a member of the community.

The model of the church as the family of God has consequential implications for mandatory celibacy of priests. In view of the respect they command and the role they play in the family, bishops and priests who fulfill the role of elders in the church as family of God ought to be married and be able to transmit life. It is unthinkable for someone to be regarded as an elder if one cannot perpetuate oneself by having children.

In Igbo traditional society, unmarried men, no matter their chronological age, do not sit in meetings where serious existential questions are discussed. Marital experience is considered a requisite if a man is to take responsibility for guiding the human community.[1] A person, regardless of his or her age, wealth, or status in the community, cannot be considered a responsible person if he or she deliberately renounces marriage and children. Therefore, it is not enough for priests and bishops to be spiritual fathers; they have to be biological fathers in the model of the church as the family of God.

As the Catholic Church maintains that Jesus' choice of men as his apostles was intentional, similar argument can be made concerning optional celibacy. One can argue that Jesus' choice of Peter, a married man, as the head of the church (Matt. 16:18-19; John 21:15-17) was not accidental. Perhaps, Jesus intended that celibacy should be optional when he chose married and single men to be his apostles.

In the course of his ministry, Jesus even paid a visit to Peter's mother-in-law who attended to their needs after receiving a cure (Matt. 8:14-15). Peter and the other apostles did not abandon their families after Jesus called them to become his apostles. If he did, what would Jesus be doing in the house of Peter's mother-in-law? Moreover, when the apostles embarked on their missionary journeys after the resurrection and ascension of Christ, their wives accompanied them (1 Cor. 9:5).

Paul in enunciating the qualifications of a bishop among other things explicitly states, "A bishop must be irreproachable, married only once, temperate, self-controlled, decent, hospitable, able to teach . . . ." (1 Tim. 3:2).

Celibacy is not a divine rule. It is a matter of church discipline. Most of the apostles and the first Christians presbyters were married. Celibacy began in the early church as an ascetic discipline among monks and hermits, but it was optional. It was rooted partly in a neo-Platonic and Gnostic-Manichean contempt for the physical world, the human body, and sex. Sex was considered debasing and impure. Married priests were strongly admonished to practice sexual continence or abstain from sexual intercourse with their wives a night before Mass. In addition, celibacy as a renunciation of sexual expression by men fit nicely with a patriarchal denigration of women in the early church. Nonvirginal women, typified by Eve as the temptress of Adam, were seen as a source of sin.[2]

The first official attempt to prohibit the clergy from marrying was made by the Council of Elvira in Spain (c. 309). The council decreed that bishops, presbyters, and deacons—indeed, all clerics who have a place in the ministry (of

---

[1] Francois K. Lumbala, *Celebrating Jesus Christ in Africa*, 107.

[2] James Carroll, "Mandatory celibacy at the heart of what's wrong," *National Catholic Reporter* (June 11, 2010), 23

the altar)—abstain from their wives and not beget children.[3] This decree was not obeyed because priests, bishops, and even popes continued to marry and have children.

Medieval politics, in addition to the church's penchant to control the intimate lives of priests and prevent families of married priests from expropriating church property at the death of priests all led to the imposition of mandatory celibacy.

In the eleventh century, under Pope Gregory VII, the quest to impose mandatory celibacy on the clergy reached a frenzy pitch. In 1074, Pope Gregory VII decreed that those to be ordained to the priesthood must renounce marriage. The pope threatened bishops with suspension if they allowed their clergy to marry and remain in office.[4] The pope reasoned that "the Church cannot escape from the clutches of the laity unless priests first escape the clutches of their wives." However, it was not until 1139, under Pope Innocent II, with the Second Lateran Council that mandatory celibacy was officially imposed on all clergy.[5] Even after the imposition, some popes were either married and had children before their election or continued to live with their wives or mistresses and fathered children during their papacy.[6] Of course, several bishops and priest ignored the decree of Second Lateran Council regarding obligatory celibacy.

Proponents of celibacy often speak of the practice in glowing terms as Christ's cherished gift to his church. Pope Paul VI called celibacy the church's "brilliant jewel." It might as well be a cherished gift, but how come Jesus chose mostly married men as his apostles if he wanted to bestow such a priceless gift on his church? Moreover, it took the church eleven hundred years to realize that a cherished gift (celibacy) has been bequeathed to her. One is left to wonder why the same gift is not bestowed on Catholics of Eastern Rite (celibacy is optional) or the married clergy of some Protestant churches (Lutheran, Anglican, etc.) who

---

[3] Council of Elvira, Canon 33: Placuit in totum prohibere episcopis, preysbteris et diaconibus vel omnibus clericis positis in ministerio abstinere se a coniugibus suis, et no generare filio: quicumque vero fecerit, ab honore clericatus exterminetur.

[4] Richard P. McBrien, *Lives of the Popes* (New York: HarperCollins, 1997), 187.

[5] Second Lateran Council, Canon 6: "We also decree that those in the Orders of subdeacon and above who have taken wives or concubines are to be deprived of their position and ecclesiastical benefice. For since they ought to be in fact and in name temples of God, vessels of the Lord and sanctuaries of the Holy Spirit, it is unbecoming that they give themselves up to marriage and impurity."

[6] Richard P. McBrien, *Lives of the Popes*, 217, 266, 267, 270. Popes who were married before or after election as popes, or lived with a mistress and had children after 1139 include: Innocent VIII 1484-1492; Alexander VI 1492-1503; Julius II 1503-1513; Paul III 1534-1549.

upon conversion to Catholicism are allowed to keep their wives after ordination to the Catholic priesthood.[7]

The question then is what is wrong with an African Rite that permits its clergy to marry if they so choose? This issue cannot be wished away if the church is serious with inculturating the model of the church as an extended family of God and if it is concerned with authentic evangelization. How could a priest function effectively in a culture where a man or woman without children is not only despised and scorned, looked at with suspicion, but also considered a waste?

The church will continue to be viewed as alien and a form of western Christian imperialism if this issue is not given a serious consideration. As an alternative, I would suggest that the church in Africa should adopt optional celibacy. While celibacy should be accepted, and perhaps even encouraged, priests should also have the option to honor the values of their African heritage by marrying and having children. My advocacy for optional celibacy in the African church does not suggest that Africans are incapable of observing mandatory celibacy, but rather simply that celibacy in Africa is a cultural aberration.

Sociopolitical Implications

The traditional African family, which forms the *locus classicus* of the extended family model, has been impacted by urbanization and globalization. The negative influences of urbanization and globalization have contributed in no small measure to the breakdown of traditional family values and morals. African families, like other families in the world, are becoming dysfunctional with untold consequences ranging from divorce, abuse of women and children, prostitution, egocentrism, fratricidal genocide, corruption, child labor, oppression, to a "culture of death" with its utter disregard of the dignity and sacredness of human life. These cancerous vices have slipped into the fabric of Africa's family values.

The question that agitates the mind here is how can the model of the church as the family of God contain further degeneration of family values? It is hoped that the recovery of traditional family values will stem the tide of desacralization of the family institution and values. Since, in Africa, marriage and family are not just about two individuals but a covenant between two families, clans, and or social

---

[7] These seem to be exceptions to the rule. However, it seems the exceptions are becoming the norm. In the United States and Europe, almost every year a small number of men who used to be married but lost their wives either through annulment or death have been ordained to the priesthood. In addition, the Vatican recently opened the priesthood to Anglican clergy (Anglican Ordinariate) who wish to convert to Catholicism. These men are permitted to keep their wives and remain priests but must promise not to remarry should their wives die or divorce them.

IMPLICATION OF THE MODEL OF THE CHURCH AS THE EXTENDED FAMILY OF GOD

groups, all the members of the extended families will work together to preserve and protect family values. Thus, the model of the church as the family of God can greatly contribute to finding an effective response to the crisis of the family in modern societies. What is required to achieve this is a greater appreciation of various customary laws of marriage and inculturate them into church laws on marriage.[8]

At the global level, the model calls for reassessment of the political and economic situation of the continent of Africa and how the global community relates with one another. Africa has been described as a continent of war, disease, famine, hunger, and high mortality rate. Without any iota of doubt, Africa is full of problems. In almost all its nations, there is abject poverty, gross mismanagement of abundant natural resources, political instability, and social disorientation. In a world controlled by rich and powerful nations, Africa has practically become an irrelevant appendix, often forgotten and neglected.[9]

The shameful African situation moved the Special Assembly for Africa of the Synod of Bishops to compare Africa to the biblical man who went down from Jerusalem to Jericho; he fell among robbers who stripped and beat him, leaving him half-dead. Africa is a continent where countless human beings—men and women, children, and young people—are slouching as it were, on the edge of the road, sick, injured, disabled, marginalized, and abandoned. They are in dire need of Good Samaritans who will come to their aid.[10] There is no doubt that the synod fathers properly articulated the hydra-headed problems of Africa. Unfortunately, the synod fathers failed to address a crucial question: who were the robbers that stripped, beat, and left Africa half-dead?

Without exculpating Africans of gross irresponsibility, the scramble for Africa by her Christian brothers and sisters from the West with the collaboration of missionaries led to the exploitation of Africa's human and natural resources, misery, and decimation of the population through slave trade, impoverishment, and so forth. Centuries of colonization and neocolonization, which have continued shamelessly to the present, are responsible for Africa's woes. Eugene Uzukwu is right when he suggests that the marginalization of Africa in the world today, the poverty, wars and distress, are not chance events. "They are not 'accidents of history,' but were planned by our conquerors to keep the continent under dependency in order to perpetuate the exploitation of its human and natural resources."[11]

The model of the church as the extended family of God brings to the fore the idea of our common brotherhood/sisterhood, interrelatedness, participation,

---

[8] *L'osservatore Romano*, # 16 weekly edition (April 20, 1994).

[9] John Paul II, *Ecclesia in Africa*, #40

[10] Ibid., #41

[11] Eugene E. Uzukwu, *A Listening Church*, 72-73.

solidarity, mutuality, reconciliation, communion between churches, etc. But how can the church be a family of God when Africans connive with their Western brethren to inflict mortal wounds on Africa? The model challenges Africans and the rest of the world, particularly the West, to view Africans as their brothers and sisters and to work toward ending the despicable orgy of violence, injustice, exploitation of Africans and their ecosystem.

Thus, in light of the new understanding of the church as the family of God, the relationship between the churches of Africa and her Christian brothers and sisters in the West assumes a new dimension in order to defend the weak and create a New World order.[12] The model calls for a conversion, a *metanoia,* on the part of Africa's brothers and sisters in America, China, and Europe. This conversion should first begin with an acknowledgement of the sins of exploitation, degradation, and depersonalization of Africans. The conversion is necessary because a great percentage of the wealth they enjoy now was built on the labor of their African brothers and sisters who were uprooted from their motherlands.

The church as the family of God also challenges the West to rethink its attitudes toward Africa. The only aid Africa urgently needs from the West is a commitment by her Christian brothers and sisters to stop exploiting, meddling in the politics of Africa, fuelling wars, and selling arms to warring countries and to acknowledge the dignity and equality of all irrespective of color, race, or religion.

Solidarity between the churches in the context of the church as family of God, based on autonomy and communion, should be translated into the sharing of sustainable human values.[13] Solidarity should not be restricted to sharing of financial aid, because it is not simply an issue of benefactor and beneficiary churches. Cultural treasures, especially spiritual treasures of humane living, of interconnectedness between humans and the environment, are indispensable for the reconstruction of society

The model of the church as the family of God equally challenges Africans to rise to the challenges posed by war, economic impoverishments, gross mismanagement of resources, corruption, and inept leaders who do not have the well-being of the people at heart.

The church in Africa is equally challenged to confront the HIV/AIDS pandemic that is threatening the very survival of the family and society. The church in Africa must not be complacent in the fight against HIV/AIDS. The social aspect of the Gospel is as important as its other facets. The church must also step up to the plate and confront other egregious conflicts that stare Africa in the face, such as, poverty, hatred, negative self-image, ethnocentrism, embezzlement and looting of the common good, and so forth.

---

[12] Ibid., 73.
[13] Ibid.

IMPLICATION OF THE MODEL OF THE CHURCH AS THE EXTENDED FAMILY OF GOD

It is hoped that a recovery of the invaluable position of the family in Africa will lead to a new appreciation of our oneness, solidarity, and communion, which should exist in the one family of God. In the same vein, the model of the church as the extended family of God challenges all to appreciate the gift of family and value of one another. It urges us to move beyond ethnocentrism to the realization of cosmic or, rather, universal brotherhood and sisterhood of all people.

CONCLUSION

In this book, I set out to propose a new model of the church as the extended family of God for the African church. I drew extensively from the Igbo concept of family, *ezi-na-ulo*, a revered and sacred institution, to lay out an ecclesiology that not only resonates with the Igbos but also promotes authentic evangelization and deep rooting of the faith worldwide. The objective of this book is not to blame past missionaries for not inculturating Igbo culture into the faith. The purpose of this book is to deepen the foundation missionaries laid in the evangelization of the Igbos and to ensure that the faith is adequately inculturated into the lives of modern day Igbo and African Christians.

The Igbo concept of *ezi-na-ulo*, with its deep sense of relationality, communality as the essence of being and existence is at the heart of our model of the church as family of God. The Igbo notion of family is inclusive. It transcends consanguine relationships or kinship bonds to embrace the totality of the cosmic order. It also highlights the inter-relatedness of all human beings and the ecosystem. *Ezi-na-ulo* is subsumed in the Igbo worldview and also embraces the social, political, economic, cultural, and religious life of the Igbos. Thus, a successful African ecclesiology and missiology must be grounded in the family model.

The theology of inculturation as a method of evangelization commits us to accept theological and liturgical pluralism as the new face of the one, holy, Catholic, and apostolic church. The Church in the twenty-first century is not monolithic. It is diverse and multicultural. Each culture has much to contribute to the building of the church on earth. There will be different approaches to understanding the mystery of the Church. The church as the extended family of God in Africa is one such approach.

The image of the church as the family of God, like all images or metaphors, cannot exhaust the reality of the mystery of the church. The image, however, highlights areas that best speak to the Igbos in their understanding of the nature and mission of the church. Since images function as symbols, any image that

CONCLUSION

does not evoke meaning cannot be accepted. It should be able to speak to people existentially and find an echo in the inarticulate depths of their psyche.[1] Since the image of the church as the extended family of God resonates with the Igbos and Africans in general, it has to be accepted together with its implications and the challenges it poses.

The image of the church as the family of God does not claim to be the final word or to be the perfect model of the church. It is fraught with ambiguity. For example, if the model is not properly inculturated, it can lead to exclusivism, segregationism, and discrimination. It could pit one ethnic group against the other in the church. Archbishop Albert Obiefuna of Nigeria articulates this ambiguity very clearly when he says, "An African Christian with his or her exaggerated ethnicism finds it difficult to accept the truth that the man or woman in India who is a Christian is much more a brother and or sisters as in the natural family." Obiefuna goes on to suggest that "this mentality is so pervasive that the saying goes among Africans that when it comes to the crunch, it is not the Christian concept of the Church as a family which prevails but rather the adage that 'blood is thicker than water.' And by water here one can presumably include the waters of Baptism through which one is born into the family of the Church."[2]

Sadly, for many Africans, consanguinity and ethnic identity is thicker than even the water of baptism. Perhaps, such a mentality accounts partly for the horrible war of attrition and genocide in supposedly predominant Christian countries (like Rwanda, Congo, Uganda, etc.) in Africa.[3] In this regard, the task of the theology of inculturation is to rouse the consciences, the minds and hearts of Africans to rediscover the universality of the family metaphor.

For the church to be truly the family of God, its boundaries must transcend ethnic or kinship bonds. The water of baptism must be stronger than the blood of narrow clannishness and ethnic identity.[4] The church in Africa and elsewhere can truly see itself as a family if we intensify our catechesis on the meaning of the church.[5] Thus, far from degenerating into sects or a theater for operation of primitive sentiments of nepotism, ethnocentrism, or racism, the church as the family of God, under the guidance the Holy Spirit, will be a caring community that is guided by solidarity to witness to the coming of the reign of God by overcoming these narrow divisions.[6]

---

[1] Avery Dulles, *Models of the Church,* 18

[2] Albert Obiefuna, "Present the Church as a Family in Africa." *L'osservatore Romano* # 17, April 27, 1994, 9.

[3] Joseph Healey & Donald Sybertz, *Towards an African Narrative Theology,* 149.

[4] Eugene E. Uzukwu, *A Listening Church: Autonomy and Communion,* 68.

[5] Albert Obiefuna, *"Present the Church as a Family,* 9.

[6] Eugene E. Uzukwu, *A Listening Church: Autonomy and Communion,* 68.

The model of the church as the family of God parallels the image of the church as the new Israel of God. Thus, the church as family of God may be called the fulfillment of the prophecy of the assembling of the nations on the mountain of the house of God devoid of divisions, humiliations, and violence, because this new family, directed by the spirit of God, walks in the light of God.[7]

Evidently, there is need to recover and emphasize the values of relationality and communality that are inherent in the African extended family model. I will then conclude this discourse by re reiterating Avery Dulles's view on images of the church:

> Because images are derived from the finite realities of experience, they are never adequate to represent the mystery of grace. Each model of the church has its weakness; no one should be canonized as the measure of all the rest. Instead of searching for some absolutely best images, it would be advisable to recognize that the manifold images given to us by scripture and Tradition are mutually complementary. They should be made to interpenetrate and mutually qualify one another. None, therefore, should be interpreted in an exclusive sense, so as to negate what the other approved models have to teach us.[8]

The image of the church as the family of God complements other images. I believe that this image will help the church in Africa to understand its nature and mission to the continent. The understanding will not only promote evangelization but also help to curb the senseless fratricidal genocide going on in different parts of the continent.

The inculturation of the model of the church as an extended family will certainly help the Igbos to hear the Gospel within the ambient of the Igbo cultural matrix. The image will serve as a catalyst for deepening the faith. Rather than being divisive, this model will promote the interrelatedness of all human beings more particularly for Christians scattered all over the world. Just as the image of the church as the people of God, despite its aforementioned shortcomings, transcends all race and culture, the extended family model crosses boundary lines to reach all peoples who value their families.

---

[7] Ibid.
[8] Avery Dulles, *Models of the Church*, 29

SELECTED BIBLIOGRAPHY

Achebe, Chinua. *Things Fall Apart.* New York: Anchor Books edition, 1994.
───. *Hopes and Impediments: Selected Essays.* New York: Anchor Books, 1990.
Afigbo, Adiele E., ed. *Groundwork of Igbo History.* Lagos, Nigeria: Visita Books, 1991.
Anderson, Jane. *Priests in Love: Roman Catholic Clergy and Their Intimate Relationships.* New York: Continuum, 2006.
Appiah-Kubi, Kofi, and Sergio Torres, eds. *African Theology En Route.* New York: Orbis Books, 1979.
Basten, George T. *Among the Ibos of Nigeria.* New York: Barnes & Noble, 1966.
Bediako, Kwame. *Jesus and the Gospel in Africa: History and Experience.* New York: Orbis Books, 2004.
───. *Christianity in Africa: The Renewal of a Non-Western Religion.* New York: Orbis Books, 1995.
Bidwell, Lee D. M., and Brenda J. Vander, eds., *Sociology of the Family: Investigating Family Issues.* Boston: Allyn & Bacon, 2000.
Bosch, David. *Transforming Mission: Paradigm Shifts in Theology of Mission.* New York: Orbis Books, 1998.
Bright, John. *A History of Israel,* 2nd ed. Philadelphia: The Westminster Press, 1972.
Burrows, William R., ed. *Redemption and Dialogue: Reading Redemptoris Missio and Dialogue and Proclamation.* Maryknoll, New York: Orbis Books, 1993.
Cahill, Lisa S. *Sex, Gender & Christian Ethics.* United Kingdom: Cambridge University Press, 1996.
Carr, Anne E. *Transforming Grace.* New York: Continuum Publishing Co., 1998.
Chadwick, Henry. *The Early Church.* Revised edition. London: Penguin Books, 1993.

SELECTED BIBLIOGRAPHY

Chauvet, Louis-Marie. *Symbol and Sacrament: A Sacramental Reinterpretation of Christian Existence*. Trans. Madigan Patrick. Collegeville, MN: The Liturgical Press, 1995.

Chibuko, Patrick C. *Paschal Mystery of Christ*. New York: Peter Lang, 1999.

Chukwu, Emmanuel U. *Ezi-Na-Ulo: The Extended Family of God: Towards an Ecological Theology of Creation, STD Dissertation*. Louvain: Katholieke Universiteit Leuven, 2002.

Chupungco, Anscar. *Cultural Adaptation of the Liturgy*. New York: Paulist Press, 1982.

_____. *Liturgies of the Future: The Process and Methods of Inculturation*. New York: Paulist Press, 1989.

Coleman, John A., ed. *One Hundred Years of Catholic Social Thought: Celebration and Challenges*. New York: Orbis Books, 1991.

Congar, Yves, and O'Hanlon D. *Council Speeches of Vatican II*. New York: Paulist Press, 1964.

Cornwell, John. *The Pontiff in Winter: Triumph and Conflict in the Reign of John Paul II*. New York: Doubleday, 2004.

Cox, James L, and Gerrie T. Haar, eds. *Uniquely African?: African Christian Identity from Cultural and Historical Perspectives*. Trenton, NJ: African World Press, Inc, 2003.

Crollius, Ary R., ed. *What Is So New about Inculturation?* Rome: Pontifical Gregorian University, 1984.

_____. *Effective Inculturation and Ethnic Identity*. Rome: Pontifical Gregorian University, 1987.

De Lubac, Henri. *The Church: Paradox and Mystery*. Translated by James R. Dunne. New York: Alba House, 1969.

Dhavamony, Mariasusai. *Christian Theology of Inculturation*. Rome: Editrice Pontificia Universita Gregoriana, 1997.

Donovan, Daniel. *The Church as Idea and Fact*. Wilmington, DE: Michael Glazier, 1988.

Doyle, Dennis M. *Communion Ecclesiology*. New York: Orbis Books, 2000

Dulles, Avery. *Models of the Church,* Expanded edition. New York: Doubleday, 2002.

_____. *A Church to Believe In: Discipleship and the Dynamics of Freedom*. New York: Crossroad, 1987.

Edeh, Emmanuel M. P. *Towards an Igbo Metaphysics*. Chicago: Loyola University Press, 1985.

Ejizu, Christopher. *Ofo, Ritual Symbols*. Enugu, Nigeria: Snapp Press, 1986.

Ezekwonna, Ferdinand C. *African Communitarian Ethics: The Basis for the Moral Conscience and Autonomy of the Individual*. Frankfurt, Germany: Peter Lang, 2005.

Fitzpatrick, Joseph P. *One Church Many Cultures: The Challenge of Diversity.* Kansas City: Sheed & Ward, 1987.

Foley, Edward. *From Age to Age: How Christians Celebrate the Eucharist.* Chicago: Liturgical Training Publication, 1991.

Forte, Bruno. *The Church: Icon of the Trinity.* Boston: St. Paul, 1991.

Gallagher, Michael Paul. *Clashing Symbols: An Introduction to Faith and Culture.* Mahwah, NJ: Paulist Press, 1998.

George, Francis E. *Inculturation and Ecclesial Communion: Culture and Church in the Teaching of Pope John Paul II.* Rome: Urbaniana University Press, 1990.

Giles, Kevin. *What on Earth Is the Church?* London: SPCK, 1995.

Grant, Brian W. *The Social Structure of Christian Families.* St. Louis, Missouri: Chalice Press, 2000.

Greinacher, N., & Mette, ed. *Christianity and Cultures.* London: MaryKnoll, 1994.

Halton, Thomas. *Message of the Fathers of the Church: The Church.* Wilmington: Michael Glazier, 1985.

Halvor, Moxnes, ed. *Constructing Early Christian Families: Family and Social Reality and Metaphor.* London: Routledge, 1997

Harmer, Jerome. *The Church Is a Communion.* New York: Sheed & Ward, 1964.

Harvey, Sindima J. *Drums of Redemption: An Introduction to African Christianity.* Westport, CT: Greenwood Press, 1994.

Healy, Joseph, and Donald Sybertz. *Towards an African Narrative Theology.* New York: Orbis Books, 1996.

Herman, Pottmeyer J. *Towards a Papacy in Communion: Perspectives from Vatican Councils I & II.* Translated by Matthew O'Connell. New York: Crossroad Publishing Co., 1998.

Hillman, Eugene. *Toward an African Christianity.* New York: Paulist Press, 1993.

Jay, Eric G. *The Church: Its Changing Image through the Twenty Century.* Atlanta: John Knox Press, 1980.

Idowu, Bolaji E. *Olodumare: God in Yoruba Belief.* New York: A & B Publishers, 1994.

_____. African *Traditional Religion: A Definition.* New York: Orbis, 1973.

Iroegbu, Pantaleon O. *Communalism: The Kpim of Politics, Toward Justice in Africa.* Owerri, Nigeria: International Universities Press, 1996.

Isichei, Elizabeth. *A History of Christianity in Africa: From Antiquity to the Present.* Grand Rapids: William B. Eerdmans Publishing Company, 1995.

Johnson, Luke Timothy. *Sacra Pagina: The Gospel of Luke.* Vol. 3. Collegeville, Minnesota: Michael Glazier Book, 1991.

Jones, Serene. *Feminist Theory and Christian Theology: Cartographies of Grace.* Minneapolis: Fortress Press, 2000.

SELECTED BIBLIOGRAPHY

Kaiser, Robert B. *A Church in Search of Itself: Benedict XVI and the Battle for the Future.* New York: Alfred A. Knopf, 2006.

Kasper, Walter. *Theology and Church.* London: SCM Press, 1989.

Katongole, Emmanuel, ed. *African Theology Today.* Scranton: University of Scranton Press, 2002.

Kelly, John N. D. *Early Christian Doctrines,* Revised edition. New York: HarperCollins Publishers, 1978.

Knitter, Paul F. *Jesus and the Other Names: Christian Mission and Global Responsibility.* New York: Orbis Books, 1996.

_____. *No Other Name? A Critical Survey of Christian Attitudes toward the World Religions.* MaryKnoll, New York: Orbis Books, 1985.

Kraft, Charles H. *Christianity in Culture: A Study in Dynamic Biblical Theologizing in Cross-Cultural Perspective.* New York: Orbis Books, 1979.

Küng, Hans. *The Church.* New York: Sheed and Ward, 1967.

_____. *Structures of the Church.* New York: Crossroad Publishing Company, 1982.

Lachance, Albert J., and John E. Carroll eds. *Embracing Earth: Catholic Approaches to Ecology.* New York: Orbis Books, 1994.

LaCugna, Catherine M., ed. *Freeing Theology: The Essentials of Theology in Feminist Perspective.* San Francisco: HarperCollins Publishers, 1993.

Latourette, René. *Theology of Revelation.* New York: Alba House, 1967.

Leeder, Elaine. *The Family in Global Perspective: A Gendered Journey.* Thousand Oaks, CA: Sage Publications, 2004.

Lonergan, Bernard. *Method in Theology.* Toronto: University of Toronto Press, 1979.

Lumbala, François K. *Celebrating Jesus Christ in Africa: Liturgy and Inculturation.* New York: Orbis Books, 1998.

Magesa, Laurenti. *Anatomy of Inculturation: Transforming the Church in Africa.* New York: Orbis Books, 2004.

Malinowski, Bronislaw. *Magic, Science and Religion and Other Essays.* New York: Anchor books, 1992.

Maura, Browne, ed. *The African Synod: Documents, Reflections, Perspectives.* New York: Orbis Books, 1996.

Mbiti, John S. *African Religions and Philosophy,* 2nd ed. London: Heinemann Educational Publishers, 1990.

_____. *Introduction to African Religion,* 2nd ed. Oxford: Heinemmann Educational Publishers, 1991.

McBrien, Richard P. *Lives of the Popes.* New York: HarperCollins, 1997.

Minamiki, George. *The Chinese Rites Controversy: From Its Beginning to Modern Times.* Chicago: Loyola University Press, 1985

Minear, Paul S. *Images of the Church in the New Testament.* Philadelphia: The Westminster Press, 1975.

Mroso, Agapit J. *The Church in Africa and the New Evangelization: A Theologico-Pastoral Study of the Orientation of John Paul II.* Rome: Editrice Pontificia Universita Gregoriana, 1995.

Murdock, George P. *Social Structure.* New York: MacMillan, 1949.

Newbigin, Lesslie. *The Gospel in a Pluralist Society.* Grand Rapids: William B. Eerdmans Publishing Company, 1989.

Newman, David M. *Sociology of Families.* Thousand Oaks, CA: Pine Forge Press, 1999

Nicholls, Bruce J. *Contextualization: A Theology of Gospel and Culture.* Downers Grove, IL: Intervarsity Press, 1979.

Nwala, T. U. *Igbo Philosophy.* Lagos, Nigeria: Lantern Books, 1985.

Njoku, John E. E. *The Igbos of Nigeria: Ancient Rites, Changes and Survival.* New York: The Edwin Mellen Press, 1990.

Obi, Celestine, et al. *A Hundred Years of the Catholic Church in Eastern Nigeria 1885-1985.* Onitsha, Nigeria: Africana-FEP Publishers, 1985.

Ogbonnaya, Okechukwu A. *On Communitarian Divinity.* New York: Paragon House, 1994.

Ogbuene, Chigekwu. *The Concept of Man in Igbo Myths.* New York: Peter Lang, 1999.

Ogbunanwata, Benignus C. *New Religious Movements or Sects: A Theological and Pastoral Challenge to the Catholic Church.* Frankfurt: Peter Lang, 2005.

Onwubiko, Oliver A. *The Church as the Family of God (Ujamaa).* Nsukka, Nigeria: Fulladu Publishing Company, 1999.

_____. *Missionary Ecclesiology: An Introduction.* Enugu, Nigeria: Snaap Press, 1999.

_____. *Theory and Practice of Inculturation: An African Perspective.* Enugu, Nigeria: Snaap Press, 1992.

_____. *African Thought, Religion and Culture.* Enugu, Nigeria: Snaap Press, 1991.

Osuchukwu, Peter. *The Spirit of Umunna and the Development of Small Christian Communities in Igboland.* Frankfurt: Peter Lang, 1995.

Parrinder, Geoffrey E. *African Traditional Religion,* 3rd ed. Westport, CT: Greenwood Press, 1970.

Perdue, Leo, et al. *Families of Ancient Israel.* Louisville: Westminster, John Knox, 1997.

Pomeroy, Sarah B. *Families in Classical and Hellenistic Greece: Representations and Realities.* Oxford: Clarendon Press, 1997.

Poupard, Cardinal Paul. *The Church and Culture: Challenges and Confrontation.* Translated by John H. Miller. New Hope, KT: St. Martin de Porres Lay Dominican Community, 1994.

Quinn, John. *The Reform of the Papacy: The Costly Call to Christian Unity.* New York: The Crossroad Publishing Company, 1999.

SELECTED BIBLIOGRAPHY

Rahner, Karl. *Foundations of Christian Faith: An Introduction to the Idea of Christianity*. Translated by William V. Dych. New York: Crossroad Publishing Company, 1978.

_____, ed. *Sacramentum Mundi: An Encyclopedia of Theology*. New York: Herder & Herder, 1970.

Ruether, Rosemary. *Christianity and the Making of the Modern Family*. Boston: Beacon Press, 2000.

Schineller, Peter. *A handbook on Inculturation*. New York: Paulist Press, 1990.

Schreiter, Robert. *Constructing Local Theologies*. New York: Orbis Books, 1993.

Shank, Howland T. *Salt, Leaven and Light, the Community Called Church*. New York: Crossroad Publishing Company, 1997.

Shorter, Aylward ed. *African Christian Spirituality*. New York: Orbis Books, 1980.

_____. *Toward a Theology of Inculturation*. New York: Orbis, 1988.

_____. *Evangelization and Culture*. London: Geoffrey Chapman, 1994.

_____. *Celibacy and African Culture*. Nairobi: Paulines Publications—Africa, 1998.

Stanford, Peter. *The Legend of Pope Joan*. New York: Henry Holt and Company, 1999.

Tanner, Kathryn. *Theories of Culture: A New Agenda for Theology*. Minneapolis: Fortress Press, 1997.

Tillich, Paul. *Systematic Theology*. Chicago: University of Chicago Press, 1951.

Tracy, David. *The Analogical Imagination: Christian Theology and the Culture of Pluralism*. New York: Crossroad Publishing Company, 1981.

_____. *Plurality and Ambiguity: Hermeneutics, Religion, Hope*. Chicago: The University of Chicago Press, 1987.

_____. *Dialogue with the Other: The Inter-Religious Dialogue*. Louvain: Peeters Press, 1990.

_____. *Blessed Rage for Order: The New Pluralism in Theology*. Chicago: University of Chicago Press, 1996.

Turkson, Peter, and Frans Wijsen, eds. *Inculturation: Abide by the Otherness of Africa and the Africans*. The Netherlands: Kok Publishers, 1994.

Uchendu, Victor C. *The Igbo of Southeast Nigeria*. New York: Holt, Rinehart and Winston, 1965.

_____. *The 1995 Ahiajoku Lecture: Ezi Na Ulo: The Extended Family in Igbo Civilization*. Owerri, Nigeria: Ministry of Information and Social Development, 1995.

Uzukwu, Elochukwu E. *A Listening Church: Autonomy and Communion in African Churches*. New York: Orbis Books, 1996.

_____. *Worship as Body Language: Introduction to Christian Worship, An African Orientation*. Collegeville, MN: The Liturgical Press, 1997.

Westermann, Dietrich, and Bryan, M. A. *Languages of West Africa: Handbook of African Languages Part II.* London: Oxford University Press, 1952.

Winters, Bartholomew. *Priest as Leader: The Process of the Inculturation of a Spiritual Theological Theme of Priesthood in a United States Context.* Rome: Editice Pontificia Universita Gregoriana, 1997.

Zizioulas, John. *Being as Communion.* New York: St. Vladimir's Press, 1985.

Dictionaries, Encyclopedias, Journals, Periodicals, and Internet sources

Abati, Reuben. "Lagos: The Domestic Violence Bill. 2004." http://www.nigeriavillagesquare.com/content/view/2857/96/

Amaladoss, Michael S. J. "Mission in a Post-Modern World: A Call to be Counter-Cultural." *SEDOS Bulletin.* Vol. 28, # 8/9 (August 15-September 15, 1996): 68-79.

Botterweck, Johanes G & Ringgren, Helmer (eds). *Theological Dictionary of the Old Testament*, vol. 11, revised edition, Trans. Willis, John T. Grand Rapids, Michigan: William B. Eerdmans Publishing Company, 1974.

Brueggemann, Walter. "Rethinking Church Models through Scripture." *Theology Today* 48, # 2 (July 1991): 128-138.

Catholic Bishops Conference of Nigeria. http://www.cbcn.org (accessed December 10, 2006).

CIA World Fact Book. "Nigeria." *https://www.cia.gov/library/publications/the-world-factbook/geos/ni.html#top* (accessed March 22, 2010).

Dowd, Maureen. "Worlds without Women," *The New York Times Sunday Opinion* (April 11, 2010), 20.

Dulles, Avery. "Christ among the Religions." *America* (February 4, 2002): 8-55.

Faniran, Joseph O. "Journeying Together into the 21st Century." *AFER* 37, # 1, (February 1995): 34-43.

Healy, Joseph et al. "Our Five Year Journey of SCCs from Dec. 1991-Oct. 1996: The Evolving Sociology & Ecclesiology of Church as Family in East Africa." *Africa Ecclesial Review* 39, # 5 & 6 (1997): 299-309.

Iroegbu, Pantelon. *African Vicious Triangle a Plea for Ohacracy: The Socio-Political Lee-way.* http://www.etes.ucl.ac.be/Publications/DOCH/DOCH%2039%20(Iroegbu).pdf

Isichei, P. A. C. and McCarron, M. "Methods in Evangelization in African Cultures." *The Nigerian Journal of Theology* 4 (1988).

Isizoh, Denis Chidi. *Dialogue with Followers of African Traditional Religion: Progress and Challenges.* http://www.afrikaworld.net/afrel/dialogue-with-atr.htm

SELECTED BIBLIOGRAPHY

Jewell, Elizabeth J., and Frank Abate, eds. *The New Oxford American Dictionary*. New York: Oxford University Press, 2001.

Knight, Philip. *The African Synod in Rome, 1994: Consequences for Catholicism*. http://www.martynmission.com.cam.ac.uk/CAfrica.htm

Komonchak, Joseph, et al. *The New Dictionary of Theology*. Wilmington: Michael Glazier Inc., 1987.

Marthaler, Berard, et al. *New Catholic Encyclopedia*, 2nd ed. Washington: Gale Group, 2003.

Merriam-Webster's Collegiate Dictionary deluxe edition. Springfield, MA: Merriam-Webster Inc., 1998.

Metzger, Bruce, and Coogan D. Michael, eds. *The Oxford Companion to the Bible*. New York: Oxford University Press, 1993.

Modras, Ronald. "In His Own Footsteps: Benedict XVI: From Professor to Pontiff." *Commonweal* CXXXIII, # 8, April 21, 2006, 12-16.

Njoku, Anthony P. C. "Requiem for Echo Theology: Globalization and the End of the Missionary Era." *Bulletin of Ecumenical Theology* 16 (2004): 53-60.

Obiefuna, Albert. "Present the Church as a Family in Africa." *L'Osservatore Romano*, April 1994, weekly edition, #17-27, 9.

Okoye, James C. The Eucharist in African Perspective, *Mission Studies* XIX, # 238 (2002): 159-173.

Sanneh, Lamin. "Why is Christianity, the Religion of the Colonizer, Growing so Fast in Africa." *The Santa Clara Lectures* 11 (May 11, 2005): 1-31.

Uzukwu, Eugene E. "Food and Drink in Africa and the Christian Eucharist." *African Ecclesial Review* # 22 (1980): 370-385.

Magisterial Documents

Canon Law Society of America. *Code of Canon Law*. Washington, DC: 1993.

Catechism of the Catholic Church. Liguori, MO: Liguori Publications, 1994.

Catholic Bishops Conference of Nigeria. *Church in Nigeria: Family of God on Mission. Lineamenta for the First National Pastoral Congress*. Lagos, Nigeria: Catholic Secretariat of Nigeria, 1999.

Cyprian of Carthage. *Epistle LXVIII. 8*. http://www.newadvent.org/fathers/0506.htm

ICEL. *The Rites of the Catholic Church*, vol. 1, Study edition. New York: Pueblo Publishing Company, 1990

———. *The Sacramentary*. New York: Catholic Book Publishing Company, 1985.

Ignatius of Antioch. *Epistle to the Symrnaeans VIII. 2*. http://www.newadvent.org/fathers/0109.htm

Justin, Martyr. *Apologia, 1, XLVI.* http://www.newadvent.org/fathers/0126.htm
Pope Benedict XV. *Maximum Illud.* 1915. http://www.svdcuria.org/public/missions/encycl/mien.htm
Pope John Paul II. *Apostolic Exhortation: Catechesi Tradendae.* Vatican: Libreria Editrice, 1979.
_____. *Familiaris Consortio: On the Role of the Christian Family in the Modern World.* Boston: Daughters of St. Paul Press, 1981.
_____. *Slavorum Apostoli.* Vaticana: Libreria Editrice, 1985.
_____. *Mulieris Dignitatem: On the Dignity and Vocation of Women on the Occasion of the Marian Year.* Boston: St. Paul Books & Media, 1988.
_____. *Redemptoris Missio.* Boston: Pauline Books & Media, 1990.
_____. *Letters to Families.* Boston: Daughters of St. Paul Press, 1994.
_____. *Apostolic Letter: Ordinatio Sacerdotalis.* Vaticana: Libreria Editrice, 1994.
_____. *Ecclesia in Africa: Post-Synodal Apostolic Exhortation.* Vaticana: Libreria Editrice, 1995.
_____. *Fides et Ratio.* Boston: Pauline Books & Media, 1998.
_____. *Message to the Fourth Centenary of the Arrival in Beijing of the Great Missionary and Scientist Matteo Ricci S.J.* http://www.vatican.va/holy_father/john_paul_ii/speeches/2001/october/documents/hf_jp-ii_spe_20011024_matteo-ricci_en.html
Pope Paul VI. *On Reconciliation within the Church: An Apostolic Exhortation.* London: Catholic Truth Society, 1974.
_____. *Evangelii Nuntiandi:* Apostolic Exhortation. London: Catholic Truth Society, 1975.
Ratzinger, Cardinal Joseph. *Considerations Regarding Proposals to Give Legal Recognition to Unions between Homosexual Persons.* Rome: Congregation for the Doctrine of the Faith, 2003.
_____. *Dominus Iesus.* Boston: Pauline Books and Media, 2000.
Synodus Episcoporum Coetus Specialis Pro Africa. *Instrumentum Laboris: The Church in Africa and Her Evangelizing Mission towards the Year 2000.* Vatican: Libreria Editrice, 1993.
The Documents of Vatican II. Abbott, Walter M., ed. Translated by Joseph Gallagher. New York: Guild Press, 1966.
The New American Bible. Washington, DC: World Catholic Press, 1987.

INDEX

A

Abraham, 84, 184
acculturation, 100
Achebe, Chinua, 82
adaptation, 101
Africanization, 125
African Rite, 175, 191
African traditional religion (ATR), 164
ali (earth goddess), 152
Amalados, Michael, 131
Ambrose of Milan, Saint, 149
anamnesis, 173
Anazonwu, Obi, 45
ancestors, 33, 36, 182-84, 187
 ecclesiology, 182-87
 proto, 81, 132, 185
Anderson, Jane, 157
antifamily, 87-88
Aquarians, 173
Aristotle, 77
Arrupe, Pedro, 103
Augustine, Saint, 49, 108
 City of God, 154
authority, 30, 72-73, 146, 181

B

baptism, 94, 131
Basden, George, 38
bayith, 83-84, 86
Bediako, Kwame, 185
Bellarmine, Robert, 52
belongingness, 34, 44
Benedict XV (pope), 120-21
 Maximum Illud, 120
Benedict XVI (pope), 147
bishops, 65, 70-72, 144
Bosch, David, 97, 108
Bright, John, 110
Bujo, Benezet, 80, 132

C

Cahill, Lisa Sowle, 131
Carr, Anne, 63, 72
Catholic Women Organization (CWO), 158
celibacy, 157, 189-90
Chinese culture, 117-18, 177
Christmas, 113
Christological confession, 48
Chukwu, Emmanuel, 81
Chupungco, Anscar, 101, 114
church

INDEX

autochthonous, 138
autonomous, 63
as bride of Christ, 66-69
as a communion, 62-66
as extended family, 79-82
as an institution, 69-70, 72-74
meaning of, 55
as a mystery, 54
as a paradox, 54
as people of God, 57, 59-61
self-understanding, 55
as a society, 69
City of God (St. Augustine), 154
civilized culture. *See* culture
Clement of Rome, Saint, 149
communality, 41-42, 80
Congar, Yves, 62
consequential implications. *See* implications
Constantine (emperor), 56
contextualization, 102-3
continuity, 37, 86, 168
corpus mixtum, 49
corruption, 191, 193
cosmic order, 32, 195
cosmology, 30, 182. *See also* ontology
Council of Elvira, 189
Crollius, Ary Roest, 97-98
Crowther, Samuel, 45
culture, 98-99
Cummings, Charles, 174
Cyril, Saint, 116-17
Cyril of Jerusalem, 51

D

Dark Continent, 162
death, 31
deicide, 59
delecta gaviora, 158
democracy, 148
dialogue, 162-67

Didaché, 113
diffused monotheism, 32
diversity, 63, 136
divination, 184
domestica ecclesia, 90
Donovan, Daniel, 61
double descent, 40
Dowd, Maureen, 155
Dulles, Avery, 166

E

Ecclesia in Africa, 92-94
ecclesiology, 51, 65, 75
ecclesio-missiology, 79
echo theology, 9, 22
Edeh, Emmanuel, 37
ekklesia, 47-48, 50
elders, 50, 70, 145
enculturation, 99-100, 108-9
ethnocentrism, 193-94, 196
Eucharist, 94, 173-75
Europe, 100, 116, 134
Evangelii Nuntiandi (Paul VI), 125
evangelization, 46, 75, 106-7
evil spirits, 33
ezi-na-ulo, 39, 89, 195

F

faith and culture, 132-35
Familiaris Consortio, 90
family, 76-79
    eschatological, 87, 89, 132, 185
    extended, 39-40, 79-82, 93
    Hebrew concept of, 85
    Igbo concept of, 36-44
feminists, 87, 155
Foley, Edward, 171
Forte, Bruno, 53
Francis Xavier, Saint, 120

G

globalization, 191
Greco-Roman culture, 113-14, 169
Gregory the Great, Saint, 135
Gregory VII (pope), 70, 190

H

Hamer, Jerome, 62
Hammurabi code, 110
hell, 33
henotheism, 32
Homily on the Pasch (Melito of Sardis), 59
hypostatic union, 174

I

identity, 88
Idowu, Bolaji, 164
igba ndu, 42
Igbos, 29-30
  beginning of Christianity among, 44-46
  concept of family, 36-37
  marriage, 37
  ontology, 32, 34-35
  peripatetic, 29
  worldview of, 36
literati, 117
ikwu-na-ibe, 42
images, 55
Images of the Church in the New Testament (Minear), 57
imago Dei, 158
implications
  ecclesial, 191
  sociopolitical, 191-94
incarnation, 105-6, 185
inculturation
  African food and wine, 170
  liturgical, 169
  meaning, 97
  in the medieval and reformation era, 115-16
  in the patristic age, 113, 115
  scriptural foundation of, 109-13
indigenous clergy, 121
individualism, 34, 41
Innocent II (pope), 190
institutionalism, 72
interdependence, 31
invisible world, 31
Isizoh, Denis, 164
Israel, House of, 83-85

J

Jay, Eric, 47-48
Jerusalem, Council of, 58, 111-12
John Paul II (pope), 92, 124-29
Justin Martyr, Saint, 113-14

K

Kaiser, Robert, 139
Kasper, Walter, 61
kingdom, 107, 125, 134
kinship, 36, 43, 84, 86
Knight, Philip, 178
Knitter, Paul, 165
Komonchak, Joseph, 54, 66
Kunambi, Bernadette, 155
Küng, Hans, 47, 56

L

latae sententiae, 158
Lateran Council II, 190
latinization, 115
leadership, 151
living dead. *See* ancestors
Lonergan, Bernard, 55, 133, 140, 161
Lubac, Henri de, 54

Lumbala, François Kabasele, 182
Lutz, Joseph, 162

M

Manson, Jamie, 159
marriage, 37-38, 191
matrilineal descent, 40
Maximum Illud (Benedict XV), 120
Mbiti, John, 30, 35-36, 183
Mediterranean agriculture, 173
Melito of Sardis, 59
   Homily on the Pasch, 59
Mesopotamia, 110
metanoia, 106, 193
Methodius, Saint, 116
Meyers, Carol, 84
Minear, Paul, 57, 75
   Images of the Church in the New Testament, 57
missio-ecclesia, 46
missiology, 57, 74, 195
Mithriac religion, 113
mmadu, 33-34
Mohler, Johann, 62
monoculturalism, 123, 174

N

Ndigbos. *See* Igbos
Niger-Congo, 30

O

Obiefuna, Albert, 196
Oduyoye, Mercy, 82
Ogbuene, Chigekwu, 34
oha, 43-44
ohacracy, 43-44
oikos, 39, 85-86
Okoye, James, 172
Onitsha, 44-45

ontology, 30, 33, 35
Onwubiko, Oliver, 97, 109, 115
oppression, 92, 191
order, 32-33
Origen (father of church), 59
Osuchukwu, Peter, 146

P

palm wine, 172
pantheist, 32
parables, 111
paternalism, 145
patriarchalism, 157
patrilineal descent, 40
Paul VI (pope), 92, 107, 125
   Evangelii Nuntiandi, 125
Pentateuchal law, 110
persona Christi, 68, 160
Pew Research Center, 46
pluralism, 135-41
   cultural, 101, 134
   liturgical, 195
   theological, 135-36
polygamy, 38
Pottmeyer, Hermann, 63
poverty, 192-93
Preface of Marriage, 95

Q

Quinn, John, 148

R

Rahner, Karl, 50, 62
Ratzinger, Joseph. *See* Benedict XVI (pope)
Reid, Barbara, 89, 159
reincarnation, 33
relativism, 138
Ricci, Matteo, 117-19, 177

rites and rituals, 168
Ross, Susan A., 68
Royal Niger Company (RNC), 44
Ruether, Rosemary, 76, 87

S

sacrament, 94, 131
Sacrosanctum Concilium, 122-23, 170
Sanneh, Lamin, 163
Schreiter, Robert J., 102, 136
sensus communium, 81
Shorter, Aylward, 97, 100, 103, 115
   Toward a Theology of Inculturation, 97
small Christian communities (SCC), 178-81
solidarity, 62, 81, 193
Stanford, Peter, 153
Stephanos II (patriarch of Alexandria), 108
substitution, 101, 113, 115
superficial adaptation, 126
Supreme Being, 32, 35
symbols, 55-56
synagogue, 47-48
syncretism, 105, 118, 127

T

taboos, 41, 152
Tanner, Kathryn, 138
theophany, 109, 111
Thiandoum, Hyacinth, 93
Thomas Aquinas, Saint, 154
Tillich, Paul, 140
Torah, 48, 110
Toward a Theology of Inculturation (Shorter), 97

Tracy, David, 136, 139, 165
tribal father, 132, 184-85
trinity, 129-30, 139
Troeltsch, Ernst, 138
"turn to the self," 35

U

ubuntu, 35
Uchendu, Victor Chikezie, 31, 39
uka fada, 142, 144
umuada, 152
umunna, 42, 89
uncanny, 140
uniformity, 76, 101, 115. *See also* diversity
unity, 35, 54, 78, 131
Urban VIII (pope), 119
Uzukwu, Eugene, 145-46, 149, 169, 174, 192

W

Waliggo, John Mary, 145
women
   and church, 152-60
   as deacon, 152
   early leadership roles, 154
   as head of church, 158
   as prophets, 159
   status of, 152

Z

Zizioulas, John, 130